Messenger International
Presents

The Bait of Satan

Living Free
from the
Deadly Trap of Offense

Student Workbook

A Complete 12-Session Video Curriculum

by John Bevere

with Neil Wilson

Table of Contents

A Word from John Bevere

I have been teaching the material found in this video curriculum for more than a decade now. The book *The Bait of Satan* was originally published in 1994. Throughout these years I have seen these truths from God's Word literally open the spiritually blind eyes of hundreds of dear brothers and sisters in Christ. Many more have seen how the light of God's principles and the darkness of Satan's strategies are continually clashing in their lives.

The testimony that touched my heart the most occurred when I ministered in Naples, Florida. Just before I spoke, a burly, middle-aged man stood up before the congregation and wept as he relayed his tragic story: "All my life I have felt like there was a wall between me and God. I would attend meetings where others sensed God's presence, while I watched detached and numb. Even when I prayed there was no release or presence. Several weeks ago I was handed the book *The Bait of Satan*. I read it in its entirety. I realized I had taken Satan's bait years ago. I hated my mother for abandoning me when I was six months old. I realized I had to go to her and forgive. I called and spoke with her for only the second time in thirty-six years. I cried, 'Mom, I have held unforgiveness toward you all my life for giving me away.' She began to weep and said, 'Son, I have hated myself for the last thirty-six years for leaving you.'"

He continued, "I forgave her, and she forgave herself; now we are reconciled."

Then came the exciting part. "Now the wall that separated me from God's presence is gone!"

At this point, he just completely lost it and wept. He struggled to get these last words out, "Now I cry in the presence of God like a baby."

I know the strength and reality of that captivity. I had been held hostage to its numb torment for years. These video presentations and *The Bait of Satan* book are not theory; they are God's Word made flesh. They brim with truths I have personally walked through. I believe they will strengthen you. As you read, watch, and listen, ask the Master to increase your faith! As you grow in faith, He will receive glory and you shall be filled with joy! May God richly bless you.

—John Bevere

Introduction

Welcome to "The Bait of Satan" a study of the biblical principles of responding God's way to the inevitable opportunities for offense.

This workbook has been prepared to help you study and apply the principles included in the book *The Bait of Satan* and in the videotaped seminar by the same title.

Getting the Most Out of **The Bait of Satan** *Study*

1. First, read the book *The Bait of Satan: Living Free from the Deadly Trap of Offense*. Make notes in the margins, underline key ideas, and mark places where you have questions.
2. Second, keep your Bible open as you read, consulting the Scriptures to make sure you are grasping John Bevere's points.
3. If you are part of a group study, preview each session in the workbook before your group time. Read the chapter summary even if you have read the book and fill out the Warm-Up questions.
4. During the video presentation, open your workbook to the first page of the lesson so you can jot notes in the Personal Notes section.
5. Continually ask the Holy Spirit to give you discernment; particularly in the way the Scriptures apply to your life.

Preparing the Lessons

Read over at least one of the lessons to become familiar with the approach to this study. If you are leading the group study, prepare for the study by reading the notes in the leader's guide before each lesson. Each lesson includes . . .

1. *Chapter Summary*—brief summary of the teaching principles in the chapters from *The Bait of Satan* that include the material being studied in the session.
2. *Personal* Notes—space for personal notes as you read the book or watch the video presentation.
3. *Warm-Up Questions*—topical questions to focus your thinking in preparation for the video presentation.
4. *Teaching by John Bevere*—the 30-minute video session with John Bevere.
5. *Teaching Review*—observation questions to help focus attention during the video session.
6. *Exploring God's Word*—study of each of the main passages used in the session. After each passage study you will find a section for *Personal Application*. Be sensitive to what God's Spirit may be telling you about that particular part of Scripture.
7. *Exposing the Truth*—questions to help reach conclusions regarding the Scriptures and insights from the session.
8. *Applying the Lesson*—specific directions for application of the principles in the session.
9. *Bait Warnings*—an opportunity for prayerful submission to the truth of the lesson.

The Bait of Satan *Quotes*

Several times in each lesson, you will find key quotes from the book that pertain to the subject under discussion. These are intended to help you remember the spiritual principles from God's Word.

May the Lord richly bless you and teach you as you discover the freedom in responding appropriately to the traps of the enemy with the wisdom of God's Word.

Lesson 1

The Bait of Offense

Then He said to the disciples,
"It is impossible that no offenses should come,
but woe to him through whom they do come!"
(Luke 17:1)

Summary of *The Bait of Satan,* Chapters 1 and 2

In the introduction to his book, John Bevere explains the significance of the title *The Bait of Satan.* The enemy of our souls desires to trap and destroy us. "He is shrewd in his operations, cunning, and crafty" (p. 1). He uses several kinds of bait to set his traps for us. One of his most deceptive and effective enticements comes in the form of *offense.*

"This book," writes Bevere, "exposes this deadly trap and reveals how to escape its grip and stay free from it. Freedom from offense is essential for every Christian because Jesus said it is impossible to live this life and not have the opportunity to be offended (Luke 17:1)" (p. 2).

The first chapter focuses on the multitude of offended believers in the church and the consequences of their offenses. Bevere clarifies the biblical meaning of "offense." He also points out that offended people fit into two significant categories: (1) those who have been treated unjustly, and (2) those who *believe* they have been treated unjustly. Then he spells out some of the dangers for those who fail to recognize their offended state and the biblical instructions for avoiding or settling offenses. The chapter closes with a challenge to see our own spiritual condition clearly.

Based on Matthew 24:10–13, the second chapter explains that the abundance of offense offers us one clear sign of the end times. Jesus' language clearly indicates that the divisions and chaos created among believers should warn those who are alert that history is drawing to a close. Meanwhile, mature believers must be on guard lest they be drawn into the many and devious schemes that Satan continuously launches. This side of eternity we can expect opportunities for offense to appear in our lives almost on a daily basis. Bevere writes urgently, "We must come to the place where we trust God and not flesh. Many give lip service to God as though He is their source. They take their own lives in their hands while they confess with their mouths, 'He is my Lord and God'" (p. 21).

Offenses are temptations to sin. Like any temptation, they are also opportunities for us to experience God's power and grace. If we take the bait of offense, we follow a course that leads to death. With Christ's help, if we resist the temptation to be offended, God leads us to victory.

Warm-Up Questions

Use the following questions to prepare your heart and mind for the personal and/or group study in which you will participate.

1. When you hear the expression "taking offense," what situations come to your mind almost immediately?

2. In the Introduction to his book, Bevere mentions nine fruits that result from offense. List them below. (See p. xiv.)

3. Read through the list you just made and place a check mark next to each fruit you have experienced as a result of offenses in your life.

4. Describe briefly how much of an impact offenses are having on your spiritual life right now.

STUDENT NOTES

_____

_____

_____

_____

Teaching by John Bevere

Watch the first session video presentation.

Personal Notes on Video Session 1

Use the following lines to keep notes as you view
the video.

_____

_____

_____

_____

_____

_____

_____

_____

_____

THE HEART'S TRUE CONDITION
One way the enemy keeps a person in an offended
state is to keep the offense hidden, cloaked with
pride. Pride will keep you from admitting your true
condition.

Once I was severely hurt by a couple of ministers.
People would say, "I can't believe they did this to you.
Aren't you hurt?"

I would quickly respond, "No, I am fine. I'm not hurt." I knew it was wrong to be offended, so I denied and repressed it. I convinced myself I was not, but in reality I was. Pride masked the true condition of my heart.

Pride keeps you from dealing with truth. It distorts your vision. You never change when you think everything is fine. Pride hardens your heart and dims the eyes of your understanding. It keeps you from the change of heart—repentance—which will set you free (see 2 Timothy 2:24–26).

Pride causes you to view yourself as a victim. Your attitude becomes, "I was mistreated and misjudged; therefore I am justified in my behavior." Because you believe you are innocent and falsely accused, you hold back forgiveness. Though your true heart condition is hidden from you, it is *not* hidden from God. Just because you were mistreated, you do not have permission to hold on to an offense. Two wrongs do not make a right!

—John Bevere, *The Bait of Satan*, p. 8.

Teaching Review

Use the following questions to consider some of the central points made by John Bevere during this video session.

5. What command did Jesus give that caused His disciples to respond with a desperate plea, "Lord, increase our faith"? forgive your brother

STUDENT NOTES

6. Bevere mentions that we get our word "scandal" from the same Greek word that is translated "offense" in our Bibles. To what did the Greek word refer?

bait stick
trap
scandalon

7. What has Bevere discovered is the first step in dealing with people who are offended?

realizing we've been
offended

You see, a hunter, in order to catch prey, has to lay a smart trap. You make the trap obvious; you're not going to catch anything. If you go down there and jump into the water when you got a hook in your hand and you got some bait in your hand and you say, "Hey fish, I'm coming to get you," he's not going to pay any attention to you.

If you walk out to your trap and you put that bait in there and make the thing obvious, the animal is not going to take it. Satan is no different. He is very cunning; he is very, very cunning, very shrewd. And he knows the very way he can get you into his captivity is not going to be by blatant, obvious traps. It is going to be by something very subtle, and it is called offense. Everybody say, "Being offended." That is the bait.

—John Bevere, adapted from Video Session 1

8. Who does Bevere identify as the people who can hurt and offend you the most? Why?

the one's who are closest at this ten. (Christians/spous, friends, etc)

Exploring God's Word

Revisit these key passages from which John Bevere develops his teaching.

Luke 17:1–5 *Then He said to the disciples, "It is impossible that no offenses should come, but woe* *to him through whom they do come! It would be better for him if a millstone were hung around his neck, and he were thrown into the sea, than that he should offend one of these little ones. Take heed to yourselves. If your brother sins against you, rebuke him; and if he repents, forgive him. And if he sins against you seven times in a day, and seven times in a day returns to you, saying, 'I repent,' you shall forgive him." And the apostles said to the Lord, "Increase our faith."*

9. Why is Jesus' statement, "It is impossible that no offenses should come" (Luke 17:1) such a crucial truth that believers must take to heart?

    Because they will come

Jesus made it very clear that it is impossible to live in this world and not have the opportunity to become offended. Yet most believers are shocked, bewildered, and amazed when it happens. We believe we are the only ones who have been wronged. This response leaves us vulnerable to a root of bitterness. Therefore we must be prepared and armed for offenses, because our response determines our future.

—John Bevere, *The Bait of Satan*, pp. 2–3

10. How many times did Jesus require His disciples to forgive a repentant offender in a single day?

   7 times (as many times it takes)

Personal Application

2 Timothy 2:24–26 *And a servant of the Lord must not quarrel but be gentle to all, able to teach, patient, in humility correcting those who are in opposition, if God perhaps will grant them repentance, so that they may know the truth, and that they may come to their senses and escape the snare of the devil, having been taken captive by him to do his will.*

11. What did Paul tell Timothy must happen to resistant people (in opposition) before they can escape the snare of the devil?

   1) repentance
   2) knowledge of gods word
   3) coming to there senses

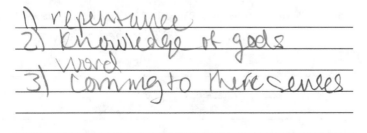

STUDENT NOTES

_____

_____

Personal Application

_____

_____

_____

2 Corinthians 10:3–5 _For though we walk in the flesh, we do not war after the flesh: (For the weapons of our warfare are not carnal, but mighty through God to the pulling down of strongholds;) Casting down imaginations, and every high thing that exalteth itself against the knowledge of God, and bringing into captivity every thought to the obedience of Christ._ (KJV)

12. In interpreting and explaining this passage, Bevere asks a question: "So, folks, what are strongholds?" How did he answer that question?

    thoughts thoughts

    _____

    _____

    _____

13. How does Bevere draw out the implications of this verse? (See also pp. 16-17 in _The Bait of Satan._)

    Under Control

    with neways are

    _____

_____

_____

_____

_____

_____

Personal Application

_____

_____

_____

Matthew 24:10–13 *"And then many will be offended, will betray one another, and will hate one another. Then many false prophets will rise up and deceive many. And because lawlessness will abound, the love of many will grow cold. But he who endures to the end shall be saved."*

14. What, according to Jesus, are the next steps that people take when offenses become part of their thinking?

___deception, betray___

___one another, hatred___

___lawlessness, cold love___

_____

_____

_____

15. How does Bevere drive home the importance of this teaching for Christians?

___concerns the ___

___of believers___

STUDENT NOTES

_____

_____

_____

_____

_____

Personal Application

_____

_____

_____

> Betrayal is when I seek my protection or my benefit at the expense of one with whom I have a relationship. Can I say that again? Betrayal is when I seek my protection or my benefit at the expense of one with whom I have a relationship. A betrayal is the ultimate abandonment of a relationship. And if a betrayal is not repented from and dealt with, it will completely sever that relationship.
>
> —John Bevere, adapted from Video Session 1

Exposing the Truth

Use the following questions to help reach conclusions regarding the Scriptures and insights from the session.

16. Bevere reports that in his conferences on *The Bait of Satan*, typically 50 to 80 percent of the attendees not only admit they are living with offenses but that they "didn't even know it until the truth came out." To what degree would you say the people in your circle of fellowship are dealing with offenses?

17. Having heard Bevere describe the walls and strongholds of offense, how would you describe these in your own experiences in relationships? (See also Proverbs 18:19.)

18. How does Bevere use the insights about predators from what he has learned from the nature programs he has watched to warn about the dangers of isolation that results from offense?

Separation if you don't need to. (Stay w/God = your safe)

Applying the Lesson

Use the following specific directions to internalize the principles in the session and put them into practice.

19. As you begin to learn about the reality and dangers of offense, what relationships in your life would you place on the "Offense Watch" list because you now realize that expectations are creating multiple opportunities for offense?

STUDENT NOTES

_____

_____

20. What relationship (or relationships) in your life has moved beyond the stage of offense to one of the others mentioned by Jesus (betrayal, hatred, deception, lawlessness)?

_____

_____

_____

21. Thinking and praying about the relationship you just listed, circle the letter of the response below that best expresses your present attitude. (Remember the danger of strongholds!)

A. _I'm just beginning to admit my own level of offense._

B. _I'm trusting that this study will give me specific tools to deal with offenses._

C. _I'm still offended and not ready to do anything about it right now._

D. _I never get offended._

E. _I've identified at least one relationship that has been seriously damaged by offenses and further separation. I intend to seek forgiveness._

F. _I'm overwhelmed by what I'm hearing and studying, but eager to know more about the danger of offenses._

Bait Warnings

A final opportunity for prayerful submission to the truth of the session.

In hunting, bait works because it appears to be something good and right. But it hides what is deadly. In the natural realm, we can't always spot Satan's bait. But God's Spirit in us is never deceived. As we explore the dangers and responses to the bait of Satan, continually pray that God will sensitize your spirit to respond to the promptings and warning of His Spirit when you are dealing with potential bait and traps.

Ask God for a humble attitude as you examine the strongholds in your own life and seek to have His truth demolish what past offenses have constructed between you and others.

Video Script for Lesson 1
The Bait of Offense

I would like you to open up your Bibles with me please to two places. Find Luke the seventeenth chapter and then go ahead and put a marker in Matthew chapter 24. That's Luke 17 and Matthew chapter 24. As you know, we are going to be doing twelve thirty-minute sessions, roughly thirty minutes, a little bit less on *The Bait of Satan*.

Now in Luke 17, I want to begin here and read just one verse. We are going to kind of backtrack in this Scripture here. In verse 5 we read, *"And the apostles said to the Lord 'Increase our faith.'"* Now, this is the latter part of Jesus' ministry and you have to understand these guys have seen Him raise the dead, they have seen Him open up the eyes of the blind, they have seen Him open up the ears of those who were born deaf. They have seen Him cause the cripple to walk; they have seen Him feed five thousand people with just a few loaves and fishes. They have watched Him calm a life-threatening storm. But, yet none of those miracles cause them to cry out and say, "Lord, we can see there is a lot of doubt, we need more faith."

What I want to ask is, what was it that caused these disciples to say, *"Lord, increase our faith"*? Now I want to be honest with you. These guys just didn't say "Jesus, please increase our faith." I believe that if you were actually standing there, Jesus makes a statement to them and after He makes the statement they go, *"Lord, increase our faith,"* out of desperation. What was that statement? Go back to the third verse and you are going to see it. Jesus said, *"Take heed to yourselves. If your brother sins against you rebuke him and if he repents forgive him."* Now look at verse 4, *"And if he sins against you seven times in a day—wow!—and seven times in a day returns to you saying, 'I repent,' you shall forgive him."* And

then the disciples cried out, *"Lord, increase our faith."* So it wasn't the miracles; it is when Jesus simply said, *"Whenever your brother sins against you, you forgive him."* Now, Jesus makes this statement in the first verse. **Then He said to the disciples, "It is impossible that no offenses should come."**

Now "offense" in the Greek is an old Greek word and that is *skandalon*. Now that is an old Greek word that was used to describe the bait stick of a trap that hunters used to catch small animals and birds in. The hunter would place the bait on the *skandalon*, the bait stick, which we would call it today, and the animal or the bird would take the bait and the cage would close and would either capture it or kill it. Thereby, an offense is the bait of Satan to pull you, the believer, into his captivity.

Now Paul confirms this when he writes to Timothy. I'm going to read to you out of 2 Timothy chapter 2, verses 24–26. Paul says, *"And the servant of the Lord must not quarrel, but be gentle to all able to teach and patient. In humility, correcting those who are at opposition, if God perhaps would grant them repentance so that they would know the truth."* Now listen to verse 26. This is 2 Timothy, chapter 2, verses 24–26. And he says, *"And they may come to their senses."* *"And escape the trap or snare of the devil, having been taken captive by him the devil, to do his will."* **So Paul says, "Those who are at opposition, those who are offended with one another, are taken captive of Satan to do his will."**

Now the scary thing is, most people that are in the trap of offense don't even know it. Because that is what Paul says, *"They may come to their senses."* If they knew they were in the devil's trap, they wouldn't stay there. I'm preaching better than you're saying "Amen" right now.

So the thing that I found out—I preach this message all around the world. I preach it in conferences, in churches and every continent except for Antarctica, I haven't preached to the penguins yet—but anyway, I found out something: that most people that are offended don't even realize they are offended. In every conference that I have preached this message, 50 to 80 percent of the people respond saying, "I'm offended," and most of them say they didn't even know it until the truth came out.

You see a hunter; in order to catch prey, has to lay a smart trap. You make the trap obvious, you're not going to catch anything. If you go down there and jump and you jump into the water when you got a hook in your hand and you got some bait in your hand and you say, "Hey fish I'm coming to get you," he's not going to pay any attention to you. If you walk out to your trap and you put that thing in there and make the thing obvious, the animal is not going to take it. Satan is no different. He is very cunning; he is very, very cunning, very shrewd. And he knows the very way he can get you into his captivity is not going to be by blatant, obvious traps. It is going to be by something very subtle, and it is called offense. That is the bait.

Now turn with me please to Matthew, the twenty-fourth chapter. Matthew 24. Now in Matthew 24 Jesus is speaking about the last days. Let me ask you, this church, this morning, how many of you believe we are living in the last days? Can I see your hands? Okay, this is something that we do not have to labor about this morning. Correct? I mean we are living in the days and the season of His return. Now the apostles or the disciples said to Jesus, they said to Him, "What's going to be some of the signs of Your second coming? What's going to be the evidence of You really coming

back?" And Jesus begins to list certain things that were going to happen in the earth, among God's people. And one of the signs that He listed I find that is so interesting is found in the tenth verse. **He said, "And then many."** Now the Greek word for "many" there is the Greek word *polus*, which means this: much, many, and great. This word in no way implies a few or some. It means a very large part of something. You got it? So what He is indicating here is: it's going to be a very large amount of people. Now I can say that I have seen this fulfilled because in all of the conferences I preached at, all over the world, I have told you 50 to 80 percent of the people respond. So look what He says, *"And then many will be offended."* Everybody say (offended). *"Will betray one another, and will hate one another."* Now this is a progression. An offense will lead to a betrayal, and a betrayal if it is not dealt with will ultimately lead to hatred. You see now where you get that from.

Proverbs chapter 18, verse 19 says this (you can look it up later, just write it down), *"A brother offended is harder to win than a strong city."* Let me say that again. *"A brother offended is harder to win than a strong city."* Now in the days of Solomon, who wrote the Book of Proverbs, what did strong cities have around them, folks? Walls. What were walls built for? Come on you are saying it. Protection, right. Those walls were built to keep out those people that you thought were against you. And they were also built to allow those people who you thought were for you, in. Correct? So what Solomon is saying is a brother that is offended is harder to win then a strong city. He is saying that a brother has built walls. Now the New Testament does not call them walls. The New Testament calls them strongholds. Second Corinthians, chapter 10, verses 3, 4, and 5 say this, *"Though we walk in the flesh, we do not war according to the flesh."* How many know we are in a war? Come on. I'm glad a third of you know that. How about the rest of you? How many of you know this is not a playground? This is a battleground. Too many people wearing a dress right now instead of putting on armor. Amen. They talk about flying away when God says, "Get ready for war." Good preaching, Amen, I'll help you this morning. I just want to make sure you are here, alright. *"Though we walk in the flesh, we do not war according to the flesh. For the weapons of our warfare,"* he goes down to say, *"are not carnal, fleshly, but are mighty in God to the pulling down of strongholds."* Everybody say (strongholds). Now are those strongholds devils in the atmosphere? No. Now that is a valid teaching. Ephesians chapter 6. There is a validity in that, but that is not what we are talking about; that is not what Paul is talking about in there. He goes on to tell what those strongholds are.

In the very next verse, verse 5 he says this, *"Casting down every imagination,"* in the literal rendering of this, every "reasoning." Casting down every reasoning. Everybody say (reasoning). Now where do reasonings occur? Point to your head. Casting down every imagination or reasoning, every high thing that exalts itself against the knowledge of God. Everybody point to your head. Where is knowledge? Oh man, you are getting it. And then he says, listen *"Bringing every thought."* Everybody say (thought). Where do thoughts occur? Everybody point to your head. Isn't this interesting? *"And bringing every thought captive to the obedience of Christ."* So now folks, what are strongholds? Strongholds are reasonings, are thought processes that are contrary to the will of God. Amen, good preaching. I'm helping you this morning. We are waking up on this nice Sunday morning, Amen. Now listen, I know what it is, you are listening real good but I just kept trying to get you to laugh because I find that a "spoonful of sugar helps the medicine go down." Amen. I found out that God can do things in your life, He can bring correction in your life and spanking in your life, and give you some honey to go with it, makes it a little bit nicer. Thought processes or reasonings are these strongholds

that are contrary to the will of God, the Word of God.

Now God's Word, listen, is a reflection of His nature. Now God's nature is love. Everybody say (He is love). Bible does not say He has loved. He is love. Good preaching. Now listen, the love of God always seeks to give, give, give. Are you with me? How many of you remember when you first got born again? Can I see your hands? I remember when I first got born again and filled with the Holy Spirit. I mean I laughed and I sang all the way home from the meeting. I woke up the next morning with a smile on my face. For the first time since I'd been a kid at Christmastime. I was so in love with everybody. I mean I don't care who you were, I was in love with you. I mean you loved everybody. You remember you even loved your mother-in-law. You remember that? And then what happened? Somebody did something to you that was not kind. Or they said something to you that was not kind. Or actually it was hurtful. They gossiped about you; they spoke against you. Now it wasn't a sinner, it was somebody in the church.

You see, I have discovered something that really isn't that big of a discovery. The person who can hurt you the most is the person who is closest to you. Why is that? Because our expectation is higher upon them. If we set up expectations on people, then if they don't meet them, they have offended me. That is why the one who can hurt you the most is not somebody that is a sinner but somebody who is in the church or even more so a husband and a wife or a pastor because our expectations are higher.

David said it like this in Psalm 55. He says this in verses 12 to 14, *"For it is not an enemy who reproaches me, then I could bear it. Nor is it one who hates me who has exalted himself against me, then I could hide from him. But it was you, a man my equal, my companion, and my acquaintance, we took sweet counsel together and we walked in the house of God and throne."* This is a guy, he's saying, I went to church with, I sat next to. The word of God ministered to both of us. He was my brother. You're the one who has lifted up yourself against me. He said, "I could've handled it a lot easier if it would have been somebody in the world." See, because the one who can hurt you the most is the one who is closest to you because your expectations are higher.

Let me show it to you like this. Let's say this is zero expectation, alright? Our expectations on the world are probably about this high. Our expectations on our Christian brothers and sisters are about this high. Our expectation on our husband and wife are about this high, and our expectation upon our pastor is about this high. If somebody only does this much, well guess what? If he's a sinner, he has been a blessing to you because he has exceeded your expectations. Now if somebody only does this much and they're in a church and your expectation was here, they would have offended you by this much. If your wife or husband would have done that much and then your expectations were here—woo!—they really offended you. If your pastor has only done this much, if he didn't shake your hand this morning when you left the church, if he didn't recognize your prophetic gift, then guess what? The offense is that big—it is huge. That's why most offended people today in the church, you know what they say?

I have been preaching on this for almost ten years. You know what they say? "Why, you know the world treats me better than most Christians?" Well that's right, because their expectation was only *that* on the world and the world did *that* much and they were like, "Well, they're nice to me." Hallelujah! Alright now, and then many we will be offended, we will betray one another, hate one another. And now remember, I said it's a progression.

An offended person is a person who builds walls. Now those walls are up, so guess what now? They're no longer seeking to give, give, give. The walls are now getting them to seek to protect, protect, protect. The focus is no longer now to give; the focus now becomes protect what I got. Now what they become is like the Dead Sea in Israel. How many of you know there are two seas in Israel? Two seas that are surrounded by the landmass in Israel. You have the Sea of Galilee and you have the Dead Sea. Now the Sea of Galilee is up north and it receives waters that originate up in the mountains near Caesarea Philippi. Now they flow down to the northern part of the Sea of Galilee. Now, the Sea of Galilee freely takes in the northern part and also freely gives out in the southern part. Freely it receives; freely it gives. The result is the Sea of Galilee is loaded with life. I mean marine life all of that. It's loaded. Now, the same living waters that come out of the Sea of Galilee flow down the River Jordan and enter into the northern part of the Dead Sea, but the Dead Sea only takes in, it doesn't give out. The result is every bit of life that comes into the Dead Sea dies because it hangs on to what it's got.

Remember Jesus said, *"Freely you have received, freely give."* You want to really enter into life? Release the life that God has given you and you will enter into life. But you see what happens to an offended person says, "I've been hurt and I don't want to get hurt again." So now these mechanisms go up in their minds, in their thoughts, in their subconscious. "I've been hurt and I'm not going to get hurt again." So they develop these thought patterns, these reasonings that are mechanisms to protect them from getting hurt again. So now we respond a little differently. We respond around the church, we respond in the church, we're quick to go into another place. Why? Because we were hurt in that place; we don't want to get hurt again. We'll get into all that later.

A person now who has the walls up is a perfect candidate for betrayal. Most people I find in the church today don't even know what betrayal is. They know very limited aspect of what betrayal is I should say. When people hear the word betrayal, you know what they think? They think Judas. Let me tell you what betrayal is. Betrayal is when I seek my protection or my benefit at the expense of one I have a relationship with. Can I say that again? A betrayal is when I seek my protection or my benefit at the expense of one I have a relationship with. A betrayal is the ultimate abandonment of a relationship. And if a betrayal is not repented of, it will completely sever a relationship. When I have built walls, if push comes to shove, if situations get a little rough, I'm going to seek to protect myself. I don't care at the expense of someone else. Proverbs 18, verse 1 says this, *"A man who seeks his own desire rages against wise judgment."* The man who has built walls will seek his own desire; therefore, he will betray if push comes to shove. And if there is a betrayal in a relationship, it will ultimately lead to hatred.

The Bible says hate your brother, you're a murderer. I want to make sure that has settled in. Can I give you the Scripture reference to that one? The Bible says in 1 John, chapter 3, verses 14 and 15, *"Whoever hates his brother."* You can see very clearly John isn't talking to sinners. *"Whoever hates his brother is a murderer."* Doesn't say he's *like* a murderer; it says he *is* a murderer. *"Whoever hates his brother is a murderer and you know that no murderer has eternal life abiding in him."* Now let me say this about hatred. You know what people think of when they think of hatred. They think of real rage and anger. That's not necessarily hatred. The Bible says that Absalom hated Amnon—those are two of David's sons. And you know what the Bible says. He neither spoke good to him nor evil to him. He controlled his hatred. Hatred means loveless, means have no love. Is the void of having the love of God. Go meditate on 1 Corinthians, chapter 13, verses 4–8. Meditate on

those verses. I don't know about you, but something that I have wanted to excel in this, especially my last couple of years, and especially in the last six months, is the love of God. I mean, I am so drawn to the love of God. It is the most powerful force in the whole universe. And I am convinced that the church that Jesus is coming back for is the church that is going to walk in exceptional, extravagant love. Amen.

Hatred is not seen necessarily by emotions, by words. It can be, of course, because out of the abundance of the heart the mouth speaks; however, it can be cleverly disguised. I'll never forget the time that the Lord exposed the hatred that was in my heart. Were in my mind, in my emotions whatever, there was a certain person I didn't like. And the Lord said to me, "How would you like to live right next to her in heaven?" When He did, I went ballistic. I said, "No! She needs to be on the other side." Well then I realized I had an offense and the offense went further.

Now watch this, verse 11. *"Then."* What does "then" mean? It means after there's massive offense and much of the offense turns into betrayal and hatred. There's stages you go through. Some of you I may be talking to right now. You may be only at the initial stage of offense. Some of you may have gone to the stage of betrayal. Some of you may be at the stage of hatred. And then Jesus says, after this, after you have a lot of offended people, He said, "Many false prophets will rise up and deceive many." Notice He is saying here that after there's massive offense, there is going to be a lot of deception. You know what the first thing Jesus said to these guys when He says, "What is going to be the sign of your second coming?" The first words out of his mouth are, "Be careful that nobody deceives you." In other words, deception is going to run rampant.

If you look in Timothy, Paul says, "There's going to be people in the church in the last days that are not only going to be deceiving people but they are going to be deceiving themselves." An offended person deceives himself. What Jesus is telling us here is, offense is the breeding ground for deception. Now you know what the problem with deception is? There is only one problem and that is this: it's deceiving. In other words, a person who is deceived really believes he is right when in reality he is wrong. That's the only problem with it.

Now, what did Jesus call false prophets? Matthew 7:15, what did He call false prophets? Wolves in sheep's clothing. Now notice He doesn't say there, "wolves in shepherd's clothing." Everybody's always looking for the false prophet behind the pulpit. Now listen, they may be there, but I find there are a lot more false prophets out there then there are in here. That's a true statement; that's not a biased statement. They're in the salons, they're in the grocery stores, they're everywhere, telling people you can't believe what pastor did.

I've learned that these predators—I'm talking about like wolves, hyenas—they travel in packs. They have a goal. You know what their goal is? To isolate the sheep from the herd. There is protection for the sheep in the herd. But if they can get the sheep to separate from the herd, they're now meat for their table.

Proverbs 18:1, *"A man who isolates himself seeks his own desire and rages against all wise judgment."* The scary thing is this: he can be in a huge church, he can have a huge family, but the isolation doesn't occur outwardly. It eventually results outwardly. Where it begins is right here.

Strongholds. Now you are a candidate for deception. Remember deception doesn't come with a black cape. It comes with angels' clothing or believers' clothing. Verse 12, *"And because lawlessness will abound, the love of many will grow cold."* You know what is really scary. The Greek word here for "love" is not the Greek word *phileo*. *Phileo* is the love that everybody has, the world, and sinner, and Christian alike in brotherly affection. There is a Greek word used for love called *agape*. *Agape* is the love of God. The world does not have it. Jesus says, *"This is the love the world cannot receive."* This is the love that is shed abroad in a believer's heart when he is born again and filled with the Holy Spirit. The word that He uses there is *agape*. What Jesus is saying there in the last days, the massive offense is not going to be in society only. But what He is talking about here is that it is going to be within the church. And He said, *"The love of many is going to grow cold, wax cold."* It means the fiery passion of the love of God in your heart is going to become very cold. It is a gradual thing.

You put a frog in a kettle and that kettle is room temperature and you turn on the fire and you boil that water, that frog will sit there and die. He will not jump out even though he can. If you threw him into boiling water, he would jump out. Let me tell you something. When the love of God begins to grow cold, it's a growing, it's not an instant, you don't notice it. Keep yourself from the offense because it is massive, it's rampant and Jesus said, "It would occur massively in the last days." That's why you are sitting here through this course, to hear the Word of God to protect you. Amen. God bless you.

Lesson 2

How Could This Happen to Me?

*Joseph said to them, "Do not be afraid, for am I
in the place of God? But as for you, you meant evil
against me; but God meant it for good, in order to bring
it about as it is this day, to save many people alive."*
(Genesis 50:19–20)

Summary of *The Bait of Satan,* Chapter 3
Bevere begins chapter 3 with a pointed question:
"If you've been genuinely mistreated, do you have the
right to be offended?" (p. 23). His answer involves a
retelling of the story of Joseph, Jacob's son.

After explaining some of Joseph's background, Bevere
details the first of several mistreatments Joseph
suffered—a betrayal by his brothers. This was followed
by the shock of being sold into slavery, transported to a
far country in chains, and then sold again to the
Egyptian Potiphar. At this point we get a glimpse of
Joseph's response to the gross injustice he suffered—he
faithfully served Potiphar and proved to be a channel of
great blessing on Potiphar's house.

The next round of suffering began when Potiphar's
wife set her sights on Joseph and hounded him with
adulterous advances. His resistance led to a false
accusation of rape and imprisonment. Bevere details some

of the thinking that Joseph must have wrestled with in the darkness of the dungeon. Given the unfair blows of the past years, it would have been natural for Joseph to seriously question, "Is God in control?" What becomes clear from Joseph's response is that he continued to trust God and resist the invitation to become offended.

Bevere describes Joseph's prison experience as a "sifting time." In spite of his holy response to the hard conditions and his willingness to help others (the jailer, Pharaoh's butler and baker), a way of escape was not soon in coming. Apparently, Joseph understood a principle that Bevere highlights: "Absolutely no man, woman, child, or devil can ever get you out of the will of God! No one but God holds your destiny" (p. 27).

As bad as Joseph's experiences became, he never fell victim to the worst trap of all, taking offense. He practiced the principle later described by the apostle Paul in 1 Corinthians 10:13, "No temptation has overtaken you except such as is common to man; but God is faithful, who will not allow you to be tempted beyond what you are able, but with the temptation will also make the way of escape, that you may be able to bear it." Bevere closes the chapter with the challenge, "Stay submitted to God by not becoming offended; resist the devil, and he will flee from you (see James 4:7)" (p. 31).

Warm-Up Questions

Use the following questions to prepare your heart and mind for the personal and/or group study in which you will participate.

1. Once again, why does Bevere insist on calling the continual temptations to take offense, "the bait of Satan"?

_____

_____

_____

_____

_____

_____

_____

2. According to Bevere, what are the two kinds of offended people he finds in the church and which group will he be discussing in this session (related to chapter 3 of his book, p. 23)?

    A. _____

    _____

    B. _____

    _____

    _____

3. If a painter asked you to suggest one scene he or she could paint that would capture the story of Joseph in the Old Testament, which scene would you choose?

_____

_____

_____

_____

_____

_____

_____

Teaching by John Bevere

Watch the second session video presentation.

Personal Notes on Video Session 2

Use the following lines to keep notes as you view the video.

_____

_____

_____

_____

_____

_____

_____

_____

_____

_____

_____

_____

ASSIGNING BLAME

How often do we hear our brothers and sisters fall into the same trap of assigning blame? For example:

"If it weren't for my wife I would be in the ministry. She has hindered me and ruined so much of what I have dreamed of."

"If it weren't for my parents I would have had a normal life. They are to blame for where I am today. How come others have normal parents and I don't? If my mom and dad didn't get divorced I would have been much better off in my own marriage."

"If it weren't for my pastor repressing this gift in me I would be free and unhindered. He has kept me from fulfilling my ministry destiny. He has turned the people in the church against me."

"If it weren't for my former husband, my kids and I wouldn't have all this financial trouble."

"If it weren't for that woman in the church I would still be in favor with the leaders. With her gossip, she has destroyed me and any hope I had of being respected."

The list is endless. It is easy to blame everyone else for the problems you have and imagine how much better off you would be if it had not been for all those around you. You know that your disappointment and hurt are their fault.

I want to emphasize the following point: *Absolutely no man, woman, child, or devil can ever get you out of the will of God! No one but God holds your destiny.*

John Bevere, *The Bait of Satan*, p. 27

Teaching Review

Use the following questions to consider some of the central points made by John Bevere during this video session.

4. Bevere began this session's presentation by referring to Proverbs 6:16–19, verses that spell out the six things God hates and the seventh that receives a

special mention as an abomination. Which one is
the abomination?

_____

_____

5. According to Bevere, what biblical principle backs up
the statement that though it is wrong to take up an
offense, we still have the right to do it?

_____

_____

_____

_____

_____

_____

_____

_____

_____

6. Summarize Joseph's two dreams. What was their
main point?

_____

_____

_____

_____

_____

_____

7. List the setbacks and offenses that Joseph had to
endure from the time of his dreams to the moment
of their exact fulfillment:

STUDENT NOTES

_____

_____

_____

_____

_____

_____

_____

_____

_____

_____

_____

_____

_____

_____

_____

_____

_____

_____

_____

_____

_____

_____

_____

_____

_____

_____

_____

_____

_____

Exploring God's Word

Revisit the key passages from which John Bevere develops his teaching.

Genesis 37:20 *"Come therefore, let us now kill him and cast him into some pit; and we shall say, 'Some wild beast has devoured him.' We shall see what will become of his dreams!"*

8. Who is speaking in this verse and what are the details of their plan? Who is the victim?

_____

_____

_____

_____

_____

_____

9. How does Bevere use Genesis 37:20 to discuss the role others may have in carrying out or preventing God's will in our lives?

_____

_____

_____

_____

_____

_____

_____

_____

_____

_____

_____

Personal Application

_____

_____

_____

_____

_____

_____

_____

_____

_____

Genesis 40:1–8 *It came to pass after these things that the butler and the baker of the king of Egypt offended their lord, the king of Egypt. And Pharaoh was angry with his two officers, the chief butler and the chief baker. So he put them in custody in the house of the captain of the guard, in the prison, the place where Joseph was confined. And the captain of the guard charged Joseph with them, and he served them; so they were in custody for a while. Then the butler and the baker of the king of Egypt, who were confined in the prison, had a dream, both of them, each man's dream in one night and each man's dream with its own interpretation. And Joseph came in to them in the morning and looked at them, and saw that they were sad. So he asked Pharaoh's officers who were with him in the custody of his lord's house, saying, "Why do you look so sad today?" And they said to him, "We* *each have had a dream, and there is no interpreter of it." So Joseph said to them, "Do not interpretations belong to God? Tell them to me, please."*

10. Describe in your own words the sequence of events in these verses.

_____

_____

_____

_____

_____

_____

_____

_____

_____

_____

_____

_____

11. According to Bevere, why did the arrival of Pharaoh's two servants represent a severe test God allowed into Joseph's life after years in prison (see Genesis 40:1–23)?

_____

_____

_____

_____

_____

_____

_____

Personal Application

_____

_____

_____

_____

_____

_____

Genesis 45:5–8 *"But now, do not therefore be grieved or angry with yourselves because you sold me here; for God sent me before you to preserve life. For these two years the famine has been in the land, and there are still five years in which there will be neither plowing nor harvesting. And God sent me before you to preserve a posterity for you in the earth, and to save your lives by a great deliverance. So now it was not you who sent me here, but God; and He has made me a father to Pharaoh, and lord of all his house, and a ruler throughout all the land of Egypt."*

Psalm 105:16–19 *Moreover He called for a famine in the land; He destroyed all the provision of bread. He sent a man before them—Joseph—who was sold as a slave. They hurt his feet with fetters, he was laid in irons. Until the time that his word came to pass, the word of the LORD tested him.*

12. How does Joseph let his brothers off the hook in these verses? What do his comments imply about his attitude toward them?

_____

_____

_____

13. After reading Genesis 45:5–8 and Psalm 105:16–19, describe the significance of the word "sent" in these two passages. Who was sent and who did the sending?

_____

_____

_____

_____

_____

_____

_____

Personal Application

_____

_____

_____

_____

_____

_____

_____

1 Corinthians 10:13 _No temptation has overtaken you except such as is common to man; but God is faithful, who will not allow you to be tempted beyond what you are able, but with the temptation will also make the way of escape, that you may be able to bear it._

14. This passage is foundational to chapter 3 in the book. What does Bevere point out about the specifics of the "escape" mentioned in this passage (see p. 31)?

(see p. 31)

STUDENT NOTES

_____

_____

_____

_____

_____

_____

_____

15. What does Bevere teach about our own circumstances, based on this verse?

_____

_____

_____

_____

_____

_____

_____

Personal Application

_____

_____

_____

_____

_____

_____

_____

Exposing the Truth

Use the following questions to help reach conclusions regarding the Scriptures and insights from the session.

16. By his use of the story of Joseph, how does Bevere settle the question he raises at the beginning of the session, "Do you have the right to be offended if you have been mistreated?"

_____

_____

_____

_____

_____

_____

_____

_____

_____

17. What made it possible for Joseph to consistently respond to offensive events by other means than taking offense?

_____

_____

_____

_____

_____

_____

_____

_____

_____

_____

_____

_____

_____

_____

_____

18. According to Bevere, how do we get into trouble
    when we assume that God responds to circum-
    stances in our lives the same way we respond?

    _____

    _____

    _____

    _____

    _____

    _____

    _____

**The way we respond to certain situations, you would
think that is exactly the way God responds. I mean,
can you just see God, looking at Jesus saying, "Jesus,
what are we going to do? Sally is thirty-four and not
married yet because I wanted her to marry Jim, but
Mary, her best friend, gossiped to Jim and then Jim
didn't marry her. Oh my goodness, do you have
another available bachelor down there for Sally to
marry? I mean, come on Jesus, there has go to be
somebody."**

STUDENT NOTES

> You think that's the way some of us respond? "Jesus, what are we going to do? Fred just got fired, oh my goodness, they gave him his last paycheck. Are there any jobs down here available for Fred? Come on, talk to me." I mean, that is the way we respond. We think, "Oh no!" And we panic and we think, "Oh my goodness, I hope heaven has got some kind of solution," and we never say it with our mouth. But the way you act is exactly the way you are saying it is in heaven.
>
> —John Bevere, adapted from Video Session 2

Applying the Lesson

The following are specific directions to internalize the principles in the session and put them into practice.

19. On the lines below, list at least two circumstances in your life about which you have been exercising the right of offense.

_____

_____

_____

_____

20. For each of those circumstances, what other rights could you have exercised instead? Identify at least one of the following for each circumstance you listed.

Instead of taking offense, I could be . . .

_____

_____

_____

_____

_____

_____

_____

_____

_____

_____

_____

21. What attitudes or perspectives would have to change in your life before you could put the above plans into action?

_____

_____

_____

_____

FEED ON HIS FAITHFULNESS

You know, David makes one statement I don't want you to miss. David said, "Feed on His faithfulness" (Psalm 37:3). I hit a couple points in my life, folks, that I am going to tell you, what I was going through was so severe that reciting the promises that He made to me weren't feeding me anymore. I had to listen, I had to feed on His faithfulness. I remember sitting at times and just saying, "God, You're faithful," and that would minister life to me; it was feeding me. See? Do you think Abraham can quote the promise when he is walking three days to put the promise to death? Abraham has got only one choice—to feed on God's faithfulness. David learned that. We can too!

—John Bevere, adapted from Video Session 2

Bait Warnings

A final opportunity for prayerful submission to the truth of the session.

If you stay free from offense, you will stay in God's will. If you become offended, you will be taken captive by the enemy to fulfill his own purpose and will. Take your pick. It is much more beneficial to stay free from offense.

We must remember that nothing can come against us without the Lord's knowledge of it before it ever happens. If the devil could destroy us at will, he would have wiped us out a long time ago because he hates man with a passion. Always keep this exhortation before you:

No temptation has overtaken you except such as is common to man; but God is faithful, who will not allow you to be tempted beyond what you are able, but with the temptation will also make *the way of escape,* that you may be able to bear it (1 Corinthians 10:13, italics added).

—John Bevere, *The Bait of Satan,* pp. 30-31

Video Script for Lesson 2
How Could This Happen to Me?

I have learned that of all the offended people that you find in the church, you can put them into two major categories, alright? Category number one are those who have been genuinely mistreated, alright? Category number two are those who think they have been mistreated, but they really haven't. Now category number two are people that usually have inaccurate information, a lot of times that come through gossip. Amen.

Do you know what is amazing? Proverbs says these six things the Lord hates and the seventh one is an abomination. Now you know that the one that is an abomination is not murder, it's not homosexuality, it's not adultery. Do you know what it is? Those who sow discord among brethren—gossip. Gossip should be treated as arsenic; it's poison. Your ears are not garbage pails, your heart is not a waste place—guard it. Be careful what you are listening to, and cut them off when they are talking to you. If they are talking about your pastor, cut them off. If they are talking about your spouse, cut them off. If they are talking about your father, cut them off. If they are talking about one of your friends, cut them off. If they are talking about another brother in Christ, cut them off. Amen. Unless they got proof, and the Bible says let there be two witnesses with proof, if it's an elder, if it's a leader. Amen.

Now, if you look at that second category of people that think they have been mistreated, usually they have inaccurate information or have accurate information but they discern incorrectly. Now you know what I have learned about discern? Discernment is rooted in the love of God, but I find that there is a counterfeit to discernment and its called criticalness. Now anybody can be critical, all you need is two eyes and a carnal brain. But true discernment is rooted in the love of God. The next time you think you are discerning something about somebody; ask yourself, would I be willing to die for them?

The reason Jesus can look at the Pharisees and call them snakes is cause He died for them. If you are offended by somebody you will not be willing to die for them. So category number two are those who either have accurate information and have discerned incorrectly or they have inaccurate information. Now I don't want to deal with category number two. I want to deal—in this session—with category number one. What if you have been genuinely mistreated? Do you have the right to be offended? Now let me say this. You got the right to do anything. God will not violate your will. How many of you really understand that? I mean God says, *"I call heaven and earth this day to record to hold against you that I have set before you that life and death; therefore, choose life."* What is He saying? If you don't choose life, you already have death. You have to make an active choice of life. Amen. God will not violate your choice. God will protect a person's right to go to hell if they want to go to hell. That's a scary thing, isn't it? I mean that is deception to the fullest, but God will protect them. Amazing, isn't it?

Do you have the right to be offended if you have been mistreated? Well to answer that let's look at the life of Joseph. Now I want to walk through Joseph's life with you. Most of you have read this story, but you know what. I want to walk you through it and I want to help highlight some things that I think are going to point out some beautiful truths out that we need to know for today. Joseph is Jacob's son; Jacob is the son of Isaac, who is the son of Abraham. Joseph is son number eleven. You know Jacob had twelve sons. I looked up at Lisa one day, you know we have four sons, and I said, "Honey, I sure would like twelve sons," I said, "because you know Joseph had twelve sons." And then she looked back at me with those beaming eyes and she said, "He also had four wives." I said, "Alright honey I got it, I got it, I'm fine with four, I'm fine with four." So anyway, Joseph the son number eleven. Now Joseph's brothers didn't like him very much. How many of you know that? Why? Because Jacob favored Joseph and he gave him the robe of many colors.

Now one day Joseph goes to sleep and God gives him a dream, and in his dream he sees all these sheaves bowing down to him, and those sheaves represent his brothers. And God showed him in his dream that he was going to be a leader and that his brothers would serve him. So when he woke up from that dream, he immediately shared it with excitement with his brothers. Now they did not share in his enthusiasm, okay. So he goes to sleep again and God gives him another dream. And this time the sun, the moon, and the stars are bowing down to him and now he wakes up and says, "Not only are my brothers going to start bowing down, but also my mother and my father." So now they are really mad. I mean they are steaming mad at him, and they hate him. So the brothers go out, the ten older brothers go out to the field and when they would go out with the herd they would go great distances. I mean we're not just talking a stone's throw away. We are talking miles away. They went out and Jacob said to Joseph, "I want you to go and see how your brothers are doing and bring us some supplies." So Joseph goes and searches for his brothers and he finally finds out where they are at. And when the brothers see him coming they say, "Oh here comes Mr. Leader. Here comes the man who is going to rule over us." So a couple of them look at each other and say, "Hey wait a minute, let's kill him. Then he won't rule over us. Let's see him try to rule over us when he is dead." So you know

what these guys do? When he comes, they grab him, tear the robe of many colors off of him, and throw him into a deep pit to die. Now for those of you who don't know, pit stands for "preachers in training." So they throw him into this pit and they are all happy now. They are delighted they say, "We don't have to put up with this brat anymore, talking about leading us and all this, hah," and they are having a great time.

Now, a few hours later they see a caravan of Ishmaelites coming down the road heading toward Egypt to do slave trading. And Judah, the fourth born, says to his brothers, "Hey guys now wait a minute, wait a minute. If we let him rot in that pit, we don't get anything out of it, but if we sell him as a slave, he will be as good as dead. Because he will be sold as a slave to another country and we will never have to see him again and we will make some money off of him." So they sold him as a slave to the caravan of Ishmaelites for twenty pieces of silver.

Now you see folks, listen, the older brothers were offended by Joseph therefore they betrayed him. Offense leads to betrayal. They were already at the hatred state, but believe me, here is the betrayal opportunity. So now Joseph is brought down to Egypt and he is sold as a slave to a man named Potiphar. Potiphar was one of Pharaoh's officers. Joseph now is a slave for the next ten years for this man named Potiphar, this Egyptian. And the thing is you got to understand, now listen to me carefully, I know most of you know this story and you know the outcome, but can you please put yourself in Joseph's shoes?

You don't know the outcome. You just know that your own brothers have just destroyed your life. Because you got to understand something folks, see, we Westerners can't really relate to this. Back then it was everything for a man to have a son. As a matter of fact men sometimes—I'm not this way, this is the way they were—almost a little depressed when they had daughters because basically you sell her for 500 camels and she's gone one day. But sons carried on your name. They carried on your inheritance. Alright, now it was everything for a son to carry on a father's name and his inheritance. It is one thing when you are born a slave and you never knew what it was like to be an heir of a wealthy man. It is another thing when you are an heir of a wealthy man who has a covenant with Almighty God and your own brothers steal that from you and now you are sold as a slave. Because when you are sold as a slave to another country, you are going to get married to a woman and she is going to be a slave, your children will be a slave. You have lost your inheritance completely. It was almost as if Joseph is a living dead man. What his brothers did to him in their mindset, in their culture, was every bit as bad as killing him because now he's got to live as a dead man. He's got to live the rest of his life thinking, what I could have had but because of my brothers it's not there.

So now he's in Potiphar's house for ten years and there is not even any indication of a rescue coming from his father. Why? Because he knows his brothers probably told his father that he was dead. He probably heard them laughing and plotting when they were dipping the robe of many colors into the lamb's blood and he is thinking, "My father thinks I'm dead. I have no hope here." Except for a dream that God gave him. That's the only thing he's got. Now I love this man because he goes ten years, there is no church, no home fellowship group, no Bible, no nothing. But we never find him complaining and we never find him disobeying. And so things begin to look up because Joseph is obeying God's Word and, you know, Potiphar starts giving him more and more responsibilities and eventually makes him charge over his whole household.

So God starts blessing him, but underneath the blessing there is something really wicked begin-

ning to brew and that is this: Potiphar's wife. She gets the hots for Joseph. She wants to commit adultery with him. She's burning in lust for him. So the Bible says she starts approaching him daily. Not once, not twice, everyday. Now, she is dressed in the best and scented in the best and has a seducing spirit up to her eyeballs. You got it. Everyday he goes, "No, no, no I will not sin against God." I love this man's fear of God. He's obeying after ten years, even when he hasn't seen one ounce of the promise come to pass yet. And so he keeps going, "No, no, no, no." Finally one day they are alone in the house, everybody's out. She grabs him by the robe, she says, "Lie with me." He says, "God forbid I sin against God and your husband," and he does what the Bible says. He flees sexual immorality, right? And when he runs out of the house, the robe tears. He runs out a naked man and she's a scorned woman. So she's mad now, so she screams, "Rape!"

So the very thing he is running from he gets blamed for. And what happens? Potiphar commits him into Pharaoh's prison or dungeon. When you think of Pharaoh's dungeon or prison, do not think of our prisons today. I have preached in many prisons and I want to tell you this. Our prisons in the United States are country clubs, compared to Pharaoh's dungeon. I have been in a Middle-Eastern dungeon, physically been in one. They were usually emptied out cisterns underneath the ground. Sometimes the ceilings were only about four feet tall. They were very damp and very dark. And you know what the Bible says in Psalm 105? *"They laid his feet in irons and his neck in chains and they hurt him with these chains."*

This is not a picnic place, he's in the dungeon for two years.

Now I want you to stop and think about this. He has hit the lowest a man can go. Twelve years ago God gave him a dream that he was going to be a leader and that his brothers would bow down to him. His brothers are the ones that are crooked, they're the ones who are perverted, they're the ones who have acted wickedly, and yet they are still enjoying all the benefits of their wealthy father. He, on the other hand, has done nothing but obey God, shared a dream that got him the pit. Then he's sold as a slave, he is a good slave, he is an obedient slave, he holds to the Word of God for ten years. He looked like he was prospering and he was, God was blessing him. But yet now he obeys the Word of God and he flees sexual immorality and it gets him into the dungeon.

So now what it appears like to this man is, "The more I obey God, the worse things get." And you know what God said in Malachi chapter 3? God says, *"In the last days, I'm going to come to My church as a refining fire."* Now how many of you know refining is not comfortable? And you know what God says, "There's going to be two groups of people in the church during this refining."

He said, "The first group is going to say, 'What good is it that we served you, God? We've obeyed your ordinances, we kept your command, but we're looking at the proud, we're looking at the wicked, and they are the ones who are laughing and giggling. They are having a great time. I'm going through one test after another test after another test. It seems the more I pray, the worse it gets. The more I obey, the worse things get.'" Did you ever hear the parable when Jesus said, *"When the Word is sown immediately they receive it with joy, but afterwards persecution, affliction arises for the Word's sake"*? These people are going to be complaining. They are going to say, "Look, these people are going to obey God. They look happy and having a great time." And God says, "Your words are harsh against me."

"And then there is going to be another group," God said, "that are going to fear the Lord. And they are going to speak to one another the Word of the Lord because they meditate on His name." These are the same people that are going through the same trials, but yet they are not complaining. They are keeping their focus on His faithfulness.

You know David makes a statement. David said, "Feed on his faithfulness." I've hit a couple points in my life folks that I am going to tell you what, what I was going through that was so severe. So severe that reciting the promises that He made to me weren't feeding me anymore. I had to feed on his faithfulness. I remember sitting at times and just saying, "God You're faithful," and that would minister life to me, it was feeding me. See do you think Abraham can quote the promise when he is walking three days to put the promise to death? Abraham has got only one choice—to feed on His faithfulness. See David learned that.

So here is Joseph in the dungeon. Can you imagine the thoughts that are going through that guy's mind? Can you imagine the thoughts he had to wrestle with? "God, all I have done is obey You and the more I have obeyed You the worse it gets. I look at my brothers, they're the ones that are wicked and yet they are the ones who are enjoying Your blessings." Can you imagine the thoughts he had to fight? You got to understand, you're in the dungeon for two years. You had a lot of time to think. Every bit of his freedom had been taken. There is only one freedom that wasn't taken. You know what it was? His ability to respond correctly. Not to get offended.

Folks, let me say this to you. Joseph could have easily entertained the thoughts of "what if." "What if I didn't have these wicked brothers? What if I never shared the dreams?" You know I run into this all the time. People say, "You know life would have been a whole lot better for me if my ex-husband wouldn't have done this. If my parents would have been normal, I wouldn't have the family problems that I have. You know if my pastor just would have received my gift, I wouldn't have the problems today that I am having. If my pastor just would have recognized me, I would be a lot better off today." Do you ever hear the people go through the "what if"? Can I make a statement? Nobody, no man, no woman, no child, no devil can get you out of the will of God. I really want that to sink in. I'm going to say that again. No man, no woman, no child can get you out of the will of God.

Joseph's brothers made the statement, I've got it quoted right here. They made the statement, they said, *"Come therefore let us now kill him and cast him into some pit. We shall see what shall become of his dreams,"* Genesis 37,verse 20. That's what they said. We are going to destroy the call of God on his life. Nobody can destroy the call of God on your life. There is only one person in your life that can do it. Everybody turn your finger around and point at you. You are the only one who can destroy the call of God on your life.

The children of Israel were called to go and inherit the Promised Land. They had been complaining, complaining, complaining for one year. Now it was in God's will that they experience the desert for one year after coming out of Egypt because one year later that is when God said to Moses, "Send the spies into the Promised Land." But you know what, for one year they're complaining. Let me say this to you. God hates complaining and you should treat complaining like poison because that is exactly what it is. Do you know what complaining says to God? "God I don't like what You're doing in my life right now and if I were You, I would do I differently." Do you know what a slam that is on His character? Do you know what you are saying? You are saying, "God, You're incompetent. You are not doing a good job. I wish I was You, I would do better." It is rebellion and it is a lack of the fear of God. You never find Joseph complaining.

See in the book of Malachi that's what people were doing. They were complaining. What good is it that we obey? It seems like the more we obey the harder things get. Well guess what? That is what the Bible says, *"When the word's sown, affliction is going to come."* Persecution is going to come for the Word's sake. I mean look at Moses when he brings the Word of the Lord to Pharaoh, what happens? Pharaoh increases their hardship. He says, "You are going to have to get your own straw now. I'm not going to provide it for you," and the people said to Moses, "Stop preaching, your preaching is making our life harder. We're going through more trials now." Well, welcome to life.

When you make the decision that you are going to go with God, guess what? The flow of the world is contrary to the flow of the kingdom and you are going to meet with resistance and opposition. How you handle that resistance and that opposition will determine your future because God's Word, His promise will always come to pass as long as you don't get offended. Joseph is in that dungeon and he could have been there sitting and thinking, "You know if it wasn't for my brothers, I'd be a leader today." Can you see the Father when those brothers threw him into the pit and then sold him to slavery, can you see the Father going, "Hey, Jesus, You got an alternate plan? We want him to be a leader and he was supposed to lead his brothers and they just sold him to slavery. Oh my goodness, this is not what I anticipated! What are we going to do?"

God already knew that they were going to do that before he ever gave Joseph the dream. He knew that they were going to do that before they were ever born because God knows the end from the beginning. But yet, the way we respond to certain situations, you think that is exactly the way God responds. I mean can you just see that God looking at Jesus saying, "Jesus, what are we going to do? Sally is thirty-four and not married yet because I wanted her to marry Jim, but Mary, her best friend gossiped to Jim, and then Jim didn't marry her. Oh my goodness do You have another available bachelor down there for her to marry? I mean, come on Jesus! There has go to be somebody!" You think that the way some of us respond, "Jesus, what are we going to do? Fred just got fired! Oh my goodness, they gave him his last paycheck. Is there any jobs down there available for Fred?" I mean that is the way we respond, we think, "Oh no!" And we panic and we think, "Oh my goodness I hope heaven has got some kind of solution," and we never say it with our mouth. The way you act is exactly the way you are saying to heaven. Good preaching, Amen.

God brings the biggest test into Joseph's life right at the end. Do you know when the greatest attack comes, just before the harvest is manifest? I mean look at David. The same day Saul is getting put to death by the Philistines, the very same day, his own men wanted to kill him. He's at the lowest he has ever been. If he would have lost it there, he would have lost his harvest. Do not be weary in well doing for you will reap, you will harvest, if you faint not. There is an "if" on there—if you faint not. That's why sometimes I had to go, "God You're faithful, God, You're faithful." Because all I knew I had to do was stay obedient to the harvest.

So God brings Joseph's greatest test of his fear of God at the very end. You know what He does? He brings two guys to minister to him. He brings a butler and a baker and these guys want ministry. Now if Joseph would have been like some people in the church and they would have said, "You got problems, I got problems. Leave me alone. You go pray. Here's a Bible, go read it." Now what is that greatest test? What's the greatest test? The greatest test is this. God brings two men to him to minister to. The test is this; can Joseph proclaim to those two men the faithfulness of God when he hasn't seen one evidence of His faithfulness in his own life in twelve years?

Come on now, twelve years ago he had a dream from heaven that said his brothers would serve him. He has not seen one ounce of it, because when you are a foreign slave and you are thrown into a dungeon for raping one of the officers of the king, you are left in there to rot. Killing you is too easy. They want you to suffer so they can give you just enough bread and just enough water so you can stay alive because they want you to suffer in a hole that is damp and laid up in chains. Can he proclaim God's faithfulness to those two men? When every time he has obeyed God it has gotten worse and yet he hasn't seen one evidence of his dreams come to pass? If he would have been like a lot of believers—bitter with God, offended with God—he wouldn't have ministered to them, he would have passed up the very ticket out. You know what is really amazing? If Joseph would have chosen to be offended with God and his brothers, if he would have chosen to be offended with his brothers, he would have sat in the dungeon saying, "If I ever get out of here, I'm going to kill them." And you know what is amazing? If he would have killed them, he would have killed ten out of the twelve tribes of Israel, and including Judah who Jesus and David came through. Do you know, you are going to see those boys in heaven?

What happens? He ministers to the butler and the baker. God restores the butler and the baker gets his head chopped off, but the butler gets restored. Time later Pharaoh has a dream. The butler says, "I remember this man, this Hebrew boy who walked with God in prison." Joseph is brought up and interprets the dream; Pharaoh makes him number two in command of all of Egypt. When the famine comes two years into it, here comes Joseph's brothers and what does he do? He blesses them. If he would have been offended with them he could have killed them and Pharaoh couldn't have cared less if he killed them because they weren't anybody to Pharaoh. He could have done it, he had the power to do it, but he used his power to serve, to bless. That's meekness, folks. What God was doing in Joseph those twelve years, was developing in him the character for him to handle the leadership that He wanted to bring him into. Don't take the bait. See you next session.

Lesson 3

My Father! My Father!

*"Moreover, my father, see! Yes, see the corner
of your robe in my hand! For in that I cut off
the corner of your robe, and did not kill you,
know and see that there is neither evil nor rebellion
in my hand, and I have not sinned against you.
Yet you hunt my life to take it."*
(1 Samuel 24:11)

Summary of *The Bait of Satan,* Chapter 4

Because offenses usually arise in personal relationships, John Bevere follows up chapter 3 and the review of Joseph's life with another example of a potentially explosive offensive relationship in which a father figure (King Saul) betrays a son (David).

Bevere traces the relationship between Saul and David, beginning with Samuel's anointing of the shepherd boy from Bethlehem as the next king. The first encounters between King Saul and king-to-be David are noteworthy: David becomes the king's designated harpist, playing in the background of the throne room. Later, David takes on and takes out Goliath the giant, winning Saul's daughter Michal and getting the attention of Jonathan, Saul's son, with whom he became a close friend. All is well.

STUDENT NOTES

Then, when Saul hears the people cheering comparisons between himself and David, a spirit of jealousy, suspicion, and hatred overtakes the king. He becomes driven to kill David. Months go by and Saul spends a great deal of effort and time attempting to eliminate David. He even persecutes and kills some of the people (like the priests of Nob) who helped David along the way. David has opportunities to kill the king but refuses to take action out of respect for the office. The cry of abandonment uttered by David in 1 Samuel 24:11, Bevere hears echoed in the lives of countless men and women today.

Eventually, Saul falls into David's hand again, and the circumstances seem to indicate that it's time for David to avenge himself. Even then, David remains faithful to God's ways. Instead, God uses the Philistines to settle matters with Saul. David responds to his sworn enemy's death with grief for Saul, compassion for Saul's family, and anger at one who sought to benefit from taking his life. Bevere draws comparisons with an experience in his own life in which God taught him lasting lessons that the desire for personal revenge often comes cloaked in a quest for justice. David's faithful loyalty, even in the face of betrayal, proved to be part of the character that God desired to develop in him. God wants to find that same loyalty in us, a passion for God that supercedes our ownership of reputation, ministry, or even well-being.

Warm-Up Questions

Use the following questions to prepare your heart and mind for the personal and/or group study in which you will participate.

1. Describe the character traits of a loyal friend.

_____

_____

_____

_____

_____

_____

2. Based on what you learned from Joseph's life in the last lesson, what would you say is the hardest part about trusting God in the face of disappointment and mistreatment?

_____

_____

_____

_____

_____

_____

_____

3. The book includes Bevere's statement, "It is one thing to experience rejection and malice from a brother, but it is entirely different to experience rejection and malice from a father" (p. 33). As you begin this lesson, how would you describe those differences?

_____

_____

_____

_____

_____

Teaching by John Bevere

Watch the third session video presentation.

Personal Notes from Video Session 3

Use the following lines to keep notes as you view the video.

_____

_____

_____

_____

_____

_____

_____

_____

_____

_____

_____

To examine an example of a father who betrayed, let's look at the relationship between King Saul and David (see 1 Samuel 16–31). Their lives touched even before they met, as Samuel, the prophet of God, anointed David to be the next king of Israel. David must have been overwhelmed with excitement, thinking, "This is the same man who anointed Saul. I am really going to be king!"

Back at the palace, Saul was being tormented by an evil spirit because he had disobeyed God. His only relief came as someone played the harp. Saul's servants began to look for a young man who could sit in

STUDENT NOTES

his presence and minister to him. One of the king's servants suggested David, the son of Jesse. King Saul sent for David and asked him to come to the palace and minister to him.

David must have thought, "God is already bringing to pass His promise through the prophet. Surely I'll win the favor of the king. This must be my entry-level position."

—John Bevere, *The Bait of Satan*, p. 34

Teaching Review

Use the following questions to consider some of the central points made by John Bevere during this video session.

4. If you got a chance to talk to David about his life, what do you think he would say were the three high points of the time between Samuel anointing him to be the next king and the death of Saul that brought about his rise to the throne?

_____

_____

_____

_____

5. What would be his three lowest points along the way?

_____

_____

_____

_____

6. What appears to have been the event that turned Saul's heart away from David (see 1 Samuel 18:5–11)?

_____

_____

_____

_____

_____

_____

_____

7. How would you describe David's attitude toward Saul throughout their relationship?

_____

_____

_____

_____

_____

_____

_____

_____

Exploring God's Word

Revisit the key passages from which John Bevere develops his teaching.

1 Samuel 24:11 *"Moreover, my father, see! Yes, see the corner of your robe in my hand! For in that I cut off the corner of your robe, and did not kill you, know and see that there is neither evil nor rebellion in my hand, and I have not sinned against you. Yet you hunt my life to take it."*

8. When you look at the context of this verse in your Bible, to what was David referring when he used the word "moreover," meaning "besides all this"?

_____

_____

_____

_____

_____

_____

_____

_____

_____

_____

_____

_____

_____

9. Why does David continue (in verses 12–15) to plead his case before Saul?

_____

_____

_____

_____

_____

_____

_____

10. What was the result of this confrontation?

_____

_____

STUDENT NOTES

_____

_____

_____

_____

_____

_____

Personal Application

_____

_____

_____

_____

_____

_____

_____

_____

_____

_____

_____

_____

_____

1 Samuel 26:8–11 *Then Abishai said to David, "God has delivered your enemy into your hand this day. Now therefore, please, let me strike him at once with the spear, right to the earth; and I will not have to strike him a second time!" But David said to Abishai, "Do not destroy him; for who can stretch out his hand against the LORD's anointed, and be guiltless?" David said further-*

more, "As the L<small>ORD</small> lives, the L<small>ORD</small> shall strike him, or his day shall come to die, or he shall go out to battle and perish. The L<small>ORD</small> forbid that I should stretch out my hand against the L<small>ORD</small>'s anointed. But please, take now the spear and the jug of water that are by his head, and let us go."

11. How is this situation different than the situation in the cave?

_____

_____

_____

_____

_____

12. What statements indicate that David has a very clear perspective on the only acceptable forms of Saul's death?

_____

_____

_____

_____

_____

_____

_____

13. How did this confrontation turn out?

_____

_____

_____

_____

Personal Application

_____

_____

_____

_____

_____

_____

_____

_____

_____

_____

_____

_____

_____

_____

2 Samuel 1:14–15 *So David said to him, "How was it you were not afraid to put forth your hand to destroy the Lord's anointed?" Then David called one of the young men and said, "Go near, and execute him!" And he struck him so that he died.*

14. Why was David's judgment on the young Amalekite immediate and severe?

_____

_____

_____

_____

_____

_____

_____

_____

15. What does the context of this passage tell us about
    the immediate response of David and his men to
    the confirmation of Saul's death?

_____

_____

_____

_____

_____

_____

_____

Personal Application

_____

_____

_____

_____

_____

_____

_____

_____

_____

_____

_____

_____

_____

_____

_____

Ezekiel 44:10–11, 15 *"And the Levites who went far from Me, when Israel went astray, who strayed away from Me after their idols, they shall bear their iniquity. Yet they shall be ministers in My sanctuary, as gatekeepers of the house and ministers of the house; they shall slay the burnt offering and the sacrifice for the people, and they shall stand before them to minister to them . . . But the priests, the Levites, the sons of Zadok, who kept charge of My sanctuary when the children of Israel went astray from Me, they shall come near Me to minister to Me; and they shall stand before Me to offer to Me the fat and the blood," says the Lord G*od*.*

16. Bevere refers to the above passage from Ezekiel to illustrate what core truth about two groups who may bear the same title, but a different role?

   _____

   _____

   _____

   _____

   _____

17. How does Bevere apply this comparison between the two groups of priests to the relationship between Saul and David?

   _____

   _____

   _____

   _____

   _____

STUDENT NOTES

_____
_____
_____
_____
_____
_____

Personal Application

_____
_____
_____
_____
_____
_____
_____
_____
_____
_____
_____
_____
_____
_____
_____
_____
_____
_____
_____
_____
_____
_____
_____

Exposing the Truth

The following are questions to help reach conclusions regarding the Scriptures and insights from the session.

18. Beneath all the details, how was David good for Saul and how was Saul good for David?

_____

_____

_____

_____

_____

_____

_____

_____

_____

_____

_____

_____

_____

19. Bevere describes one of the potential uses of offenses, mistreatment, and unfairness as "stepping stones," which they become when we choose not to take offense. Using this same picture, what other kinds of stones might those hardships represent if we choose to respond to them by taking offense?

_____

_____

_____

_____

_____

_____

_____

_____

_____

_____

_____

_____

20. During the months when Bevere was under intense pressure because of the supervisor's attempts to have him fired, what seems to have been the most difficult choice Bevere had to make?

_____

_____

_____

_____

_____

_____

What I find is that every single person who is receiving adverse treatment from a leader goes through this constantly, "What have I done to turn his heart against me? What have I done? What sin have I committed? What wrong have I done?" Folks, sometimes you haven't done anything wrong.

Now, that isn't always the case—matter of fact, most of the time, the child or the follower *has* made a mistake—but there are times when leaders' characters must be built or developed and God will use other

STUDENT NOTES

> **people, with their actual or perceived shortcomings, as purifying vessels in a leader's life.**
>
> —John Bevere, adapted from Video Session 3

Applying the Lesson

Use the following specific directions to internalize the principles in the session and put them into practice.

21. Take a moment to review the *Personal Application* notes you made during the Exploring God's Word section. Summarize the main lesson you want to apply to your life as a result of this session.

_____

_____

_____

_____

_____

_____

22. What hardships in your life right now would take on a whole different value if you began to think of them as tools God is using to shape your character?

_____

_____

_____

_____

_____

_____

23. What has it done or will it do to your relationship with God to realize that He allows even very

difficult events into your life because of the good they can bring about?

_____

_____

_____

_____

_____

Bait Warnings

A final opportunity for prayerful submission to the truth of the session.

> Oh yeah, I can look back at those times and I can say, "I remember they were difficult, they hurt, they brought questions, and a lot of pain in my heart." I've looked back now and I treasure those times because, I will be honest with you . . . nothing is worse than unfair treatment especially from a leader. The hardest times in my life, as I look back now, were also the greatest stepping stones—the greatest times of growth I have ever encountered. But the sad thing is how many people don't get the blessing because they don't see the working of the Holy Spirit in their lives in those times.
>
> —John Bevere, adapted from Video Session 3

Video Script for Lesson 3
My Father! My Father!

Luke 17, verse 1, Jesus made this statement, *"It is impossible that offenses will not come."* Now let me make this really clear. If you breathe air, if you drink water, if you eat food, you will have the opportunity to be offended. What you do with the offense will determine your future. Either you will become stronger or you will become bitter. You will never remain the same after encountering an offense. Everybody say (I will never remain the same after encountering an offense, and Father, in Jesus' name help me to choose Your way). Amen.

Now in the last session we talked about being betrayed by brothers, brothers being offended with us and betraying us. And we saw in the last chapter how Joseph was betrayed by his brothers but yet he chose not to be offended with them. And so then when God did bring forth His promise in Joseph's life, he blessed them. He did not curse them, he blessed them because Joseph realized that nothing could happen to him in his life without God approving it and as long as he stayed obedient. Amen.

No one can get you out of the will of God; no man, no woman; no child can get you out of the will of God. Joseph's brothers tried to do it. They said, "Let's kill him. Let's see if he ever leads us." Correct, however; they could not do it because God knew before they ever, ever were born, before He ever gave Joseph the dream what his brothers would do. And in fact Joseph said, "It wasn't you who sent me here." He said, "It was God who sent me here." Joseph said that, we read that in Genesis and we also read it in the book of Psalms. The psalmist said, "God sent a man before me." It does not say his brothers sent a man before him.

When you really understand that nothing can come into your life without God allowing it, it really sets you free because anything you go through, God will use it as a stepping stone of your life if you respond in obedience. I want to read to you a direct quote "Often the thing that looks like an abortion of God's plan actually ends up being the road to its fulfillment if we stay in obedience and free from offense." Children of Israel became offended, they aborted the plan, and they aborted their call. Joseph chose to stay sweet; he chose to stay obedient and God fulfilled the plan of God in his life.

Now it is one thing to be betrayed by a brother, it is an entirely different thing—now listen to me carefully—to receive unfair treatment or even betrayal by a father or a leader. I said in the first session that the ones who can offend you the most are the ones that you have the greatest expectations on. It is natural that we have greater expectations on leaders because we expect leaders to nurture us, to help us to grow into the kind of people that God has called us to be.

David experienced rejection from a father. I want to talk about David. When David was a young man, his life and Saul's life met before they ever met. And that was Samuel came to David's home and Samuel anointed David to be the next king of Israel. All seven of David's older brothers were all passed by and God said, "There is the one I am chasing." You know it's one thing—for us to pursue God and it's another thing having God pursue us. And you know, I don't know about you, but I would love to be someone who God is chasing. And God was chasing David and He sent the prophet to his house and the prophet went through all the ones who looked like perfect candidates to be the next king and God, "Uh ah, this is a little ruddy one feeding the sheep. That's the one I'm chasing." Amen.

So now David is anointed to be king. Can you imagine the thoughts that are running through David when the oil is coming down and he's thinking, "Now this is the senior prophet, the senior prophet of Israel, the one who anointed King Saul. And he is saying I will be the next king." Well time goes by, and back at the palace Saul is being tormented and the men of Saul, his surrounding aides said, "We have to go find a skillful musician who can play and minister to you." And they said, "Hey, we know about this son of Jesse who is excellent on the harp." And so they bring David in and David begins to minister to Saul musically. And David thinks this is phenomenal. "It is my entry level position."

So later on, the Philistines and Israel are at war and they had been at war for quite some time and David's father said, "I want you to bring some supplies and see how your brothers are doing." When he comes, he finds all the warriors hiding behind rocks, hiding from a giant that is about nine feet nine inches tall. And when he comes up to his brothers and looks at them and says, "Who is this uncircumcised Philistine?" they get angry. And David says, "This is the call for me being here," and moves on from his brothers to the king and says, "I'll get him." And David asks in the process, "What will be given to the man who kills the giant?" And they said, "The king's daughter's hand in marriage." And David goes, "Oh boy!" So David says to the king, "I'll get him," and David goes out and kills Goliath. And so King Saul's daughter Michal is given to David in marriage. Now King Saul asks him to move into the palace. David befriends Jonathan. He is now eating at the king's table and the king, King Saul, actually makes David his armor bearer. So David is sitting there pinching himself. He is going, "This is phenomenal! What God prophesied is actually coming to pass. I have been brought into the king's palace; I eat at his table; I have favor with his sons; I am his armor bearer; and I've got his daughter's hand in marriage. This king is going to

mention me one day and put me on the throne. Wow, the plan of God is unfolding right before my eyes!"

Well, they come back from a battle and you know what happens. The women begin to proclaim. They say, *"Saul has killed his thousands and David has his ten thousands."* Now Saul is angry and he is jealous. And so now David is ministering to the king a couple times in the palace and the king grabs a javelin and tries to pin David to the wall. And after the second time, David does what any smart person would do. He said, "I'm getting out of here or I am going to become a wall hanging here." Okay. And so he leaves.

For the next fourteen years—David no longer lives at home in the comfort of his own bed, the shelter of his own parents and brothers. He now has to live in caves and deserts and wildernesses. His life now has totally changed. He is the age of sixteen years old and all the way until he was thirty this is where he has got to live. Now these are the prime years of a person's life. And it is all because of one reason: because his leader is trying to kill him. Now in 1 Samuel 24, Saul discovers that David is in the wilderness of En Gedi, and when Saul comes out, he comes out with three thousand of Israel's finest warriors to do one thing folks, to kill David. Now can you imagine if you were a person and your leader is out to absolutely destroy you? Now listen, we are talking about a leader that God put you under. The devil didn't put David under Saul, the Lord did. Saul comes with his three thousand warriors and they go into the cave of En Gedi. Inside the cave there is a pool and Saul and his men take off their armor. What are they doing taking a bath and using the restroom, you know what I am talking about. And so they are completely disarmed. Now David and his men are in the back part of the cave and his men go, "Hey, David this is it. God has given you your enemy. God has literally brought them into your hands. They have disarmed. We can go out there and kill every single one of them like that. No sweat. We won't lose a man." And what is David thinking, David is thinking, "Somebody has lied to my leader. Somebody has turned his heart against me. Somebody has told him that I am in rebellion and I am going to take his throne and ministry away from him."

How many of you know that there are good leaders, gentle leaders, and harsh leaders? How many of you know that to be true? How many of you know that God ordains both? Now He doesn't make the bad leader bad, but He places His authority on a leader who may have a bad personality. But He will use that.

So here is David. He's underneath a leader like this and his men are encouraging him. But what I find is that every single person who is receiving adverse treatment from a leader goes through this constantly, "What have I done to turn his heart against me? What have I done? What sin have I committed? What wrong have I done?" Folks, sometimes you haven't done anything wrong. Now that's not always the case; matter of fact most of the time, many times, it's that the son or the person who is following them makes the mistakes. But there are times leaders are just characters not built or developed and God will use these people in our lives as what? As purification vessels. Amen.

And so David's thinking, "What have I done that has caused Saul to turn against me? I know what I will do; I'll prove me innocence to him. I will prove to him that I am not rebellion, that I am not trying to take his life, and I am not trying to take his ministry." So David goes and cuts off a corner of Saul's robe and he takes it and he and his men go a great distance. And when Saul comes out of the cave, David cries out with a loud voice. He says, "Saul, my father! my father!" Let's just read from there; well let's just read the whole thing, verse 5. *"Now it happened afterward David's*

heart troubled him because he had cut Saul's robe." You know what I love about this in the King James? It says David's heart "smote him." David was so tender toward God that even when he cut the robe of his leader, his heart convicted him for cutting his robe. That's how tender his heart was toward his leader—and this is a leader that has been trying to kill him and has been causing his life to be turned upside down for a few years.

Verse 6, and he said to his men, *"May the Lord forbid that I should do this thing to my master the Lord's anointed to stretch out my hand against him seeing he is the anointed of the Lord."* Verse 7.

"So David restrained his servants with these words and did not allow them to rise against Saul and Saul got up in the cave and was on his way. David also rose afterwards went out of the cave and called to Saul saying, 'My Lord the King.' When Saul looked behind him David stooped with his face to the earth and bowed down. David said to Saul, 'Why do you listen to the words of these men who say indeed David seeks your harm? Look this day your eyes have seen that the Lord delivered you into my hand in the cave, someone has urged me to kill you, but I spared you. But I said I will not stretch out my hand against the Lord for my Lord he is the Lord's anointed.'" Verse 11, *"Moreover, my father."* Now do you see what David is doing? He's crying out, "Please be a father to me, please be a leader to me. I just want to be your son." *"Moreover my father see yes to the corner of your robe in my hand for in that day I cut off the corner of your robe and did not kill you. Know and see that there is neither evil, nor rebellion in my hand and I have not sinned against you yet you hunt to take my life."* Saul looks at David and says, *"David, you are more righteous then I am. May God bless you,"* and Saul leaves. Now can you imagine the relief that David is feeling folks? He has proven his innocence to his leader. So now he is thinking, "Alright, now he isn't going to hunt

my life anymore and possibly now he will restore me because he can see that I am not out to destroy him or take his ministry."

However, two chapters later, David is in the hills of Hakilah, Saul hears about it and Saul heads out with the same three thousand warriors in 1 Samuel 26. Now when he does—this is where it gets good—God puts the whole army into a deep sleep from the Lord, alright. Now David knows this. So this is not an ordinary sleep. God literally knocks these guys out. When God knocks you out, nothing is going to wake you up, alright. So David says, "Hey man! God has put them all in a deep sleep." God reveals this to David. David looks at his men. He says, "Alright, I want to go over to Saul's camp. Who's going to go with me?" And the Lord picks the perfect guy—Abishai, who is Joab's little brother, who is bloodthirsty. You understand? Abishai would kill you if you looked at him wrong.

So Abishai and David, they sneak over to the camp and they go all the way to the center of the camp where Saul and Abner were. And there, Saul knocked out, Abner beside him knocked out, and Abishai picks up the spear and Abishai says, "Alright David, just give me the word, just give me the command and I will run this thing through him and he will never get up again. David?" David's not saying anything. I mean he is not saying nothing and Abishai turns around and looks at him and goes, "What are you doing? Just give me the command." David doesn't say anything. Abishai says, "What is wrong with you man? Listen David, he is out to kill you and you proved your innocence to him two chapters ago, David. This is self-defense; if you don't kill him, he is going to kill you. This will stand up in any courtroom David; now just give me the word. David, David what is wrong with you?"

Look, God brought him into the cave two chapters ago and we didn't do anything and he gave us a chance to save our nation. This you got to understand folks; this guy is a murderer. Do you want to know why I know that? Because it is in the Bible. There were eighty-five priests in the city of Nob. David came to that city to get some bread and those priests gave him bread and they prayed for him and gave him Goliath's sword that David had taken. When Saul heard that they had given David assistance, Saul killed eighty-five of those priests.

Now with those priests, he killed their wives and he killed their little babies and as a matter of fact he had the whole sword put to the city of Nob. The very judgment that he was suppose to execute on the Amalekites he brought on the city of Nob. He murdered in cold blood eighty-five priests. I don't know about you but I have never had a leader who has murdered eighty-five priests, eighty-five ministers. Matter of fact, I don't know anybody in America that is in the ministry that has killed eighty-five priests. So let me put it to you this way. David's leader, David's pastor so to speak, is worse than any leader I know of in America and you know of, as far as that goes.

So Abishai looks at him and goes, "He's a murderer. He murdered the entire city of Nob. He murdered those little kids. He murdered those priests. God has given him to us to deliver our nation; he is going to destroy our nation. Don't you understand?" And David's not saying anything. Finally Abishai puts his spear down and says, "Wait a minute David. Why do you think God has put this army into a deep sleep? He has put this army into a deep sleep because God wants our nation delivered from this murderer." And then David looks at Abishai. You know what he says? "Don't touch him." Do not touch him.

Look at verse 9. But David said to Abishai, *"Do not destroy him for who can stretch forth his hand against the Lord's anointed?*—other translations say leader—and be guiltless. David said furthermore,

"As the Lord lives the Lord should strike him or his day should come to die or he should go out into a battle and perish. The Lord forbid that I should stretch out my hand against the Lord's anointed. But please take now the spear and jug of water that are by his head and let us go." So again he wants to show his innocence to Saul. Abishai looks at him and goes, "Okay," and they walk out.

Why does God put that army into a deep sleep and why does God allow David to sneak right into the center? It was not for David to deliver Israel.

There were times in my life, well let me tell you something, I could have exposed a leader because how many of you know that very few people live through life without a harsh leader? There are good leaders and there are gentle ones. Thank God He has given you a good one here, isn't that right? But there are harsh ones and you know what? I think everyone experiences harsh ones because God uses the good ones to nurture us and God uses the harsh ones to refine us. They both serve a purpose in God's plan. And there were times when I could have exposed a harsh leader.

I had a leader that was wanting me fired in the church that I was in. He did everything that he could to get me fired and I remember my senior pastor—he was my immediate supervisor—my senior pastor told me, "Listen if there is anything that is going on between you and him, you come straight to me." And I remember I had evidence, evidence to destroy this guy. And I remember I was praying forty-five minutes saying, "Now God, how do I share this with the senior pastor? This has got to be exposed." I had written documented evidence of the way the guy was behaving and the Lord and I kept wrestling and wrestling and wrestling and wrestling. I said, "Lord, the guy is wanting to fire three of the pastors on staff. I said he is doing this and doing that and he is doing all this stuff to the congregation. How do you want me to share this with the senior pastor?"

And finally after wrestling for forty-five minutes I looked up and I said, "You don't want me to show this to him do you?" And the peace of God went *bam*! I went, "What?" And I tore up the evidence and I thought I was either crazy or I heard from God, but I tore it up. Now you know what is amazing is, a month later, I was out praying and I saw this guy. I was out praying in a church parking lot an hour before the office is open and I saw this guy and the Lord spoke to me and said, "Matthew 18. I want you to go apologize to him." I said, "Apologize to him! I haven't done anything! He's trying to fire me." So I prayed about something else.

I started praying about missions. You talk about dry. And finally twenty minutes later, after this dry twenty minutes I said, "Lord what are you saying right now?" He said, "Matthew 18. I want you to go and make it right. Apologize." So I went, and you know I walked into his office and I said, "You know I was out praying when you came in this morning. The Lord dealt with me." I said, "I have been very critical and judgmental of you and I've been wrong, so would you forgive me?" He said, "Sure." I mean, he was surprised. Here is a guy that has been trying to fire me.

Well, six months later I was out of town and you know what David said? *"Let the Lord judge between him and me."* Six months later I was out of town for one weekend. Everything the guy was doing got exposed. It was so severe the senior pastor could have had him prosecuted and thrown in jail for years. But the senior pastor had mercy and immediately fired him and kept the evidence of what he had done in a sealed envelope in the attorney's office.

David looks at Abishai and said, *"Let the Lord judge between him and me."* Why? Because God is the one that put Saul over David and David is saying, "God, you are the one who is able to take care of the leaders if they are acting wrong." See when we judge a leader what we do is say, "God, we don't trust in what You are doing, so we are going to take over from here." That's why God said to Miriam, "Why were you not afraid to speak against Moses? He is the one I appointed over you. Why are you judging him? You are taking My place."

Why did God put the army into a deep sleep? I will tell you why—to test David, to find out if he's going to be another Saul, if he's going to take matters in his own hands, or if he's going to remain a man after the heart of God. See you will look at the difference between Saul and David; there is a very fine line that separates them. David constantly waited on God and inquired of the Lord; Saul took matters in his own hands. That was the only difference. Saul would protect what God gave him. When he sensed there was a young man, he felt it was a threat to his ministry. He sought to kill him. However David, when Absalom rose up to take his throne, David's attitude was, "My reward, God, not that throne. He can have it, I can have my reward out in the middle of the desert."

See there are two kinds of ministers, folks. There are those who love their ministry and there are those who love God. Those who love their ministry will protect what God has given them. Those who love God, they don't have anything to worry about because nobody can take God away from me. If you read in the book of Ezekiel, chapter 43, there are two kinds of priests. There are Zadok priests and there are the others. Zadoks are the ones God says, "I am their reward." The other ones, that's not the case.

So David and Abishai walk out and you know what happens? Very shortly after, God judges Saul and who does he use? He uses the Philistines. Usually God will use the world to judge his servants. And the Philistines put Saul to death. When the Philistines put Saul to death, David does not go, "Man, he got what he deserved.

About time. Ruined about fourteen years of my life. Sleeping with rocks as pillows. About time God got him." That's an offended man.

See Jesus said, *"Out of the abundance of the heart the mouth will speak."* What does David do when Saul is judged by God? He teaches all the men of Judah a love song to sing to Saul. And he says, "Hey, don't proclaim it in the streets of Ashkelon lest the daughters of the Philistines rejoice." He said, "Oh Saul, you were lovely." And he teaches all the men to sing a love song to Saul.

And then a young man comes and reports to David—I'm actually backtracking—when he reports to David that Saul is dead in the battle, the young man thinks he is going to get brownie points with David. And David said, "How do you know he is dead?" He said, "Because he had been wounded severely to the point of death and he didn't want to be tortured so he asked me to run the sword through him and I did it." And David said, "How could you not be afraid to stretch out your hand against the Lord's anointed?" And David executed the man that he thought he was going to get brownie points. Because that man thought, "Wow, if I'm the one who tells him that I was the one who finished him off, this guy is going to be next king and he's going to give me a good place." Uh-uh. The very thing he thought he was going to get he didn't.

And then David hunted for one of Saul's descendants to bless him and he gave him land and he gave him a place at the king's table. Now does that sound to you like an offended man? David realized that the fourteen years he was running from Saul and the fourteen years of the persecution that he went through from Saul were actually the years God was training him to become the shepherd of Israel.

You see you have to understand this. God has placed dreams in every single one of you. You will run up against adversity. I remember one time the Lord showed me my spirit while I was praying. He said, "This is the dream that I have called you to." He said, "And here is where you are right now. And you think, John, all you have to do is go *zip* and you are there." He said, "No, no, no I send you through this wilderness, this crucible, this fiery, refining furnace, this wilderness, this desert, and then you go all the way around through all these places and then you end up here." And He said, "But son, you realize that you needed to go through this crucible, you need to go through this refining pot, you needed to go through this wilderness, and this and go through this and this and this in order to have the character to handle here." Saul never went through a wilderness, folks. He never went through a refining time. He didn't have the character to handle the leadership position he was given.

David in the desert, his character was developed. When Saul was persecuting and his own leader was not treating him right, turned that around instead of becoming offended ended up making it a stepping-stone in his life. Instead of an offense, which is a stumbling block in his life; he even ended up turning the very treatment that was out to kill him and destroy him and made it into a stepping-stone, which brought him to greatness.

Folks, let me make this really clear. I can't stress this enough. If God knows the very hairs on your head that are numbered, He knows the treatment that you have gotten from either another brother or sister or from a leader. There is no treatment that is ever come to you that has gone outside of God's attention. And how you handle that treatment is either how you are going to grow or you are going to become bitter and defiled. And the thing that is so sad is that all of heaven is cheering you on. All of heaven is saying, "I'm rooting for you. I want you to handle this right because if you could only see what's on the other side of this unfair treatment, if you could only see what's on the other side of this offensive treatment, if you could only see what I have for you; you would just go, 'Nothing to it.'"

Oh yeah, I can look back at those times and I can say, "Yeah, I remember they were painful, they hurt, they brought questions, a lot of pain in my heart." I've looked back now and I have treasured those times because, I will be honest with you, a hardest time in my life—and I don't know about you—but nothing is worse then unfair treatment especially from a leader. The hardest times in my life, I look back now they were the greatest stepping-stones, the greatest times of growth I have ever encountered. But the sad thing is, how many people don't get the blessing because they don't see the working of the Holy Spirit in their life in those times.

I was talking with a dear friend last night, Kevin, and I said to Kevin, I said, "Kevin, I am finally convinced one step of obedience when there is no feeling is worth far more than a thousand steps of obedience where there is feelings. Heaven will reveal it." Amen.

Lesson 4

How Spiritual Vagabonds Are Born

*And he said to his men, "The LORD forbid that I should do
this thing to my master, the LORD's anointed,
to stretch out my hand against him, seeing he is
the anointed of the LORD." So David restrained
his servants with these words, and did not allow
them to rise against Saul. And Saul got up
from the cave and went on his way.*
(1 Samuel 24:6-7)

Summary of *The Bait of Satan,* Chapter 5

When we hear or read the word "vagabond" we most
often think about wanderers, rootless people without a
home base. Combined with the word "spiritual," the
term vagabond indicates a person who has lost his or
her connection with God. This chapter begins by
expanding the lessons from David's life discussed in the
last chapter and illustrating the long-term dangers
found in taking up offense. David and many other
biblical people from Cain to Paul teach us that those
who hold offenses become spiritual wanderers.

Bevere moves from highlighting David's honor for a
harsh ruler to the parallel story of Samuel's service for
God under the corrupt leadership of Eli and his sons.
These attitudes of submission to authority contain

many lessons about our own responses to church leadership and God's standards for staying in or leaving churches. This section highlights the dual principles of sinking roots where God plants you and allowing the conditions God permits to have their healthy effects. John Bevere illustrates from his own life how easily we can be pulled into what seems to be a better spiritual situation when God clearly wants us to remain where things are more difficult.

Using a combination of principles from Genesis 4, Psalm 1, and Mark 4, this chapter demonstrates how the pursuit of an easier or more comfortable life often takes us away from God's will. The idea of spiritual vagabonds flows out of the clear teaching of God's Word. God's purposes cannot be summarized by a picture of the godly life as a life without trouble. In God's will, storms are often tools He uses to make us strong and drive our roots deeply into Him. Those, like Cain, who insist on ignoring what God has made clear will discover that God takes extraordinary measures to get their attention, and that the lessons become harder when they try to resist by taking offense. Meanwhile, lessons that we must learn may add to the suffering of those around us. The death of Abel offers us a shocking reminder of how much pain we can bring into the lives of others when we insist on taking offense. Our own actions cut us off from our spiritual home and we become vagabonds in the world.

Warm-Up Questions

Use the following questions to prepare your heart and mind for the personal and/or group study in which you will participate.

1. Up to this point, what would you say is the most challenging biblical insight you have gained from these sessions on *The Bait of Satan*?

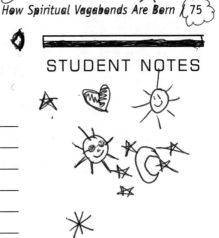

STUDENT NOTES

_____

_____

_____

_____

_____

_____

2. How would you describe the personal benefits of being able to read Bevere's presentation in the book and then watch him talk through each section on the videotape?

_____

_____

_____

_____

_____

3. If someone asked you to define what "taking offense" means, how would you summarize what you have been learning?

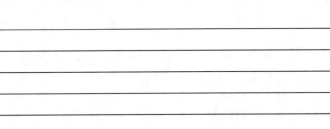

_____

_____

_____

_____

_____

Teaching by John Bevere

Watch the fourth session video presentation.

Personal Notes on Video Session 4

Use the following lines to keep notes as you view the video.

_____

_____

_____

_____

_____

_____

_____

_____

_____

_____

_____

As David stood over the sleeping Saul, he faced an important test. It would reveal whether David still had the noble heart of a shepherd or the insecurity of another Saul. Would he remain a man after God's heart? Initially it is so much easier when we take matters into our own hands, rather than waiting on a righteous God.

God tests His servants with obedience. He deliberately places us in situations where the standards of religion and society would appear to justify our actions. He allows others, especially those close to us, to encourage us to protect ourselves. We may even think

STUDENT NOTES

we would be noble and protect others by avenging ourselves. But this is not God's way. It is the way of the world's wisdom. It is earthly and fleshly.

—John Bevere, *The Bait of Satan*, p. 46

Teaching Review

Use the following questions to consider some of the central points made by John Bevere during this video session.

4. Bevere begins the session by drawing our attention to Romans 12:17. What is the first observation he makes about the character of Paul's statement, "Repay no one evil for evil"?

_____

_____

_____

_____

5. According to Bevere, what are the two groups of people that Jesus specifically singled out for prayer (Matthew 5:43–48 and Luke 6:27–36)?

_____

_____

_____

_____

6. Which of the following three passages best explains the kind of joy that Jesus experienced as He faced

the cross on our behalf: Philippians 4:4–7; Hebrews 12:1–2; or James 1:2–8? Why?

_____

_____

_____

_____

_____

_____

7. What picture of healthy spiritual life do Psalms 1 and 92 have in common?

_____

_____

_____

_____

_____

Exploring God's Word

Revisit the key passages from which John Bevere develops his teaching.

Romans 12:17–21 *Repay no one evil for evil. Have regard for good things in the sight of all men. If it is possible, as much as depends on you, live peaceably with all men. Beloved, do not avenge yourselves, but rather give place to wrath; for it is written, "Vengeance is Mine, I will repay," says the Lord. Therefore "If your enemy is hungry, feed him; if he is thirsty, give him a drink; for in so doing you will heap coals of fire on his head." Do not be overcome by evil, but overcome evil with good.*

8. This passage not only commands us not to avenge ourselves, it tells us what to do instead. What specific actions are we supposed to take toward those who treat us with evil?

9. How does Paul explain the command "give place to wrath," and how does that fit with our desire for vengeance?

10. Although the passage above is at the end of Romans 12, what does Bevere point out about the

===========

STUDENT NOTES

next chapter that gives us a good idea of what Paul had in mind as he wrote these verses?

response to
authority, have
respect

_____

_____

_____

_____

Personal Application

_____

_____

_____

_____

_____

_____

_____

_____

_____

_____

1 Samuel 3:1–4 _Now the boy Samuel ministered to the LORD before Eli. And the word of the LORD was rare in those days; there was no widespread revelation. And it came to pass at that time,_ *while Eli was lying down in his place, and when his eyes had begun to grow so dim that he could not see, and before the lamp of God went out in the tabernacle of the LORD where the ark of God was, and while Samuel was lying down, that the LORD called Samuel. And he answered, "Here I am!"*

11. Write out a brief description of each of the people through whom God worked in this part of Scripture: Hannah, Eli, Samuel, and Hophni and Phinehas.

A. Hannah — ~~drunk~~ drunkedness

B. Eli — ineffective as a father used mom to confirm hannas prayer, gave samuel advice.

C. Samuel — turned out good

STUDENT NOTES

D. Hophni & phinehas —

12. What significant points does Bevere draw from the relationship between Samuel and Eli?

Personal Application

STUDENT NOTES

Now don't get me wrong. The Bible is very clear that if the leader tells you to sin, you are not to obey the leader. But that's the only time you are not to obey a leader. But even if he tells you to sin, you still are to keep a submitted heart. In other words, you are still to honor him and respect him.

Shadrach, Meshach, and Abed-Nego looked at Nebuchadnezzar when he told him them to sin by bowing down to the idol and they said, "Your majesty, we will not do that." They spoke with respect. They didn't say, "You're a jerk. Who do you think you are?" They said, "Your majesty, we will not do that." They did not obey the command to sin, but they kept their respect for him (see Daniel 3).

—John Bevere, adapted from Video Session 4

Isaiah 55:12 *For you shall go out with joy, and be led out with peace; the mountains and the hills shall break forth into singing before you, and all the trees of the field shall clap their hands.*

13. Take a moment to review all of Isaiah 55 and note the subjects that were part of Isaiah's prophecy.

_____

_____

_____

_____

_____

_____

STUDENT NOTES

14. Bevere shares that this verse helped him see a key indication of how God moves us from one place to another, particularly one church to another. What points does he make from this verse?

joy & peace (are we enjoying God's)

Personal Application

Psalm 92:12–15 *The righteous shall flourish like a palm tree, he shall grow like a cedar in Lebanon. Those who are planted in the house of the LORD shall flourish in the courts of our God. They shall still bear fruit in old age; they shall be fresh and flourishing, to declare that the LORD is upright; He is my rock, and there is no unrighteousness in Him.*

STUDENT NOTES

15. Notice how many times the word "flourish" is used in these verses. What does it mean?

positive Synonym Synonym "Grow"

16. When David writes about "those who are planted in the house of the LORD," what kind of life is he talking about?

⊕ Stability

17. How do these verses compare to the message of Psalm 1?

location of planting from house to the law of Lord

STUDENT NOTES

_____

_____

_____

_____

_____

Personal Application

_____

_____

_____

_____

_____

_____

_____

_____

_____

_____

_____

_____

_____

_____

_____

Genesis 4:9–15 *Then the LORD said to Cain, "Where is Abel your brother?" He said, "I do not know. Am I my brother's keeper?" And He said, "What have you done? The voice of your brother's blood cries out to Me from the ground. So now you are cursed from the earth, which has opened its mouth to receive your brother's blood from your hand. When you till the ground, it shall no longer yield its strength to you. A fugitive and a vagabond you shall be on the earth." And Cain* *said to the LORD, "My punishment is greater than I can bear! Surely You have driven me out this day from the face of the ground; I shall be hidden from Your face; I shall be a fugitive and a vagabond on the earth, and it will happen that anyone who finds me will kill me." And the LORD said to him, "Therefore, whoever kills Cain, vengeance shall be taken on him sevenfold." And the LORD set a mark on Cain, lest anyone finding him should kill him.*

18. Read Genesis 4:1–8. How did God give Cain a clear opportunity to avoid the terrible choice he made in killing his brother?

    he didn't repent

19. What two descriptive words does God use in verse 11 (and Cain picks up in verse 14) that summarize the kind of life he will have because of his actions?

    ~~fugg~~ fugitive & vagabond

    pursicution complex

STUDENT NOTES

Personal Application

Exposing the Truth

Use the following questions to help reach conclusions regarding the Scriptures and insights from the session.

20. How would you explain to someone the concept Paul summarized with the statement, "Do not be overcome with evil, but overcome evil with good" (Romans 12:21)?

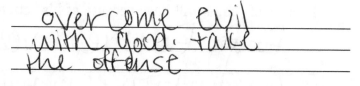

overcome evil with good. take the offense

21. Why do you think that Cain chose to kill his own brother rather than heed God's direct warnings that sin desired to possess him?

he was his brother was there doing right.

22. According to Bevere, why do the terms "fugitive" and "vagabond" clearly describe the experience of a person (like Cain) who decides to take up and hold an offense?

STUDENT NOTES

> The thing Cain feared the most, to be rejected by God, he brought as a judgment on himself. The very medium through which he tried to win God's approval was now cursed by his own hand. The bloodshed now brought a curse. The ground would no longer give up its strength to him. Fruit would come only through great effort.
>
> —John Bevere, *The Bait of Satan*, p. 54

Applying the Lesson

Use the following specific directions to internalize the principles in the session and put them into practice.

23. Although God's Word tells us to become like trees planted, it does not guarantee that such a life will be easy or always wonderful. What difficulties can you imagine that someone living like a godly, planted tree might have to endure and overcome?

_____

_____

_____

_____

_____

_____

_____

_____

_____

_____

24. As you think about your life at this moment, in what ways are you living as "a tree planted" and in what ways are you trying to be a tree that keeps transplanting itself?

_____

_____

_____

_____

_____

25. In what areas of your life are you hearing God speak to you about becoming more like a tree planted? What do you think that will take?

_____

_____

_____

_____

_____

Bait Warnings

A final opportunity for prayerful submission to the truth of the session.

> There are numerous spiritual fugitives and vagabonds in our churches today. Their gifts of singing, preaching, prophesying, and so on are not received by the leadership in their previous church, so off they go. They are running aimlessly and carry an offense, looking for that perfect church that will receive their gift and heal their hurts.

STUDENT NOTES

They feel beat up and persecuted. They feel as if they are modern-day Jeremiahs. It is "just them and God," with everyone else out to get them. They become unteachable. They get what I call a persecution complex: "Everyone is out to get me." They comfort themselves that they are just a persecuted saint or prophet of God. They are suspicious of everyone. This is exactly what happened to Cain . . .

God never created us to live separately and independently of each other. He likes it when His children care for and nurture each other. He is frustrated when we sulk and feel sorry for ourselves, making everyone else responsible for our happiness. He wants us to be active members of the family. He wants us to get our life from Him. An isolated person seeks only his own desire, not God's. He receives no counsel and sets himself up for deception.

I am not talking about seasons in which God calls individuals apart to equip and refresh them. I'm describing those who have imprisoned themselves. They wander from church to church, relationship to relationship, and isolate themselves in their own world. They think that all who do not agree with them are wrong and are against them. They protect themselves in their isolation and feel safe in the controlled environment they have set up for themselves. They no longer have to confront their own character flaws. Rather than facing the difficulties, they try to escape the test. The character development that comes only as they work through conflicts with others is lost as the cycle of offense begins again.

—John Bevere, *The Bait of Satan*, pp. 54-55

Video Script for Lesson 4
How Spiritual Vagabonds Are Born

We are in lesson 4 of *The Bait of Satan* video curriculum. I want you to open up your Bibles with me to Romans the twelfth chapter and also, to save time, let's put a marker in 1 Samuel, chapter 3. Romans chapter 12 is where we are going to begin.

Now, in the last lesson we saw how that David encountered hardship from a leader that God had placed over him. And we saw that David refused to avenge himself. I want to read here from verse 17, Romans chapter 12. Paul says, *"Repay no one evil for evil."* That was a good place to say, Amen. *"Have regard for good things in the sight of all men if it is possible."* In other words, sometimes it is not possible, okay. *"If it is possible, as much as depends on you,"* in other words, in your end of the deal, *"live peaceably with all men."* Verse 19, *"Beloved do not avenge yourselves."*

Is that a suggestion? Is it a recommendation? Is it a command? You will find this throughout the Scripture. It is an unrighteous thing for God's people to avenge themselves.

It is an unrighteous thing for God's people to avenge themselves. It is a righteous thing for God to avenge His people. Amen. The question is, will you wait? *"Beloved do not avenge yourselves but rather give place."* Make room for—alright, make room wrath, *"for it is written, vengeance is Mine, I will repay,"* says the Lord. Therefore if your enemy, now who's your enemy? That is the person who you would like to take vengeance on. If your enemy is hungry what does God say to do? Feed him. If he is thirsty, give him a drink. Do you know I was at an altar call just recently at a huge conference. I just got done ministering on how to handle unfair treatment and all the people before me, and something came out of my mouth and my

head had never thought of in my life. I said, "Folks," I said, "Jesus didn't tell us anywhere in the Gospel to pray for our wives and our husbands. He didn't tell us to pray for our parents in the Gospels. He didn't tell us to pray for our children." See, the only people that I know that He told us to pray for are your enemies and those who abuse you. *"Love your enemies and pray for those who despitefully use you and abuse you. Do good to those who mistreat you."* Your enemy—that's the person you would like to take vengeance on—is hungry feed him; if he is thirsty, give him a drink. *"For in so doing you will heap coals of fire upon his head."* What does it mean when he says, "You will heap coals of fire upon his head"? You will speed up the judgment process of God. You will slow down the judgment process of God by trying to take vengeance yourself.

Now, whenever somebody hears judgment, you know what they think of: hell, fire, and brimstone. Judgment simply means in the New Testament, it means decision. You know what God's decision may be—they may get saved or delivered. I mean, that was what Jesus was hoping for when he hung on the cross. Everybody's saying, "Father, wipe them off for putting me on this cross. Just let them have it. I feed them, do miracles among them, and look what they give me. Just let them have it."

You know that joy that was set before Him was that you get saved, I get saved. That was His joy. He didn't take offense. Aren't you glad? Because He could have said, "Father, send me six legions of angels right now and get me out of here, and let them all go to hell with the devil," and He would have been perfectly just. He said it, He said, "Do you not realize I could call six legions of angels right now and I could check out." That's not His attitude. He said, *"Father forgive them for they do not know what they are doing."* Now He wasn't just talking about that Roman solider in the Sanhedrin. He was talking about the next generation and the next generation and the next generation, because you and I put Him on that cross with our sin.

"Do not be overcome by evil but overcome evil with good." Now, Paul is not finished. He didn't write in chapter and verse the translators put it in. A lot of times people will miss what God is continuing to say by stopping at the end of the chapter and the next day picking up at the beginning of the next. They miss the transition. Isn't it interesting that the very next thing he says is, *"Let every soul be subject to the governing authorities, for there is no authority except from God and the authorities that exist are appointed by God."* So Paul is immediately talking about vengeance, being mistreated, and then immediately talks about, "There is no authority that is not appointed by God." Everybody say this with me (all authorities are appointed, not elected, they are appointed by God). Now that is a true statement. God is the one who appoints leadership. Nobody gets into leadership without God knowing about it. Amen.

Now isn't it interesting that Paul is talking about vengeance and then goes right into leadership? Now we saw that with David. God, not the devil, is the one who put David under Saul. Isn't that true? So the question we have to ask today is this: Why does God place His servants, His children, underneath leaders who make serious mistakes and even some that are wicked?

Now I will tell you, one guy who's a good example of that is Samuel. How many of you remember Samuel? Samuel, when he was a young boy, his mother dedicates him to the Lord. The Lord puts on his mother's heart to do that. And she puts

him under the leadership of Eli. Now Eli was the head priest and judge in Israel at this time. The ark of God was in Shiloh and Eli had leaders underneath him and two of his leaders were two of his own sons named Hophni and Phinehas. Now these guys were so corrupt, they're so wicked, that Hophni and Phinehas are literally going to bed committing adultery with women that are assembling at the door of the tabernacle. Not the gate, the door. The door is the entrance to the Holy Place. The gate is the entrance to the outer place. That's how corrupt these guys are. They are taking offerings by force. Eli is fat. You know when a person's fat, a lot of time the Scriptures make a point to make it and it means he is into himself.

Eli is so out of the Spirit, if you want to say it like that, Hannah is praying and Eli says, "Woman, you are full of wine. You are drunk." Now can you imagine if you come to a church, okay, and the head pastor looks at you while you are pouring your heart out to God and says, "You're full of wine; you are a drunk." Can you imagine? How many people in America would have responded to him, "You call yourself a pastor? I'm leaving. I am going to go to a church where they recognize when someone is praying and crying out to God." She would have left. But you know what is amazing to me is God used that corrupt priest to answer her prayer. Because when he found out she was praying he said, "May the God of Israel grant your petition after years of crying out to God." Now her prayer got answered because one year later she has a baby boy in her hands and his name was Samuel. And the thing that is amazing is she didn't get offended with him calling her a drunk because she brings Samuel back and puts him underneath him.

So, here's all this corruption going on, and Samuel's growing up and he's becoming a young man. Now what I find interesting is Samuel does not develop a committee and says you know what?

Eli's fat, he takes offerings by manipulation of force; his sons are committing adultery. Let's get up a committee and get him out and let's get somebody who seeks God into this pastorate.

Samuel doesn't do that. You know what the Bible says? This is the most amazing thing. Look at 1 Samuel, chapter 3. Look what the Bible says here. Verse 1, chapter 3. *"Now the boy Samuel ministered to the Lord before"—Eli."* In other words, Samuel ministered to the Lord and was completely submitted to Eli. He ministered to the Lord before him. He was submitted to his leadership. Now folks this is an amazing thing. Samuel did not pick up the offense. Why? Because he knew it was not his place to judge God's leader. It is not our responsibility to correct fathers; it is father's responsibility to correct children.

But I am amazed in my travels. Now folks, I travel in churches all around the world to conferences. I am amazed at how quickly today men and women will leave churches. It is an amazing thing. They didn't like the way the offering was taken; they didn't like the way the songs were sung; they didn't like what the pastor said; they didn't like the way the ushers treated them; they didn't like the way they were treated out in the parking lot.

To me it is an amazing thing how easily people leave churches today in the ministry teams. I have been born again for years and the last twenty-one years of my life I have been a member of three churches and I have lived in three different states. I don't understand this business of going from church to church to church to church, and I want to tell you something. In those churches that God has placed me, I have had tremendous, tremendous opportunities to get offended. And I am going to say this: In looking back, most of those opportunities of getting offended wasn't the problem of my leader, it was my immaturity.

I remember when I worked for my first pastor, when I was working for him I was his executive assistant. I felt he treated me harsh and I felt like he was making some wrong decisions. One day the Lord spoke to me and the Lord said, "I have a question for you." Now anytime God says, "I have a question for you," you're had, okay? Just remember that if you hear the Holy Spirit say that to you. He said, "Who put him in that leadership position, Me or you?" I said, "You did." He said, "You're right." And He said, "Therefore, I will show him things that I will on purpose keep hidden from you, just to see if you will follow him as he follows Me."

Now don't get me wrong the Bible is very clear that if the leader tells you to sin, you are not to obey the leader. But that's the only time you are not to obey a leader. But even if he tells you to sin, you still are to keep a submitted heart. In other words, you are still to honor him and respect him.

Shadrach, Meshach, and Abed-Nego looked at Nebuchanezzar when he told them to sin by bowing down to the idol and they said, "Your majesty, we will not do that." They spoke with respect they didn't say, "You jerk, who do you think you are?" They said, "Your majesty, we will not do that." They did not obey the command to sin, but they kept their respect for him.

Now in my experiences that I have gone through, I have had tremendous opportunities to be offended and leave. And I remember in one of those experiences, the Spirit of God spoke to me and He told me, He said, "Son, this is the way I ordained for my children to leave a ministry team or a church."

It is found in Isaiah 55, verse 12. I'm going to read it to you, you can look it up later. God says, *"For you shall go out with joy and be led out with peace."* Should I read it again? *"For you shall go out with joy and be led forth [or out] with peace."* Whenever God tells you to leave, you will go out with joy. Now it may be chaotic, you may have a situation that maybe a pastor has done something and God has said; "Now it's time to leave." I mean, let me tell you something. Whenever God exposes a leader's sin, that is usually the time when God says, "It is time to go." God will actually protect the leader for a long time trying to minister to that leader, to get him out of the sin, but he will protect you in the midst of it. Or when the sin gets exposed, that is God saying, "It's time to go." Even in those situations, even as grieved as you are at what happened, you will still leave with a peace in your heart knowing that the Holy Spirit now is telling you to go.

Now I remember there was a time because, let me tell you that most people, I would say 90 percent of the people today, when they leave ministries or churches, is because of offense. Very, very few times people leave ministries today because of not being offended. And I remember when I was in one of the churches that I was in, it just got to the place where it was getting very difficult. I was traveling, I felt like my wife and children were not getting pastored, and there was a couple that were friends. And they were kind of offended by the pastor and we were offended by the pastor, alright?

Now I have noticed that offended people will gravitate toward each other. It's amazing; they will find each other and gravitate. Then you think they're your best friends. And I thought these guys were my best friends because whenever I came back from a trip, I tell you one time when we came back from a trip, our refrigerator was filled. They filled our refrigerator, they prayed for us, they loved us, and they left and started a church about sixty miles away. And they said to Lisa and I, "We want you to come and we want you to be in our church. We want you to be one of the elders because we know there is a call of

God in your life to the nation. We want you to travel in and out of our church, and we will let you speak here whenever you are home, and we will really pastor your wife and kids. I tell you I was like, 'Hah! This is what we need.'"

So I remember leaving the church that God had put me in and I went over to their church for four months, my wife and children. When we were in their church, it was wonderful how we were getting treated, but I wasn't feeling right in my spirit. Then as time went by, things started getting uncomfortable with them. Just things weren't jelling.

So after four months, I looked at this friend and I said, "You know what?" I said, "I feel like I really need to return back to our other church where we left." And he wasn't real happy about it, but he said, "Alright if that's what you really feel to do." And I will never forget this as long as I live folks. I have been away from my church for four months and I went back and the moment—this is the most amazing thing—the moment my foot stepped in the sanctuary, I walked through the lobby of the church and the moment my foot stepped inside the sanctuary, the Holy Spirit shouted this on the inside of me. He said, "I never told you to leave." And I went, "That's it." Wait a minute. I mean just lights went off in the inside of me. I said, "Lord, You were the one who spoke to me to come to this church and You never said leave."

See folks, let me tell you something. I've learned this. When God is not speaking, He is speaking. You know what He is saying? "Don't change anything. Keep doing what you are doing."

See, I have an announcement this morning. This may be a real revelation to some of you. You don't get to choose where you go to church. I'm glad a couple of you got that. Shall I say that one again? You don't get to choose where you go to church.

You know what my Bible says in 1 Corinthians 12? Listen to me, "God has set the members in the body as He pleases." It does not say, "God allows the members to go wherever they please." God has set the members in the body as He pleases.

Now there is a fabulous Scripture found in Psalm 92. It's so good. Psalm 92, verse 13. *"Those who are planted." "Those who are planted"*—oh man, this is good—*"in the house of the Lord shall flourish in the courts of our God."* Those that are planted, flourish. Now it doesn't say those who are transplanted. What happens to a tree, a fruit tree, if you uproot it and transplant it every couple of months? The root system begins to dwarf. Are you with me? The roots system begins to dwarf and eventually it stops producing fruit, and eventually, if you keep transplanting it, it dies.

Do you know what folks? Do you know what trees use to send their roots down? Trees will use adverse weather to send their roots down deeper. Adversity causes trees to grow deeper. But if the farmer listened to the tree, if the tree could speak, the tree would say, "Get me out of here, I hate this." And if the farmer transplanted it, guess what? It would rob a tree from the opportunity to send its roots deeper. Why? Because in a drought that tree has to go deeper to find water.

I have a friend who lives in the area of a country that went through a severe drought, and all of a sudden their toilets all stopped working. So they called the Roto-Rooter man out. The Roto-Rooter Man came out and said, "Yep, just what I suspected. A root from a tree sensed the moisture from inside the PVC pipe and went right through it." What caused that tree to have the kind of tenacity? The adversity.

So what happens is, people start running from church to church to church to church. Because the first time you leave out of an offense it's going to be easier the next time to leave out of offense. Why? Because your root system is dwarfed. Psalm chapter 1, write this down, and Psalm 119:165. Psalm 1, verses 1 and 2, said, *"Blessed is the man whose delight"*—now I'm leaving a few parts out there—*"Blessed is the man whose delight is in the law of the Lord [the word of God], and in His law he meditates day and night."* Psalm 119:165 says, *"Great peace have they which love [or delight] in Your law."* *"Great peace have they which love [or delight] in Your law and nothing shall offend them."* Nothing shall offend them. Now watch, Psalm 1 goes on to say, *"He shall be."* Who's he, who delights in the law? Who loves the law of the Lord? Nothing shall offend him. *"He shall be like a tree planted by the rivers of the water that brings forth fruit in its season, whose leaf does not wither and whatever he does prospers."* So what is God saying to us in those two scriptures? He's saying a person who likes the law of the Lord is the one who's rooted and grounded. His roots go down deep and, even in adversity, he will produce fruit.

And do you know what I find amazing? You know we lived in Florida for twelve years. Do you know what I found out? In Florida, the juice of the oranges does not get sweet until you have cold, until you have adverse weather. Then the juice becomes sweet.

If we allow the adversity, if we allow the Holy Spirit to work in our lives the way He wants to, when adversity comes we would become sweeter in our fruit. Amen.

Listen to what Jesus says in Mark, chapter 4, verses 16 and 17. I am going to read it to you out of the King James; just look up and listen. He said, *"And these are they likewise that are sown on stony ground who when they have heard the word immediately receive it with gladness."* So we aren't talking about a sinner here. Sinners do not receive the Word with gladness. We are talking about people on Sunday mornings, Sunday nights, Wednesday nights, who go, "Wow, Pastor Rob that is so good." *"Who immediately receive the Word with gladness and have no root."* No root in themselves and so endure for a time, but afterwards, when affliction or persecution arises for the words sake, they immediately are offended. Why are they offended, they have not allowed the roots to go down. You want to find shallow trees? Just send a hurricane through Florida, you will find all the shallow trees. They're gone; they're uprooted. But you want to find all the strong trees.

I remember when I was in Florida I went by this Cypress tree that was around when Moses was around. They had a sign on it that says how old he was. He was a four thousand year old Cypress tree. Let me tell you, plenty of hurricanes went through there and didn't do a thing to him. Why, he's rooted.

When you leave out of an offense, your root system dwarfs, so the next time it is easier to leave again. And the next time it is even easier to leave again. And the next time it is easier to leave again. Whether it is a marriage or a church or whatever it is, it is easier to leave again, it's easier leave again, it's easier to leave again. If you don't deal with the offense, your root system keeps getting short and you know what happens? You become a spiritual vagabond. You know what a vagabond is? A wanderer. You wander from ministry to ministry, to church to church to church.

Now there was another guy who was a vagabond. His name is Cain. Go to Genesis, chapter 4. Now, I find an amazing thing here folks. Now whenever you think of Cain and Abel, the problem is because of the outcome. We always think, Cain is, oh man, this guy was wicked sinner. He represents the guy in the bars, and all this stuff. No, no, no, no—read carefully. These are two sons of Adam and Eve, and both of them are diligently

working to bring an offering to the Lord. I have news for you people out there in the bars not bringing an offering to the Lord this morning, who were out there last night, Saturday night, are not here Sunday morning bringing their offerings. We are talking about two guys who are diligently working to bring their offerings to the Lord. In fact, if you really think about it, Cain's working harder. I know a little about farming, I know a little about shepherding, but I know enough to know this: farming is harder work. Shepherding you take care of the animals in the morning and afternoon, but you can sit underneath a palm tree and sip on a cool one during heat part of the day. Farming you have to operate the whole day. So Cain's working harder, but yet when he brings an offering the Bible says God rejects Cain and his offering. Why does God not accept Cain's offering? Well, you have to go back to the parents to find out. When Adam and Eve sinned in the Garden, the first thing that they notice is they are naked. So what do they do? They attempted what? Clothe themselves. What did they use? Fig leaves, fruits of the ground. God comes in the Garden and says, "No, no, this is not my way. This is my way." He kills an animal and clothes them.

Now Adam and Eve were ignorant. Cain and Abel weren't. Cain and Abel had learned from their mom and dad what was acceptable to God and what was obedience. So when Cain brings this fruit of the ground, it represents a disobedient offering. He is serving God his own way. And so when God rejects him, God says to him, "Look at this."

Look at verse 4. *"Abel brought of the firstborn of his flock and of their fat, and the Lord respected Abel and his offering but he did not respect Cain and his offering."* See, there is a lie that the charismatics have propagated, that is God will accept you just the way you are. Wrong. God will accept you just the way you are if you repent.

See, tell Ananias and Sapphira that God will accept them just the way they are. It's too late.

Verse 5, *"But He did not respect Cain and his offering and Cain was very angry and his countenance fell."* Okay, offense has just come in. So the Lord says in verse 7, hey Cain, *"If you do well [in other words if you obey me], will you not be accepted just like your brother? But if you do not obey me, sin lies at the door."* Oooh, so we see offense is the doorway into sin.

Now watch this. *"And its desire is for you but you should rule over it."* Well folks, you know what happened? Cain doesn't obey, right? His offense turns to what? Rage. His rage turns into betrayal, and his betrayal turns into murder. And he murders his brother. Here is a guy who starts out serving God, he ends up murdering his brother.

Now, God then pronounces the judgment that is upon Cain and I want you to look at the eleventh verse. God says, *"So now you are cursed from the earth which has opened its mouth to receive your brother's blood from your hand. When you till the ground it shall no longer yield its strength to you. A fugitive and a vagabond you will be on the earth."* God says, "Now because you have picked up the offense, you disobeyed, now you are going to become a vagabond, a wanderer."

Look at Cain's reaction to the judgment. Verse 14, *"Surely you have driven me out this day from the face of the ground. I should be hidden from your face, I should be a fugitive and vagabond on the earth and it will happen that anyone who finds me will kill me."* "Anyone who finds me will kill me." You know what Cain now has developed? A persecution complex: "Everybody's out to get me." That's exactly what happens to people when they get offended. They become spiritual wanderers because they think, "Everybody's out to get me. It's me and God." It's almost like Jeremiah thing, you know. "Well, nobody really understands, but God knows what I am doing because He spoke unto me." And they isolate themselves because they have a persecution complex, everybody's out to get me. Now I know I am ending this on a very heavy note but listen. You need to think about it because, unfortunately, there are countless, countless people outside of churches and people that are running from church to church to church today because they have a persecution complex because they picked up an offense. Don't pick-up the bait. Amen.

Lesson 5

Hiding from Reality

*[They are] always learning and never able to come
to the knowledge of the truth.*
(2 Timothy 3:7)

Summary of *The Bait of Satan,* Chapter 6

In this chapter, John Bevere begins to outline some of
the hidden dangers that arise when we fail to recognize
that we have taken up an offense. For example, people
who leave ministry positions often give as their primary
reason their need to "survive." They explain their
decision to depart as "self-preservation." Often, the
feelings people call "the need for self-preservation" are
actually feelings that flow from taking up an offense.

When we use hardship and discomfort as reasons for
removing ourselves from a situation, we may actually
demonstrate that we do not understand how God
operates in our lives. According to Bevere, we can gain
a perspective on this misunderstanding by looking at
the way God uses the two Greek terms for "sons" in the
New Testament. One (*teknon*) has to do with a biological
fact of sonship. The other (*huios*) describes a father-
child relationship based on character and appearance. In
other words, a *teknon* is known by others as his or her
father's child by birth, while a *huios* looks and acts so
much like his father, that people automatically conclude
they are father-child.

STUDENT NOTES

Bevere uses a number of biblical examples, like Balaam and Elijah, to illustrate the two kinds of relationships with God. He also describes how that understanding plays itself out in his own relationship with his children as well as with those with whom he ministers. All of these illustrations have as their underlying lesson the warning of what can happen when we fail to recognize the results of taking offense in our lives.

When we try to hide from the reality of our past experiences and relationships by not dealing with them in godly and biblical ways, we find that our new relationships are complicated by the baggage we carry with us. Taking up an offense is a lot like picking up a heavy suitcase. If we insist on carrying it with us, even though it contains nothing of eternal value to us, it will slow us down and wear us out.

Warm-Up Questions

Use the following questions to prepare your heart and mind for the personal and/or group study in which you will participate.

1. Scientists point out that the root system of a healthy tree is often as large and as deep below the ground as the tree stands and spreads its branches and leaves above the ground. Since passages like Colossians 2:7 indicate that we're to think of ourselves as spiritual trees, what have you learned about what causes our roots to grow deep into Christ?

_____

_____

_____

_____

_____

2. What are the primary ways God uses to give us direction?

    _____

    _____

    _____

    _____

    _____

    _____

    _____

3. How do you think believers should handle those situations when the directions they are receiving seem to be contradictory? If your feelings tell you one thing, your friends another, your pastor another, and God's Word doesn't seem to have a specific direction, what do you do?

    _____

    _____

    _____

    _____

    _____

Teaching by John Bevere

Watch the fifth session video presentation.

Personal Notes on Video Session 5

Use the following lines to keep notes as you view the video.

There is an old parable that fits this situation. Back in the days when the settlers were moving to the West, a wise man stood on a hill outside a new Western town. As the settlers came from the East, the wise man was the first person they met before coming to the settlement. They asked eagerly what the people of the town were like.

He answered them with a question: "What were the people like in the town you just left?"

Some said, "The town we came from was wicked. The people were rude gossips who took advantage of innocent people. It was filled with thieves and liars."

The wise man answered, "This town is the same as the one you left."

They thanked the man for saving them from the trouble they had just come out of. They then moved on further west.

Then another group of settlers arrived and asked the same question: "What is this town like?"

The wise man asked again, "What was the town like where you came from?"

These responded, "It was wonderful! We had dear friends. Everyone looked out for the others' interest. There was never any lack because all cared for one another. If someone had a big project, the entire community gathered to help. It was a hard decision to leave, but we felt compelled to make way for future generations by going west as pioneers."

The wise old man said to them exactly what he had said to the other group: "This town is the same as the one you left."

These people responded with joy, "Let's settle here!" How they viewed their past relations was their scope for their future ones.

The way you leave a church or a relationship is the way you will enter into your next church or relationship. Jesus said in John 20:23, "If you forgive the sins of any, they are forgiven them; if you retain the sins of any, they are retained."

—John Bevere, *The Bait of Satan*, pp. 61-62

Teaching Review

Use the following questions to consider some of the central points made by John Bevere during this video session.

4. Bevere begins this session talking about the number of times he is asked, "When should I leave a church

or ministry team?" How does he answer that question?

_____

_____

_____

_____

5. How does Bevere explain his statement, "When God is not speaking, He is speaking"?

_____

_____

_____

_____

_____

_____

_____

_____

_____

6. Before Bevere takes us on a quick tour of 1 Peter, how does he describe the purpose of that letter from the chief of the apostles?

_____

_____

_____

_____

_____

7. What were the central lessons you got from John's story of the insurance executive who was passed over for an important promotion he clearly deserved?

_____

_____

_____

_____

_____

_____

_____

_____

_____

_____

_____

_____

_____

There are two kinds of persecutions: self-inflicted and persecution for righteousness's sake. Self-inflicted persecution is when we do what is wrong and God has set up authorities over us to punish us for it, or discipline, or correct us, or train us. Now there is a real easy way to get rid of that persecution totally and that is change your behavior. Get wisdom and change your behavior. And then there is persecution for righteousness's sake. That is when you do what is right and you get treated unfairly because of it. The Bible says, "Just have a party, whirl and twirl, because great is your reward in heaven!"

—John Bevere, adapted from Video Session 5

Exploring God's Word

Revisit the key passages from which John Bevere develops his teaching.

> **Romans 8:14–17** *For as many as are led by the Spirit of God, these are sons of God. For you did not receive the spirit of bondage again to fear, but you received the Spirit of adoption by whom we cry out, "Abba, Father." The Spirit Himself bears witness with our spirit that we are children of God, and if children, then heirs—heirs of God and joint heirs with Christ, if indeed we suffer with Him, that we may also be glorified together.*

8. The two terms "sons" and "children" are used in these verses to indicate that there are two different Greek words behind them, though each one could be translated "sons." How does the phrase that includes the word "sons" show the relational, character traits of the Greek term *huios* that Bevere explained?

_____

_____

_____

_____

_____

_____

_____

_____

9. How does the phrase that uses "children" twice
   convey the sense of basic "spiritual birth" that we
   receive by adoption in Christ (see the extended
   discussion in *The Bait of Satan,* pp. 58-59)?

_____

_____

_____

_____

_____

_____

_____

_____

Personal Application

_____

_____

_____

_____

_____

_____

_____

_____

_____

STUDENT NOTES

When Addison was first born, you couldn't tell who was my son in that nursery. But years went by and when he was about six or seven years old, I remember my wife and I went away on vacation and my mom watched Addison and Austin. At that time just the two of them were born. I remember when we came back, my mom was laughing hysterically.

She said, "That boy is so much like you. He is a spitting image of you." She said, "John, he is doing things you that you used to do when you were born that you don't even do anymore."

Now it's amazing thing, but the older he gets the more he becomes like me. You can tell now that he is John Bevere's son because he acts a lot like me. Sometimes I get upset because I am looking at things that I realize are just a big part of me and I don't like them. I'm thinking, "Do I really act like that?"

And Lisa goes, "Oh yeah you do."

And so now you can tell he is John Bevere's son because he looks more like me and he acts a lot more like me. But, listen. As he displays my character, hopefully he is going to imitate maturity. And the older he becomes, the more mature he becomes; therefore, the more responsibility I can give him.

—John Bevere, adapted from Video Session 5

Matthew 5:43–45 *"You have heard that it was said, 'You shall love your neighbor and hate your*

*enemy.' But I say to you, love your enemies, bless
those who curse you, do good to those who hate
you, and pray for those who spitefully use you and
persecute you, that you may be sons of your Father
in heaven; for He makes His sun rise on the evil
and on the good, and sends rain on the just and
on the unjust."*

10. What four actions does Jesus spell out that
    contribute to our becoming "sons of our Father in
    heaven"? Write these on the blanks below. Circle
    the letter of the one that you find personally most
    challenging to carry out.

    _____

    _____

    _____

    _____

    _____

11. What insight does Bevere draw out of Jesus'
    explanation behind His statement—"for He makes
    his sun rise on the evil and on the good"?

    _____

    _____

    _____

    _____

    _____

    _____

    _____

    _____

STUDENT NOTES

Personal Application

_____

_____

_____

_____

_____

_____

_____

_____

_____

_____

_____

_____

_____

_____

_____

_____

Now, how many of you know that you do not become a child of God by your works? It is by grace that we are saved. But when you understand the two different Greek words for sonship, you understand what Jesus is saying in Matthew 5:44–45. He is saying, "When you start living like this, you will become like your Father." You will become mature sons. You will display His character because He causes His sun to shine on the wicked just like He does the just. Are you seeing this? He feeds the wicked just like He feeds the just.

—John Bevere, adapted from Video Session 5

1 Peter 2:20–22 *For what credit is it if, when you are beaten for your faults, you take it* *patiently? But when you do good and suffer, if you take it patiently, this is commendable before God. For to this you were called, because Christ also suffered for us, leaving us an example, that you should follow His steps: "Who committed no sin, nor was deceit found in His mouth."*

1 Peter 3:9 *Not returning evil for evil or reviling for reviling, but on the contrary blessing, knowing that you were called to this, that you may inherit a blessing.*

1 Peter 4:1 *Therefore, since Christ suffered for us in the flesh, arm yourselves also with the same mind, for he who has suffered in the flesh has ceased from sin.*

12. What theme do these verses from 1 Peter have in common?

_____

_____

_____

_____

_____

13. How does 1 Peter 3:9 present the case for the correct response to unfair treatment and what does it promise as a result?

_____

_____

_____

STUDENT NOTES

_____

_____

_____

_____

_____

_____

_____

_____

_____

Personal Application

_____

_____

_____

_____

_____

_____

_____

_____

_____

_____

_____

I will never forget the time there was a person who had authority in my life and they were making all kinds of statements against me. I was frantically defending myself and the offense was building in me as I defended myself. Why? Because when you defend yourself, you forfeit your spiritual right of protection. You elevate that person's influence in your life because the very fact that you have to answer them makes them your judge. You don't have to answer anybody except your Judge and the authority that God puts over you. (Chew on that one for a few minutes.) And the Spirit of God spoke to me and said, "Son, as long as you defend yourself, I'm doing this." And I saw the Lord standing with His hands behind His back. He said, "But the moment you stop defending yourself, I'll be at work on your behalf." This is what Jesus did. Why? Because Jesus knew the Father would judge His case. His behavior caused Pilate to marvel.

—John Bevere, adapted from Video Session 5

Hebrews 5:8 *Though He was a Son, yet He learned obedience by the things which He suffered.*

14. Based on what you have learned about the two kinds of sonship (*huios*—intimate, mature, and *teknon*—basic and factual), which kind of sonship does this verse attribute to Jesus?

STUDENT NOTES

_____

_____

_____

_____

_____

_____

_____

15. So, according to this verse, does intimate sonship between us and God come before or after suffering? Why?

_____

_____

_____

_____

_____

_____

_____

_____

Personal Application

_____

_____

_____

_____

_____

_____

_____

_____

_____

_____

_____

Exposing the Truth

Use the following questions to help reach conclusions regarding the Scriptures and insights from the session.

16. Summarize what Bevere has been teaching about the importance of "staying put" when the pressures and suffering come and the temptation is to expect God to release us.

_____

_____

_____

_____

_____

_____

_____

_____

_____

_____

_____

17. What exactly is the "reality" that Bevere is referring to in this session?

_____

_____

STUDENT NOTES

_____

_____

_____

_____

_____

_____

_____

_____

18. What blessings have you noticed in this session
that can flow when we respond to opportunities for
offense by blessing and overcoming evil with good?

_____

_____

_____

_____

_____

_____

_____

_____

_____

_____

_____

_____

_____

_____

"As Christ suffered for us"—what was he talking
about? He was talking about unfair treatment. Let's
take the whole chapter in context. He said, "Arm

yourself with the same mind." Most believers are not armed to suffer. That's why they are so easily offended. So, because they are not armed, they react instead of act. They go into a state of shock. They go into a state of bewilderment or amazement when they are mistreated. The offense is easily picked up and now they are reacting instead of acting.

Let me show you the difference between someone who is armed and someone who is not. I fly two hundred thousand miles a year. I'm on a lot of commercial jets. I have learned that every six months the companies send those commercial pilots to practice in flight simulators. These are huge machines filled with computers, but you would never know if you were in a real plane or not in a real plane. What they do for three days is throw every single problem that could happen to a plane at those guys. And I mean they will crash, crash, crash and then they start acting properly. Are you with me?

So they are arming those guys. So in a real crisis in a real plane you can have the people in the back screaming, and the pilots are calmly acting. There may be chaos in the cabin with the passengers, but when the investigators listen to the black boxes they hear the pilots acting like they are in a simulator. "Do this. Pull up. Check that indicator. Push that. Check, check, check, check." They're acting in total control because they are armed by practice and preparation.

—John Bevere, adapted from Video Session 5

Applying the Lesson

Use the following specific directions to internalize the principles in the session and put them into practice.

19. Just as Jesus "learned obedience through what He suffered" so to, we don't learn the meaning of obedience until we put ourselves at risk of suffering. What in particular held offense or broken relationship in your life needs to undergo an examination of obedience? Entirely apart from what the other person has done toward you, to what extent have you responded like Christ toward him or her?

_____

_____

_____

_____

_____

20. What specific blessing or good could you give that person or do for that person that would be a conscious action of overcoming evil with good?

_____

_____

_____

_____

_____

21. What have you discovered is the most difficult aspect of learning to respond to offensive situations without taking offense?

_____

_____

_____

_____

_____

_____

_____

Bait Warnings

A final opportunity for prayerful submission to the truth of the session.

> Intellectual growth, is it limited to time? No, we have fourteen year olds that have graduated from high school. We have fifty year olds that haven't. Intellectual growth is not a function of time. It is a function of what? Of learning. You go from first to second to third, but you can do it fast or slow.
>
> Spiritual growth, is it a function of time? No, we have people that have been born again twenty years but they still wear spiritual Pampers and make the most noise in the church. Spiritual growth is not a function of time. You have other people that are born again one year but they are giants. It's not a function of time. Is it a function of learning? No. If the Pharisees can quote the first five books of the Bible but they can't recognize the Son of God who's casting the devil out in front of their faces, then spiritual growth is not a function of learning. What is spiritual growth a function of? Suffering. "He who has suffered in the flesh has ceased from sin."
>
> —John Bevere, adapted from Video Session 5

Video Script for Lesson 5
Hiding from Reality

Romans 8, I want to look at the fourteenth verse. Paul says, *"For as many as are led by the Spirit of God, these are the sons of God."* Now let's say that together. ("For as many as are led by the Spirit of God, these are the sons of God.") Now can I ask you a question? Is everybody you know in the church led by the Spirit of God? No. I know a lot of people that are led by their emotions, by their feelings, by their offenses but yet God clearly says there, *"For as many led by the Spirit of God, these are the sons of God."*

Now to really understand this verse you have to understand there are two Greek words translated "sons" and "children" in the New Testament, two major Greek words. The first Greek word is *teknon*. Now *teknon* is found here in Romans chapter 8, verse 16. *"The Spirit himself bears witness with our spirit that we are children of God."* That is the Greek word *teknon*. Now I went to Kenneth Wuest, who is an expert in Greek New Testament words, and Kenneth Wuest makes a statement on the Greek word *teknon*. He says, *teknon*, a real good definition of it is the way it is used in the New Testament is one who is a son or daughter by mere fact of birth.

Now sixteen years ago my wife had our firstborn son named Addison. And I remember as a real happy, excited, proud new dad, I ran into the nursery and there was the big glass window and it was all these little babies in there in these little plexiglass cribs. And you know what? I looked at every single one of those Caucasian babies and all of them looked the same. They all looked alike. I did not know which one was my son. It wasn't until I spotted the word "Bevere" above the little plexiglass crib and I said, "There he is! That's my son." He was my son by mere fact that he came out of Lisa.

Now, that is a good rendering of the word *teknon*. You will find the word *teknon* used in John chapter 1, verse 12. *"For as many as received Him, He gave the power to become sons of God."* The word "sons" there is *teknon*. You were a son by mere fact of birth.

Now the second word here we find in the New Testament that is used in translating the word "sons" is the Greek word *huios*. Now Vine's says this about *huios*. He says the way this is used in the New Testament is one who can be identified as the son because he displays the character of the parent. In other words, you can tell he's the son because he displays the character of the father and mother. Addison, when he was first born, you couldn't tell who was my son in that nursery. But years went by and when he was about six or seven years old I remember my wife and I went away on vacation and my mom watched Addison and Austin. I remember when we came back—my mom was laughing hysterically. She said, "That boy is so much like you. He is a spitting image of you." She said, "John, he is doing things that you used to do when you were a boy that you don't even do anymore." Now it's an amazing thing, but the older he gets the more he becomes like me. You can tell now that he is John Bevere's son because he acts a lot like me. Sometimes I get upset because I am looking at things that I realize that are just a big part of me and I don't like them. I'm thinking, "Do I really act like that?" and Lisa goes, "Oh yeah you do." And so now you can tell he is John Bevere's son because he looks more like me and he acts a lot more like me. As he displays my character, hopefully he is going to imitate my maturity. And the older he becomes, the more mature he becomes; therefore, the more responsibility I can give him.

So if you really want to come down with a simplistic term, *teknon* means immature sons. *Huios* is used to describe mature sons. Now when Paul says here, *"For as many as are led by the Spirit of God these are the sons of God."* The Greek word there, "sons," is the Greek word *huios* which means mature sons. So you can tell a mature son by the fact that he is what? Led by the Spirit of God. You can tell by the character of the heavenly Father which he displays.

Now we see this very clearly in Matthew chapter 5, verses 44 and 45. Listen to what Jesus said. He said, *"But I say to you, love your enemies." "Bless those who curse you."* Wouldn't it be wonderful if we lived this? *"Do good to those who hate you."* Find everybody that hates you and do the best you can for them and pray for those who spitefully, wow, use you and persecute you. *"That you may become sons* [Greek word *huios*] *of your Father in heaven."* Now how many of you know that you do not become a child of God by your works? It is by grace that we are saved. But when you understand the two different Greek words, you understand what Jesus is saying. He is saying, "When you start living like this, you will become like your Father." You will become mature sons; you will display His character because He causes His sun to shine on the wicked just like He does the just. He feeds the wicked just like He feeds the just.

Now go to 1 Peter, chapter 4. First Peter, the fourth chapter. Now one of the ways that my son grew—Addison grew—is by facing difficult situations. How many of you know as a parent whenever your kids face difficult situations sometimes you want to step in and help them out? But you know as a wise parent, you learn you don't step in. You let him grow off of his difficult situations, Amen.

Well, the Bible says this in Hebrews, chapter 5, verse 9. *"Though he was a son he learned obedi-ence by what he suffered."* Jesus didn't bring obedience to the earth He learned it. And how did He learn it? By that which He suffered.

Now when you come to the book of 1 Peter, I love this book. First Peter is a book that describes to us believers how to handle difficult situations, unfair treatment, etc. How many of you have ever received unfair treatment? Every one of you. Now this is what happens: you have a chance to either pick up an offense when you incur unfair treatment or you have the chance to let God defend you.

In 1 Peter chapter 2, Peter is talking about receiving unfair treatment. And he makes this statement here. He says in verse 20 of chapter 2, *"What credit is it if you are beaten for your fault, you take it patiently."* In other words, when you are doing what's wrong and authority beats you for it or punishes you for it or disciplines you for it; don't act like you are being persecuted. You're getting what you deserve. In other words, when the red lights are flashing, blue lights are flashing, in your rearview mirror, don't bind the devil. You just got a speeding ticket. You got what you deserve. Amen.

There are two kinds of persecutions: self-afflicted and persecution for righteousness' sake. Self-afflicted persecution is when we do what is wrong and God has set up authorities over us to punish us or discipline or correct us or train us. Now there is a real easy way to get rid of that persecution totally, and that is change your behavior; get wisdom and change your behavior. And then there is persecution for righteousness' sake and that is when you would do what is right and you get treated unfairly because of it and the Bible says, "Just have a party, whirl and twirl because great is your reward in heaven." Amen. So he goes on to say in verse 21, *"For to this you are called."* Now as a preacher many times people come up to me and they say, "You know, pastor, what am I called to do?" Well guess what? Here it is in black and white. This is your calling. Some people go to Bible school for four years to find out what they are called to do. Here it is right there in black and white. This is my calling.

For to this you are called because Christ also suffered for us leaving us an example that you should follow in His steps. Now I want to read this out of the Amplified. It is a little clearer. *"For even to this you are called. It is inseparable from your vocation. For Christ also suffered for you leaving you his personal example so that you should follow in his footsteps."*

What was His personal example? Verse 22, *"Who committed no sin nor was deceit found in His mouth who when He was reviled or insulted, did not revile in return. When He suffered He did not threaten,"* but what did He do? Here is the key. *"But He committed Himself to Him who judges righteously."*

Peter is talking about when Jesus was in the courtroom with Pilate. The leaders of the nation were bringing violent, railing accusations against Him. But Jesus didn't answer a word and didn't defend Himself. Why? Because He left the judgment in the hands of the Father who would judge righteously. He knew God would judge His case.

I will never forget the time there was a person who had authority in my life and they were making all kinds of statements against me. I was frantically defending myself and the offense was building in me as I defended myself. Because when you defend yourself you—you forfeit your spiritual right of protection. You elevate that person's influence—you elevate that person's influence in your life because the very fact that you have to answer them makes them your judge. You don't have to answer anybody except your judge and the authority that God puts over you. Chew

on that one for a few minutes. And the Spirit of God spoke to me and said, "Son, as long as you defend yourself I'm doing this," and I saw the Lord standing with His hands behind His back. He said, "But the moment you stop defending yourself," He said, "I'm at work on your behalf." This is what Jesus did. Why? Because Jesus knew the Father would judge His case. His behavior caused Pilate to marvel.

So Peter goes on to say, look at this third chapter because the whole book is about this. He says, *"Finally, all of you be of one mind having compassion for one another, love his brothers, be tenderhearted, and be courteous."* What Peter is doing here is giving you the formula on how to keep yourself from becoming offended.

Verse 9, *"Not returning evil for evil, or reviling for reviling, or insult for insult."* Folks let me say this. I can't emphasize this enough. When you defend yourself, when you give in to a quarrel and strife with somebody, you create an atmosphere in your heart. A condition of your heart that makes you a prime candidate for offense. So he says, *"Not returning evil for evil—verse 9—not reviling for reviling, but on the contrary blessing."* When you are insulted, he said, "Bless back, knowing that you are called to this." See folks you need to understand this. We heard this in the last lesson. That Paul said in Romans chapter 12, *"Do not repay evil for evil."* Isn't that right? Then Jesus says, *"Do not repay evil for evil."* Why? So that you may become sons of your Father, mature sons. Now here's Peter saying, "Don't return evil for evil." Is the message starting to get across? He's saying return blessing. Why? Because that is what a mature son does. Because knowing that you are called to this. Now why has God called us to this? Look at the next word: *"That you may inherit a blessing!"* The next time you are being unfairly treated, you can dance, you can do a jig, have a party because God is setting you up to get blessed!

"IF" you handle it correctly. You know how many blessings you have passed up because they didn't handle it correctly? They picked up the offense. They just got a sourpuss heart instead of a blessing.

You know I will never forget the time one of my board members told me this. A very good friend of mine, Pastor Al, was preaching to his church about five thousand people in Dallas, Texas. He was preaching along this line and after the Sunday morning service, one of the members of the church came up to him and said, "Now Pastor Al, I need to talk to you." And Pastor said, "Sure." "Sir," he said, "I am a junior executive of a very large insurance company here in Dallas, Texas." And he said, "I was next in line to be promoted to vice president." He said, "The position came open." And he said, "They gave it to another man." And he said, "There was only one reason that they gave it to another man." And Pastor Al said, "Why?" He said, "Because I am black and he is not." And he said, "That is discrimination." And he said, "Now Pastor Al, I have legal recourse." And he said, "In fact, I was getting ready to pursue the legal recourse this week but after you just preached this message this morning you messed me up." So Pastor Al looked at him and said, "Well do you want to do it God's way or your way?" He said, "I want to do it God's way." He said, "That's why I am up here talking to you because I love God with all my heart." So Pastor Al said, "Good. Let me pray for you because God is going to take this case and judge it." He said, "That is going to keep you from being offended."

So you know what this guy does the next morning? Now this is a mature son, watch. He walks into the office of the guy who got the promotion, the job he should have gotten. He looks at him and says, "I just want you to know that I am going to be your best worker and I want to congratulate you on your promotion." Well this guy said kind of like thanks, and he is very uncomfortable because he is looking at the man that should have gotten the promotion.

Now nothing happened for several weeks. How many of you know that God delivers but it usually comes later then you think? Amen. So for several weeks nothing is happening. Several weeks later this guy gets a call from a very, very, very, large insurance company in Dallas. They are actually based out of Norfolk but have a huge operation in Dallas and they said, "You know, our executives have watched how you handled some accounts because we have done mutual things together and we are very, very impressed with you and we want to talk to you." He said, "I'm not interested, I don't like change." He said, "I have been with this company for years, I have benefits built up, the people know me, my reputation is here, my integrity is here, I have clients. Nope, I'm not interested." They said, "Please would you give us one lunch." He said, "Yeah I will give you a lunch, but I'm telling you that I'm not interested." They said, "Just let us talk to you."

So he goes to lunch with these guys and they go through the whole spiel again on how badly they want to hire him. He said, "Look I'm not interested I told you. You are wasting your time. I do not like change. I'm a very stable man." He said, "I've got clients, I've got benefits, I've got a reputation. I don't want to start that all over again. I am not interested." They said, "All right, look. This is what we want you to do. We want you to go home and talk to your wife for the next week and you guys determine a salary you would like us to pay you." So he says, "Alright."

So he goes home. Now he lets this thing go for the whole week and finally the night before they lunch again he's looking at his wife and he is just going, "I don't want to change. I don't like change. I'm not interested." She's just listening to him. And he is talking this through and finally he says, "You know what I want to do, honey?" He said, "I am going to do just the most ridiculous thing I can think of"—"I am going to multiply my salary by three times." You got to remember that he is a junior executive okay? He said, "I am going to multiply my salary by three times. That will shut them up as soon as they see that and it will all be done with."

So he types up the letters saying how much he wanted to make and multiplied his existing salary by three times and he puts it in his *lapel* pocket and he goes to lunch. So he's at the lunch and they say, "Did you come up with a figure that you and your wife want us to pay you?" He said, "Oh yeah I did." And he starts pulling the letter out of his *lapel*. They said, "No, no, no we don't want to see your letter. We want to show you first what we want to pay you." So they slide this letter across the table. He picks up the letter. They want to pay him four times. Four times! He's looking at this letter in shock and he's just speechless. Well, they think because he is speechless that it isn't enough. So they up it a bunch more and add more benefits. Well, he is just in shock. So he finally gets his composure, he says, "Gentlemen, I am a Christian. I want to take this home and pray about it with my wife." They said, "Fine, fine, just let us know."

Well, he goes home and he and his wife pray and the Lord speaks to them both. He says, "Son, you turned this over to me. You didn't pick up on the offense. This is my vindication. This is my promotion, take it!" And do you know now today fifteen years later, he is one of the top executives there at that corporation in Norfolk, Virginia, and doesn't live in Dallas anymore.

This is what Peter is trying to tell us. "If you only knew that God was in control and you act like a mature son, then guess what?" He goes on to say, look at verse 13, *"And who is he who will harm you if you become a follower of what is good?"* What Peter is saying, "How can anybody hurt you,

when you get this into your life: there is nothing anybody can do to you."

You know a couple years ago, several years ago there was a man that made a statement about me that was an absolute lie. He made a statement to two major, major ministries. And that one statement within a couple of days cost our ministry ten thousand dollars. Now that is a lot of money to me, okay, was back then too. I mean it's still a lot but it was a really a lot then. And my administrator called me at the airport and he said, "Listen, John, this is just what happened." I about hit the ceiling. I said, "What?" So I was so glad I was getting ready to get on a plane and fly to Sweden because I couldn't do anything and I always found that if God couldn't talk to you when you are awake he will talk to you when you are asleep.

So when I arrived in Sweden the thought comes to me. "What are you doing, John?" Because, man, I was really having to fight to keep from being offended by this man, and I am battling it big time. And I land in Sweden and the thought comes to me, "What are you doing?" I can look at this as I have been stolen from and you know what the Bible says? If you are stolen from you can demand on the Spirit sevenfold return. It's a thief's call. Now I can do that, but I still have the sting that I have been stolen from. I said, "Or I can give this money to that man." And I said, "If I give it to him," I said, "there is a hundredfold return and there is no sting." And I started thinking and I said, "Man, this is good." So I called Lisa, she liked it. I talked to my pastor he liked it. So we prayed my wife and I and we said, "Lord, we have blessed him, we have sown it, we have sown the joy in Jesus' name." You know joy hit my heart, I was so excited and you know what happened? Ten days later a couple comes to my front door who lives in Texas—we live in Colorado—and they hand me a card and I opened the card and there was a check for ten thousand dollars for our ministry. I said, "Look at this a one-fold, ninety-nine to go. Isn't this great?"

See? "Who is he who can harm you when you become a follower of this? This is what Jesus is talking about when He says, "Hey, they want your coat? Give them this shirt also or the other way around. They want your shirt give them your coat. They want you to go one mile, hey man, go two." See because back then the Romans took a look at a Jew and said, "Hey man, you got to walk my horse one mile." And Jesus, what He is saying is, He is saying, "How can they steal that from you when you give them two? How can they steal your shirt when you were giving your coat too?" When you get this into you, who is he who can harm you? This is called kingdom living. This will keep you free from offense.

So now look what he goes on to say in chapter 4. *"Therefore since Christ suffered for us in the flesh, arm yourselves also with the same mind for he who has suffered in the flesh is ceased from sin."* Boy, there are so much in that verse that I don't know if I could finish it in the session.

"As Christ suffered for us." What was he talking about? He was talking about what? Unfair treatment. Let's take the whole chapter in context. He said, *"Arm yourself with the same mind."* Most believers are not armed to suffer. That's why they are so easily offended. Did you get that? So, because they are not armed, they react instead of act. They go into a state of shock, they go into a state of bewilderment or amazement when they are mistreated. The offense is easily picked up and now they are reacting instead of acting.

Let me show you the difference between someone who is armed and who is not. An airline pilot. I fly 200 thousand miles a year; I'm on a lot of commercial jets. I have learned that every six months that they send commercial pilots to do these flight simulators. They are big, big huge

machines filled with computers that you would never know that if you were in a real plane or not in a real plane. What they do for three days is throw every single thing that could happen to a plane at those guys. And I mean they will crash, crash, crash and then they start acting properly.

So they are arming those guys. So in a real crash, so in a real crisis hits a plane, you can have the people in the back screaming, they are reacting. In the cabin with the passengers, but when the pilots listen to the black boxes they do this pull up check, do this, push that check, check, check, check all the way until the crash. They are totally in control because they are armed.

This is what Peter is trying to say to us. As Christ suffered, arm yourselves with the same mind. *"For he who has suffered in the flesh has ceased from sin."* What does he mean "ceased from sin"? He means they have reached complete spiritual maturity. You see folks, physical growth is limited to time. You never see a two-year-old six-feet tall. It's limited to time.

Intellectual growth—is it limited to time? No, we have fourteen year olds that have graduated from high school. We have fifty year olds that haven't. Intellectual growth is not a function of time; it is a function of what? Of learning. You go from first to second to third, but you can do it fast or slow.

Spiritual growth—is it a function of time? No, we have people that have been born again twenty years but they still wear spiritual Pampers and make the most noise in the church. Not a function of time. You have other people that are born again one year but they are giants. It's not a function of time. Is it a function of learning? No. If the Pharisees can quote the first five books of the Bible but they can't recognize the Son of God who's casting the devil out in front of their face, that is not a function of learning. What is spiritual growth a function of? Suffering. He who has suffered in the flesh is ceased from sin. There is another key element because I know people that have suffered that are bitter, offended. The key element is Hebrews 5, verse 9 which says, *"Though he was a son he learned obedience by what he suffered."* I said, So what happens? God says, "I know what you can handle." And He only allows what we can handle to come by us. Spiritual growth is this. When we encounter unfair treatment, when we encounter offensive behavior and we choose to obey God's Word in the midst of it rather than react and defend ourselves, avenge ourselves or return evil for evil that's done to us, God says when we do that, that is when we grow.

I kind of see it almost like weightlifting. Seven years ago a WWF wrestler lived right next door to me started training me in the gym. And I found out something from these guys. It's not when you are doing fifteen reps when you grow; it's only when you are doing about three reps because you put a lot of weight on there and you lift heavy weight and you get to the third rep and everything in you says, "I can't lift again." I watched these guys yell at each other and their blood vessels start showing and something in them pushes it up one more time. That's when muscle starts to grow.

Well, when I started weightlifting I could only bench a 125. Then I went to one 135, 145, 55, 65, 75, 85 and I got stuck at 185 for years. A couple years ago I was in Fresno, California and a pastor looked at me at the conference and said, "John, you can bench 225." I said, "You are crazy. I can't do that." He said, "Yeah, put it on. I will spot you." And you know what? I lifted up 225. I looked at him later and I said, "Man you are like the Holy Spirit." And he did exactly what you did—he started laughing. He says, "What do you mean?" I said, "Because the Bible says God will not allow any temptation to pass us which He knows we can't handle."

Thirteen years ago I faced trials that were about all I could handle. I remember a man was slandering me and my home church. And I mean that was spreading all over because he was a man that had authority over me, a position of authority. And I mean it was about all I could handle. But now just a couple of years ago, I heard my name slandered not just in one church but I heard it slandered on three different continents by one man. Now if that would have happened back in 1987, it would have been like putting 250 pounds on the bar and that would have crushed me. I wouldn't have gotten the thing down, let alone up. It would have just collapsed on me.

Do you remember when Paul said, *"By this time you ought to be teachers?"* That is the Spirit of God almost weeping saying, "You know, I was hoping by this time you would be at the 185 level but we have start all over again at the 105 level." Because somebody spoke bad about you, so you spoke bad back. You defended yourself. You returned evil for evil. And God keeps saying, "I tried to get you back to 125 level, I'm trying to get you to the 135 level, but every time I bring the 125 level up you just scream, cry, complain, you react like the world is like an unsaved man." He said, "You got to go back to the 105." He says, "The problem is I got some 155, 165 jobs and I can't send you in there because you are not mature enough to handle it." So folks let me say this to you. When an offensive behavior comes at you, you can rejoice, you can shout because God is, number 1, setting you up to be blessed and, number 2, setting you up to grow.

Lesson 6

The Sure Foundation

Therefore thus says the Lord GOD:
"Behold, I lay in Zion a stone for a foundation,
a tried stone, a precious cornerstone, a sure foundation;
whoever believes will not act hastily."
(Isaiah 28:16)

Summary of *The Bait of Satan,* Chapter 7

This chapter could be titled, "A Firm Answer to Instability." Bevere begins by illustrating from the lives of Jesus' disciples how important it is for us to arrive at certain, settled conclusions about God and His relationship with us. Those conclusions will never be settled as long as they rest on the opinions of others or on our personal feelings. The sure foundation doesn't even depend on our attitude toward Scripture or our superficial knowledge of what God's Word says—which can easily be a little more than head knowledge. A certain, settled confidence in God's place in our lives flows out of experiencing the Word of God as a living revelation in us. Bevere quotes Psalm 119:130, "The entrance of Your words gives light; it gives under-standing to the simple," to point out that the content of God's message to us may not always be exactly what we are hearing a minister say at the moment. His role may simply be to expose us to the Word.

Bevere goes on to describe, using his own marriage and another couple's experience, how crucial the sense of God's call affects a couple's ability to overcome the kinds of stresses and difficulties that are natural by-product of living in a fallen world. John freely admits that it wasn't the feelings about God's promises or even his ability on some days to "see" God's promises fulfilled in their marriage that kept them moving ahead—beyond these things were facts like God's faithfulness and God's unchanging nature. Our feelings about God's will may vacillate and fluctuate from day to day, but the fact of God's will remains like a solid rock we can depend on and build upon.

Bevere includes some important biblical counsel (1 Corinthians 7:10–11, 24) for his readers who entered marriage before they were saved. He even includes those who may have sensed they were marrying the wrong person, but did it anyway. To all of these, John has words of hope and direction.

The chapter concludes with a number of biblical passages to point out the dangers of instability and the deep security that flows from knowing that when everything else may seem unstable, we have an unshakeable rock to which we have anchored our lives. Life has a way of revealing whether or not we have made that commitment. As John writes on page 77, "I often say that trials and tests *locate* a person."

Warm-Up Questions

Use the following questions to prepare your heart and mind for the personal and/or group study in which you will participate.

1. Think of one or two examples of unforgettable sermons you have heard. What made them so memorable?

   _____

   _____

   _____

   _____

   _____

2. Briefly describe one occasion when God spoke or communicated to you in a special and personal way. How has that experience affected your life?

   _____

   _____

   _____

   _____

   _____

3. This lesson is titled "The Sure Foundation." What example would you use to illustrate for someone what it takes for a building to have a sure foundation?

   _____

   _____

   _____

   _____

   _____

Teaching by John Bevere

Watch the sixth session video presentation.

Personal Notes on Video Session 6

Use the following lines to keep notes as you view the video.

_____

_____

_____

_____

_____

_____

_____

_____

Jesus waited until they finished, then He looked at them and asked them point-blank, "But who do you say that I am?" (Matthew 16:15).

I'm sure there was a confused, fearful look on most of the disciples' faces as they pondered this, mouths half open and speechless.

Suddenly the men who were so eager to speak, airing others' opinions, were silenced. Perhaps they had never seriously asked this question of themselves. Whatever the case, they now realized they had no answer.

Jesus did what He does so well. He located their hearts with a question. He brought them to a true realization of what they did and did not know. They were living off the speculations of others, rather than establishing in their own hearts who Jesus really was. They had not confronted themselves.

—John Bevere, *The Bait of Satan*, pp. 67-68

Teaching Review

Use the following questions to consider some of the central points made by John Bevere during this video session.

4. Right at the beginning of the session, Bevere referred back to the illustration of pilot training when he explained the significance of the Isaiah 28:16 phrase, "will not act hastily." What point did he make?

_____

_____

_____

_____

_____

_____

5. How did Bevere explain the difference between head (or soul) knowledge and revealed knowledge?

_____

_____

_____

_____

_____

_____

_____

_____

_____

6. What was the character trait in Peter (that all growing believers share) that determined God's action in giving him revealed knowledge?

_____

_____

_____

_____

_____

_____

_____

_____

_____

_____

7. Explain the connection between the title of this lesson, "The Sure Foundation," and the importance of revealed knowledge.

_____

_____

_____

_____

_____

_____

_____

_____

I have often told congregations and individuals when I am preaching to listen for God's voice within my

voice. So often we are so busy taking notes that we only record everything that is said. This yields a mental understanding of the Scriptures and their interpretations—head knowledge.

When we possess solely a head knowledge, two things can happen: 1) we are easily susceptible to hype or emotionalism, or 2) we are bound by our intellect. But this is not the sure foundation on which Jesus builds His church. He said it would be founded on the revealed Word, not just memorized verses.

When we listen to an anointed minister speak or as we read a book, we should look for the words or phrases that explode in our spirits. This is the Word God is revealing to us. It conveys light and spiritual understanding. As the psalmist said, "The entrance of Your word gives light; it gives understanding to the simple" (Psalm 119:130). It is the entrance of His Word into our hearts, not minds, that illuminates and clarifies.

—John Bevere, *The Bait of Satan*, p. 69

Exploring God's Word

Revisit the key passages from which John Bevere develops his teaching.

Isaiah 28:16 *Therefore thus says the Lord GOD: "Behold, I lay in Zion a stone for a foundation, a tried stone, a precious cornerstone, a sure foundation; whoever believes will not act hastily."*

8. How many times is the word "stone" used in this single verse, and what is a "tried stone"?

_____

_____

_____

_____

_____

_____

_____

9. In his book, Bevere comments on the last line of this verse when he writes, "A person who acts hastily is an unstable person because his actions are not properly founded. This person is easily moved and swayed by the storms of persecutions and trials" (p. 71). Write down at least three examples of what a "hasty act" might be:

_____

_____

_____

_____

_____

_____

_____

_____

_____

_____

_____

_____

STUDENT NOTES

_____
_____
_____
_____

Personal Application

_____
_____
_____
_____
_____
_____
_____
_____
_____
_____
_____
_____
_____
_____

Matthew 16:13–18 *When Jesus came into the region of Caesarea Philippi, He asked His disciples, saying, "Who do men say that I, the Son of Man, am?" So they said, "Some say John the Baptist, some Elijah, and others Jeremiah or one of the prophets." He said to them, "But who do you say that I am?" Simon Peter answered and said, "You are the Christ, the Son of the living God." Jesus answered and said to him, "Blessed are you, Simon Bar-Jonah, for flesh and blood has not revealed this to you, but My Father who is in heaven. And I also say to you that you are Peter, and on this rock I will build My church, and the gates of Hades shall not prevail against it."*

10. When the disciples reported all the different ways in which people were identifying Jesus, what title was conspicuously left out?

_____

_____

_____

_____

_____

_____

_____

_____

11. How does Bevere explain the significance of Jesus' statement to Peter, "and on this rock I will build My church"?

_____

_____

_____

_____

_____

_____

_____

_____

_____

_____

_____

_____

_____

_____

_____

_____

_____

Personal Application

_____

_____

_____

_____

_____

_____

_____

_____

_____

_____

_____

_____

Mark 4:16–17 *These likewise are the ones sown on stony ground who, when they hear the word, immediately receive it with gladness; and they have no root in themselves, and so endure only for a time. Afterward, when tribulation or persecution arises for the word's sake, immediately they stumble.*

12. How does the lack of root in this passage relate to the importance of a sure foundation that is the theme of this lesson?

_____

_____

_____

_____

_____

_____

13. Review the parable itself (Mark 4:3–9). Using the picture in the parable as well as Jesus' explanation, describe what's actually happening to the person's life who is like stony ground, and describe their response to the Word.

_____

_____

_____

_____

_____

_____

_____

_____

_____

_____

_____

_____

Personal Application

_____

_____

_____

_____

_____

_____

_____

_____

_____

_____

_____

_____

_____

_____

John 6:60–69 *Therefore many of His disciples, when they heard this, said, "This is a hard saying; who can understand it?" When Jesus knew in Himself that His disciples complained about this, He said to them, "Does this offend you? What then if you should see the Son of Man ascend where He was before? It is the Spirit who gives life; the flesh profits nothing. The words that I speak to you are spirit, and they are life. But there are some of you who do not believe." For Jesus knew from the beginning who they were who did not believe, and who would betray Him. And He said, "Therefore I have said to you that no one can come to Me unless it has been granted to him by My Father." From that time many of His disciples went back and walked with Him no more. Then Jesus said to the twelve, "Do you also want to go away?" But Simon Peter answered Him, "Lord, to whom shall we go? You have the words of eternal life. Also we have come to believe and know that You are the Christ, the Son of the living God."*

14. These verses record a definite shift in Jesus' popularity among His followers. Why does He ask the

STUDENT NOTES

disciples a question, "Does this offend you?" when He already knows the answer? Why didn't His knowledge cause Him to soften or change His message?

_____

_____

_____

_____

_____

_____

_____

_____

_____

15. What is the significance of Peter's response to Jesus' challenge?

_____

_____

_____

_____

_____

_____

_____

_____

_____

_____

Personal Application

_____

_____

STUDENT NOTES

_____

_____

_____

_____

_____

_____

_____

_____

_____

_____

Exposing the Truth

Use the following questions to help reach conclusions regarding the Scriptures and insights from the session.

16. According to Bevere, what are the differences between good, biblical preaching and revealed knowledge?

_____

_____

_____

_____

_____

_____

_____

_____

_____

_____

_____

STUDENT NOTES

_____

_____

_____

_____

_____

17. How did Bevere's application of the principle of revealed knowledge in his story about doing pre-marital counseling with his secretary and her fiancé highlight the significance of revealed knowledge?

_____

_____

_____

_____

_____

_____

_____

_____

_____

_____

_____

_____

_____

_____

_____

_____

18. Bevere uses Jesus' closing parable in the Sermon on the Mount (Matthew 7:24–27), in which He

describes the two possible responses from those who hear His words—a life built on sand or a life built on the rock. How does that parable illustrate the central theme of this lesson, "The Sure Foundation"?

_____

_____

_____

_____

_____

_____

_____

_____

_____

_____

_____

_____

You can have a house built on sand that is five stories high and beautiful, decorated with the most elaborate materials and craftsmanship. As long as the sun is shining, it looks like a bulwark of strength and beauty.

Next to that house you can have a single-story plain house. It is almost unnoticeable and possibly unattractive compared to the beautiful edifice next to it. But it is built on something you can't see—a rock.

As long as no storms strike, the five-story house looks much nicer. But when it encounters a severe

STUDENT NOTES

storm, the five-story house collapses and is ruined. It may survive a few minor storms but not the hurricane. The plain, one-story structure survives. The larger the house, the harder and more noteworthy its fall.

—John Bevere, *The Bait of Satan*, p. 77

Applying the Lesson

Use the following specific directions to internalize the principles in the session and put them into practice.

19. Describe in a few sentences what you consider to be the foundation of your life.

   _____

   _____

   _____

   _____

   _____

20. In what ways has that foundation been tested?

   _____

   _____

   _____

   _____

21. Write down one of the key statements of revealed knowledge that allow you to respond to life's biggest challenges with Peter's simple words, "Lord, to whom shall we go? You have the words of eternal life" (John 6:68).

_____

_____

_____

_____

_____

Bait Warnings

A final opportunity for prayerful submission to the truth of the session.

> Some people in the church are like the disciples who were so quick to speak in Caesarea Philippi, but only later to be exposed. They may look like five-story Christians, the picture of strength, stability, and beauty. They may weather a few minor and midsize storms. But when a mighty storm blows in, they are relocated.
>
> Be sure that you build your life on God's revealed Word, not what others say. Keep seeking the Lord and listening to your heart. Don't do or say things just because everyone else does. Seek Him and stand on what is illuminated in your heart!
>
> —John Bevere, *The Bait of Satan,* p. 77

Video Script for Lesson 6
The Sure Foundation

Isaiah 28 tonight for lesson 6. I just want to read one verse of Scripture. I want to read the sixteenth verse out of Isaiah 28. *"Therefore, thus says the Lord God, 'Behold I lay in Zion a stone for a foundation'—'a tried stone, a precious cornerstone, a sure foundation. Whoever believes will not act hastily.'"* In the last session we talked about the difference between acting and reacting. If you recall I told you that pilots, when they are in severe conditions, when a plane is in trouble, will always act because they have been trained and they are armed to do it. Passengers, on the other hand, will react; they will scream and panic.

Isaiah says here very clearly whoever believes is someone who will never act hastily. A person who acts hastily is a person who is unstable because his actions are not properly founded. Now instability is not a good thing. How many of you know that? It's true for a natural house; it's true for our lives. We need a solid foundation, Amen?

Now to get a really good example of this and a picture of this, I want you to go to Matthew 16. We are going to see a real classic example in the life of a man named Simon Peter. In Matthew 16 I want to look at the thirteenth verse. *"When Jesus came into the region of Caesarea Philippi he asked his disciples saying, 'Who do men say that I the Son of man am?'"* So now Jesus does right now what He always does so well and that is He locates people's hearts with a question. So He looks at His disciples and He says, "Hey what are they saying about Me guys? Who are they saying I am?" And so now the answers start coming quite readily. Verse 14, so they say, *"Well some say John the Baptist."* Then somebody else spoke up and said, *"Some said, Elijah."* Then another guy spoke up and said, *"Well others are saying you are Jeremiah or one of the prophets."* So these guys, these dis-

ciples start throwing out all the popular opinions of who Jesus is. I'm sure Matthew spoke up, Philip spoke up, Bartholomew spoke up. They're all just saying this is what they are saying, this is what this group is saying, this is what the Jews are saying, this is what the Sanhedrin are saying.

They are getting all this out and Jesus lets them get it all out. And then He looks at them in the next verse and He said to them, *"But who do you say that I am?"* Now I just love this. They just gotten out what everybody else is saying and then Jesus looks at them, right at them, and says, *"But who do you say I am?* It doesn't matter what this group is saying, that group's saying, and that group's saying. Who do you say that I am?" And now all of a sudden they had given all the popular opinions out and they are kind of just standing there with their mouths wide open. But, Simon Peter then opens up his mouth and look what he says. Verse 16, Simon Peter answered and said, *"You are the Christ, the Son of the living God!"* So out of Simon's mouth comes the statement, "You're the Christ, You're the Lord, You're the Son of the living God."

Now look at what Jesus says. In verse 17 Jesus answered and said to him, *"Blessed are you Simon Bar-Jonah, for flesh and blood has not revealed this to you."* In other words, you have not been taught this in your natural senses. Somebody did not speak this to you, write it on chalkboard, you didn't learn it at a seminar, a university, it has not been taught to you. It has not been revealed to you by flesh and blood, but look what He is going on to say. He says, *"But my Father who is in heaven has revealed it to you."* Jesus now is saying, "The rest of you are giving Me what everyone else is saying. You are giving Me your thoughts, your opinions. But when Simon blurted out, 'You are the Christ, the Son of the living God,' that came deep within his being." And Jesus said, "You know what? Nobody told you this, nobody taught you this." He said, "My Father in heaven revealed it to you."

Then He makes this statement to Simon, which I love. In verse 18 He says, *"I also say to you that you are Peter and on this rock I will build my church and the gates of Hades shall not prevail against it."* Now I want to take this slowly. He says, *"And also I say to you that you are Peter."* Peter is from the Greek word *petros* which simply means this—"a stone." Now the word "Simon" on the other hand is from a Greek word which means "to hear." So in other words, "Your name meant that you are a hearer but now I'm calling this, you're a rock, a stone." *Petros* means "a small stone."

Now He goes on to say, *"And upon this rock."* Now that Greek word is a different Greek word. It is the Greek word *petra* which means this—"a large massive rock." Jesus is saying to Peter, *"You are Simon."* In verse 18, *"And I also say to you that you are Peter"*—which means a little rock—*"and on this rock"*—petra, massive rock—*"I will build my church and the gates of Hell shall not prevail against it."*

Now the rock that He is talking about folks, I want to make this very clear, is not the rock of just the Lordship of Jesus. Now I want you to understand what I am saying here. Of course He is the foundation of the church, He is the cornerstone; however, He is the living Word of God. He is the Word made flesh. Now, it is not the written Word that changes us. The written Word can be taught to be communicated to our senses. What Jesus is saying is the rock that I will build My church on is the revealed Word of God.

Let me give you an example. When I preach I often tell people this. "Don't just take notes and write down everything I say. Rather listen for the voice within my voice." That's the voice of the Holy Spirit. The beauty of the ministry is this. Here I am preaching to probably what, twelve, thirteen hundred people tonight? I'm preaching one message to thirteen hundred people but listen, this message is being heard thirteen hundred different ways, if you are hungry. Because the Holy Spirit is exploding different things in each one of you.

Now I have been in services where a man is preaching and the very words that he says go off like a bomb on the inside of me. That's revealed knowledge. It's no longer *his* words; they now have been revealed to me. It's a revelation that the Spirit of the Lord has given me. That's what He says, "I build my church on."

Now I also have been in a service before and there is a man or woman preaching and they are speaking about something and all of a sudden the Holy Spirit will use that to explode something else totally different than what they are saying off on the inside of me. They are maybe going in this direction but all of a sudden an explosion off in this direction goes on the inside of me. That's revealed knowledge. You didn't hear it so to speak with your physical ears; you heard it with your spiritual ears. You didn't see it with your physical eyes; you saw it with the eyes of your spirit.

That's why Jesus says, *"Thomas you have seen me, but how much more blessed are those that have not seen, and yet believed."* What He is simply saying to Thomas is this, "Revealed knowledge is more powerful and enduring than even sense knowledge. You have physically touched the holes in My hands and have put your hand on My side, but that is not what would cause you to be stable. What causes you to be stable," He said, is what? "The revealed knowledge of God."

You see when you look at the garden—I think it is an amazing thing if you look at Adam and Eve.

God says to Adam, you know He says, *"You shall eat from every tree of this garden except for the tree of knowledge of good and evil,"* right? Well when the serpent comes to Eve, I think it's an amazing thing. The serpent says, "Can you eat from every tree of the garden?" She says, "Well," she goes on to say, "we cannot." She says, "We cannot eat or touch of the tree of knowledge of good and evil." Well, first of all, you see, in Eve it's more communicated knowledge than revealed knowledge. First of all she says, "We cannot." That sounds like the rules, doesn't it?

Now this is what happens to people when they come to church and they are listening to people out of their heads, preachers out of their head. You get a bunch of rules, regulations, and guide-lines. I can do this; I can't do that. I can do this; I can't do that. And when you hear Eve's words, if you go back and study it out, you almost hear the same thing coming out of her. It is very obvious that she didn't inquire of the Lord. It is obvious because when God gave the command, Eve wasn't around yet. It is very obvious that one day when Adam and Eve were walking through the garden, Adam just basically proba-bly said, "The Lord does not want us to touch that tree." And now it was a communicated knowledge not a revealed knowledge. It was not something that she heard from the mouth of God. She probably did not inquire of the Lord and seek Him to get that revelation knowledge. And so when the enemy came, he was easily able to get her off because it wasn't revealed knowl-edge.

See let me make this statement. You can take a man who has one, one word of revelation knowl-edge in his spirit, and take another man who has the entire Bible memorized. The man with the one word of revelation knowledge of the Lordship of Jesus will stand more than the man who has the entire Bible memorized who has no revelation knowledge.

Now you say, "Then why do you stand up here and teach and preach to us?" Because my confidence is not in my ability to articulate. My confidence is in the fact that when I speak, I'm speaking living words. Life-giving words with the Holy Spirit to those of you who are hungry is taking and exploding on the inside of your being which brings the change that we want to see. That's part of the process; that's how it works. Because some-body will say to me, "Then why should I even go to church?" The reason you go to church because there is a corporate anointing there and that explosion of revelation knowledge happens.

Now I find that it's an amazing thing to me. I can go into a church, I can go into a conference, and I can preach a message and one person sit-ting there leaves with their life absolutely transformed. The other person sitting next to them goes, "Well he's a little bit long and a lit-tle bit loud." They both got the same informa-tion, but one man was hungry, the other man wasn't.

See, revelation knowledge comes to those who are extremely hungry. If you look at Peter, he is the one who is constantly asking the questions, constantly speaking up, talking almost out of turn, making a bunch of dumb mistakes, but the thing—beyond all of that—is absolute, intense hunger. God is drawn to hunger. To be very hon-est with you folks, the level of your hunger indi-cates how healthy you are. I mean look at the natural, folks. What is the indication that some-body is sick? They lose their appetite. I mean anybody in here ever have the flu before? When you had the flu did you want to eat? No, I mean eating a piece of steak when you had the flu looked about as good as eating a shoe. You have no appetite. People that have cancer go down to seventy-five, eighty pounds. Why? They lose their appetite. They are sick. A sign of being sick is a loss of appetite. That's actually the first sign.

The sign of health is a strong appetite. Well, it's the same way spiritually. God is drawn to hunger. See, backsliding does not begin when a guy finds himself in bed with some strange chick he didn't marry, okay? It happened months or years earlier when he lost his passion for God. When the hunger began to wane and now watching the ball game was more exciting than hearing the Word of the Lord. Sleeping in sounded a whole lot better then getting up and seeking God.

I'm going to be honest with you; my eyes pop open every morning between probably around 4:30 or 5:30. Every morning my eyes open like this. I jump out of bed because it is the most exciting part of my day. The most exciting part of my day is going outside and being alone. It's dark at the school next to our house, and when I go up to that parking lot and pray, I love it. It's my favorite time of the day. Why? Because I anticipate meeting God. I'm hungry for Him and I know He is drawn to hunger and will come. I know when I call upon His name, He's coming. And God is drawn to that hunger. That is when revelation knowledge will abound—in atmospheres where there is hunger. That's why it is so fun to teach this church, because when I come to this church I find the people are just so hungry. They are on the edge of their seats, many of you got your notebooks out and you know what? You're not writing everything I'm saying. I'm watching you go "Wow" and all of a sudden it's like *dint, dint, dint*. What is that? That is something that has exploded inside of you and that nobody can ever take from you. Because when God reveals something to you, nobody can ever take that from your life. Amen.

You see Jesus never said this. Jesus never said, "Man shall live by every word that proceeded out of the mouth of God." He said, *"Man shall live by every word that proceeds."* That's present tense, so what God is saying right now. Because He's not what Paul calls a dumb idol or dumb god, He speaks.

I'm slipping over to what God has been dealing about me lately but a couple weeks ago. Now I am going to get real intimate here. Some of you may get a little shocked when you hear what I am about to say. A couple of weeks ago I was out praying. I was in prayer and I said, "Lord, if I can't have *intimacy* with you," I said, "then take me home. I want out of here." I said, "I don't want to live here." I said, "If I can't have *intimacy* with you, I don't want to be here."

Listen to what David says. Psalm 28—*"To You oh Lord I will cry." "Do not be silent to me."* Now listen, *"Lest if You are silent to me I become like those who go down to the pit."* David said, "If You're not talking to me, if You're not communicating to me, I'm no different then a sinner going to hell." I about hit the ceiling; there it is right there. You want to communicate to me.

Right around that same time period I was driving down the road and the Spirit of God spoke to me and said, "Pull off, pull off." I said, "Okay." Now I've learned when God says to do something I just do it. And there was a rest area right up just about a mile from me so I pulled off into the rest area—now as soon as I obeyed—see here is an amazing thing.

When the burning bush was burning, Moses made the statement, *"I will turn aside and see His great side."* He is busy watching his flocks, but when he sensed God was moving he said, "Forget this, I'm turning aside." And you know what the Bible says, *"When God saw that he turned aside then God spoke to him."* If he wouldn't have turned aside, God wouldn't have spoken. I pulled off in the rest area; the Spirit of God spoke to me just like that. He said, "Son, I told you to pray without ceasing." I said. "Yes Sir, you did." He said, "Son, prayer is not a monologue; it is a dialogue. It's not a one-way conversation; it's a two-way conversation." I said, "Yes Sir, I know." He said, "Son therefore, if I say, 'Pray without ceasing,' that means I am communicating without ceasing." I went, "Wow!"

Now listen, it may not always be a voice. How many of you know this? My wife can look and give me one look and I can write you three pages of what she just said with that one look. She just communicated with me without saying anything to me and a lot communication—you know what I mean, you understanding what I am saying? See now this is the thing. If we're sensitive, that's the way He will communicate to us. It may not be a word inside of our heart, but He does want to communicate to us. That's how much He desires us.

Now this is what Peter was hungry for. You see in Peter hunger above all the other guys. I mean, he is the guy who says, "Hey, I want to come walk on the water." You know, everybody's always getting down on Peter because he sank. Well you know what? What about the other eleven guys? They were all on the boat. At least he got out and walked. That's the kind of hunger this guy's got and God is drawn to it. Now when you got that kind of appetite for God, your heart becomes a place for revelation knowledge will begin to abound.

Now not only does it apply to the Scriptures, it applies to God communicating to us in our lives. For an example, you cannot find chapter or verse who it is you are supposed to marry. You can't find chapter or verse what you are called to do in this life. It does not say, "John Bevere shall preach the gospel to the nations" in the Scriptures. Are you with me?

So when seeking God, God will reveal things to us and when He does, that is what we live off of. Let me give you an example. When I was a youth pastor, I remember on a Sunday night my secretary was in service and so was I and she had been dating this guy and they were lovey-dovey and all

that stuff, and they got a prophecy by the minister that they were supposed to be married. Well, everyone in church was *dint, dint, dint*. Big church and most people knew because they worked on staff. Oh, everybody's excited. And I mean she came floating into the office the next day, okay? "Oh Pastor John, it's so exciting. Would you marry Mike and I?" And I said, "Well, yeah, I'd love to marry you guys," I said, "but we need to go through some counseling." She said, "Okay."

So I remember the first counseling appointment. I felt uncomfortable in my spirit. I mean something was wrong and I couldn't figure it out. But I've learned you just keep walking it through, God will show you.

So when they came walking into my office the very first thing I said is, I said, "Now Tanya, tell me, is Mike the man God has called you to marry?" She just beamed and said, "Yes, he's the man God's called me to marry." And I looked at Mike and I said—now Mike, is an interesting guy; he looks like Pete Sampras's twin brother—I looked at Mike and I said, "Now Mike, is Tanya the girl that God has called you to marry?" He just looked at me and he dropped his head. I said, "Mike?" He didn't look up. I said, "Mike, look at me." I said, "Is she the woman that God's called you to marry?" He just bowed his head again. I said, "Guys, counseling's over. There will be no marriage." I said, "There is no way I am going to marry you guys if you do not know that this is the woman that God has called you to marry." I said, "Because when the first major storm comes against your marriage," and I said, "believe me, it will come." I said, "The first thing you're going to think is, 'Well, was the guy wrong with the prophecy? Did I marry the wrong girl?' or *dat da dat da dah*." I said, "You will have no stability." I said, "You can leave the office, end of discussion." Woo, was she mad at me! My! I mean the next week was very uncomfortable with my secretary. I will never forget that.

So three weeks go by, and one day she comes beaming into my office again. She says, "We want to meet with you again." I said, "Okay, fine." So they both come into my office. The first thing I did was I looked at Mike. I said, "Mike," I said, "is this the woman God's called you to marry?" He goes, "Yes, sir, she sure is." I said, "Now we can proceed."

And you know what? They got married, they had beautiful little children, they're happily married. Why? Because they—listen—you build your life off that revealed knowledge.

Now let me say this to you. Some of you say, "Well I got married before I got saved." Well, guess what? You're married in the will of God. Stay together. The Bible says it specifically—are you with me—but I'm saying, when you go into a job, your career, you go into, you know, into what you're called to do, you go into who you're going to marry, you've got to have that revealed Word. That brings stability in your life. And that stability keeps you from what? Being offended! Why? Because—let me read this Scripture again. Mark 16, excuse me, Mark 4, verses 16 and 17, *"And these are they likewise which are sown on stony ground. Who when they have heard the Word, immediately receive it with gladness and have no root in themselves."* Now folks, what is a root? Another word that we can substitute for root is foundation! Right? *"They have no foundation. But endure but for a time. Afterward when affliction and persecution arises, for the Word's sake, immediately they are offended."*

What did Jesus say? He said, "Look," He said, "Here's a guy that's building his house on the sand, and here's a guy that's building his house on the rock." Now you know what's amazing is you can build a five-story house, beautiful, on sand. And you can build a little shack on a rock. And as long as the sun is shinning, you know what, the big, beautiful five-story house over-

powers the little shack on the rock. But when the hurricane comes, the bigger it is, the harder it's falling. And then all of a sudden you look at the little shack and it endured the storm. Why? Because it is built on the rock—the revealed Word. People that seek God to build their lives off of what He speaks to their heart are people that will not act hastily.

John's Gospel, the sixth chapter. Now I want to show you the stability that building your life upon the rock brings. Now in Jesus' ministry you will find out that in John chapter 5, verse 16, the religious leaders wanted to kill Him. Now when they're wanting to kill your boss, that means that you're in it, okay? So things were getting a little unstable for these guys, these disciples. But then in John chapter 6, verse 15, they were so happy with Jesus they wanted to come and make Him the king. And when they wanted to make Him the king, do you know what He did? He got out of town. I think this is amazing. And so the disciples are going, "Wait a minute. You know they wanted to kill You last chapter. Now this chapter they want to make You king and You're running from that and You're supposed to be the Messiah, and You're supposed to establish Your earthly kingdom. What are You doing?" So things are starting to get a little shaky here, okay? So then we come into John chapter 6. And now Jesus starts preaching—I mean things—that are just outright difficult. I mean hard, hard, words. Because He makes this statement in John chapter 6. He said, *"Unless you eat my flesh and drink my blood, you don't have anything to do with me."* I mean this is a really strong statement.

Look at John chapter 6, verse 60. *"Therefore many of his disciples, when they heard this"*—heard what? When He said, "You don't eat My flesh, drink My blood, you have no life in Me." He said, *"When many of his disciples heard this they said, 'This is a hard saying. Who can understand it?'"* Verse 61:

"When Jesus knew in himself that his disciples com-plained about this, he said, 'Does this offend you?'" I love this. You know how many preachers today water it down, trying to make it easier. Jesus just says, "Oh yeah, does this offend you?" And then you know what He does? He preaches it stronger. Looks right at them and says, *"Does this offend you?"* And then He starts telling it stronger. So now look at this. Look at verse 66. He said, from that, the Bible says, well, you know what, look at verse 64 because this is all so good. He said, *"But there are some of you who do not believe."* So He's just being point-blank with them now. For Jesus knew from the beginning who were, who did not believe, and who would betray Him. So He knew both who did not really believe and who would betray.

Verse 65: And He said, *"Therefore I have said to you, no one can come to me unless it has been granted to him by my father."* Verse 66: *"From that time many of his disciples went back and walked with him no more."* Now the Greek word there for "many" means a "very large part." Now look up at me. Can you imagine half of your staff just walked out? And just think about this. How many preachers would turn to the other half of the staff and say, "Guys, we just lost half of our staff. We really need to buckle up here. Our sup-port has just really gone down. I need you guys to give me double time." Right? But look what He does instead. He turns in verse 67: *"And Jesus said to the twelve, 'Do you also want to go away?'"* I mean, He looks right at the rest of them and says, "You want to go away too?" But look who speaks up. Verse 69, verse 68: *"But Simon Peter answered him."* He's the one that speaks up. *"Lord, to whom should we go? You have the words of eternal life."* In other words, Peter is saying, "I don't like so much what You're saying either." But watch this, verse 69: *"Also we have come to believe and know that you are the Christ, the Son of the living God."* What kept him from leaving? The revealed knowledge! Those other guys, they stumbled, they acted hastily, and left. But it had been revealed to Peter that He was the Christ, the Son of the living God. And what comes out of his mouth? The very thing that is revelation. "How can I go anywhere else? I don't like what You're saying, but where else can I go? Because You are the Christ, the Son of the living God."

Lesson 7

All That Can Be Shaken Will Be Shaken

He has promised, saying, "Yet once more I shake not only the earth, but also heaven." Now this, "Yet once more," indicates the removal of those things that are being shaken, as of things that are made, that the things which cannot be shaken may remain.
(Hebrews 12:26–27)

Summary of *The Bait of Satan*, Chapter 8

If it hasn't become apparent already, the same opportunities for offense that allow Satan to bait us also allow him to sift us. Closely related to this experience is another the Bible calls shaking. This chapter delves into God's purposes in permitting difficulties into our lives. The process of spiritual sifting finds one of its clearest biblical examples in the testing of Simon Peter during the night Jesus was betrayed. Jesus told Peter that he was about to be "sifted as wheat."

Although, as Bevere points out, sifting and shaking are not pleasant experiences to go through, they are necessary. They are certain of God's purposes in our lives that can only be accomplished through these means. Deeply imbedded pride and self-confidence often resist all other forms of correction. We see this illustrated repeatedly in the life of Simon Peter.

Because the shaking or sifting process can have very different results, two somewhat parallel lives are compared in this chapter—Simon Peter and Judas. They were both called by Jesus as disciples, even though the Lord knew each of them intimately, including the outcome of the events in which they would have a role. They both failed miserably, in spite of the training and exposure they had to the Son of God; yet one came through the test as a real man of God while the other took his own life. The first was bettered from the sifting; the other was sifted and found wanting.

Bevere shows us that even in ideal situations such as the Garden of Eden, for example, Satan always works his baiting and sifting to turn our attention away from God. Whether in Eve's experience, or Peter's humbling, or the shaping of the young man whose story ends the chapter, God always gives us more than enough of His faithfulness and grace to match any adversity that life sends our way. These examples remind us that our biggest dangers come when we try to face the sifting and shaking events in our lives using our own strength rather than clinging that much more closely to our heavenly Father. We can't determine when or how we will be sifted and shaken, but those times will come. We can decide each day to remain humbly dependent on the One who will make sure that, in the end, we "remain."

Warm-Up Questions

Use the following questions to prepare your heart and mind for the personal and/or group study in which you will participate.

1. Whether or not you've ever been in an earthquake, what do you think the experience is like?

   _____

   _____

   _____

   _____

2. List below your choices for the three most stressful situations a person can pass through and explain briefly why you think those situations are particularly difficult.

   A. _____

   B. _____

   C. _____

3. What do you think are the three most valuable resources people can have when they face a difficult situation?

   A. _____

   B. _____

   C. _____

Teaching by John Bevere

Watch the seventh session video presentation.

Personal Notes on Video Session 7

Use the following lines to keep notes as you view the video.

_____

_____

_____

_____

_____

_____

_____

_____

_____

_____

THE PURPOSE OF SIFTING

Even though Simon Peter had received abundant revelation of who Jesus was, he was not yet walking in the character and humility of Christ. He was building his life and ministry with past victories and pride. Paul admonished us to take heed how we build on our foundation in Christ (1 Corinthians 3:10).

Simon Peter was not building with the materials necessary for the kingdom of God but with supplies such as a strong will and personal confidence. Though unaware, he was still awaiting the transformation of his character. His reference was from the "pride of life" (1 John 2:16).

Pride would never be strong enough to equip him to fulfill his destiny in Christ. If not removed, this pride would eventually destroy him. Pride was the same

> character flaw found in Lucifer, God's anointed cherub, causing his downfall (Ezekiel 28:11–19).
>
> —John Bevere, *The Bait of Satan*, p. 81

Teaching Review

Use the following questions to consider some of the central points made by John Bevere during this video session.

4. During his message, what does Bevere compare one word of revealed knowledge to?

_____

_____

_____

_____

_____

_____

_____

_____

_____

_____

_____

5. On the night Jesus was betrayed, He gave two prophecies about Peter's future. What were they?

_____

_____

_____

_____

_____

_____

_____

_____

6. Based on the last question and some of Peter's other actions and words, how does Bevere counteract some of the assumptions that people make about Peter's courage?

_____

_____

_____

_____

_____

_____

_____

_____

_____

_____

7. Two other Bible figures besides Peter are prominent in this session—Judas and Eve. In contrast to Peter, what did these two other people lack that caused their sifting to turn out badly for them?

_____

_____

_____

_____

_____

_____

Exploring God's Word

Revisit the key passages from which John Bevere develops his teaching.

Luke 22:21–34 *"But behold, the hand of My betrayer is with Me on the table. And truly the Son of Man goes as it has been determined, but woe to that man by whom He is betrayed!" Then they began to question among themselves, which of them it was who would do this thing. Now there was also a dispute among them, as to which of them should be considered the greatest. And He said to them, "The kings of the Gentiles exercise lordship over them, and those who exercise authority over them are called 'benefactors.' But not so among you; on the contrary, he who is greatest among you, let him be as the younger, and he who governs as he who serves. For who is greater, he who sits at the table, or he who serves? Is it not he who sits at the table? Yet I am among you as the One who serves. But you are those who have continued with Me in My trials. And I bestow upon you a kingdom, just as My Father bestowed one upon Me, that you may eat and drink at My table in My kingdom, and sit on thrones judging the twelve tribes of Israel." And the Lord said, "Simon, Simon! Indeed, Satan has asked for you, that he may sift you as wheat. But I have prayed for you, that your faith should not fail; and when you have* *returned to Me, strengthen your brethren." But he said to Him, "Lord, I am ready to go with You, both to prison and to death." Then He said, "I tell you, Peter, the rooster shall not crow this day before you will deny three times that you know Me."*

8. How does Bevere explain the shift in the discussion from who would betray Jesus ("It wouldn't be me!") to an argument about who was the greatest?

_____

_____

_____

_____

_____

_____

_____

_____

9. What did Jesus say to settle the argument between the disciples and shift the discussion back to His earlier point?

_____

_____

_____

_____

_____

_____

_____

_____

_____

_____

_____

_____

Personal Application

_____

_____

_____

_____

_____

_____

_____

_____

_____

_____

_____

_____

_____

Picture this: Jesus told them He was about to be turned over to the chief priests to be condemned to death and delivered to the Romans to be mocked, scourged, and killed. The one who would do this was sitting with Him at the table.

The disciples questioned who it was, and it ended up in an argument about which of them would be the

STUDENT NOTES

greatest. It was dishonorable—almost like children arguing over an inheritance. There was no concern for Jesus, but a jockeying for power and position. What unimaginable selfishness!

If I had been in Jesus' position, I might have asked if they had heard what I had said or if they even cared. We see from this incident an example of how the Master walked in love and patience. Most of us, if in Jesus' place, would have said, "Every one of you, get out! I am in My greatest hour of need, and you're thinking of yourselves!" What an opportunity to become offended!

—John Bevere, *The Bait of Satan*, p. 86

Matthew 26:14–16 *Then one of the twelve, called Judas Iscariot, went to the chief priests and said, "What are you willing to give me if I deliver Him to you?" And they counted out to him thirty pieces of silver. So from that time he sought opportunity to betray Him.*

Matthew 27:3–5 *Then Judas, His betrayer, seeing that He had been condemned, was remorseful and brought back the thirty pieces of silver to the chief priests and elders, saying, "I have sinned by betraying innocent blood." And they said, "What is that to us? You see to it!" Then he threw down the pieces of silver in the temple and departed, and went and hanged himself.*

10. What aspects of Judas's character does Bevere highlight that distinguish him from Peter, even though the two of them had a number of characteristics in common?

_____

_____

_____

_____

_____

_____

_____

_____

_____

_____

_____

_____

_____

_____

_____

_____

_____

_____

11. In what way does Judas's statement to the priests when he brought back the money reveal his complete lack of understanding of Jesus?

_____

_____

STUDENT NOTES

_____
_____
_____
_____
_____
_____
_____
_____
_____
_____
_____
_____
_____
_____
_____
_____
_____
_____
_____

Personal Application

_____
_____
_____
_____
_____
_____
_____
_____
_____
_____
_____

Genesis 2:16–17 *And the L*ORD *God commanded the man, saying, "Of every tree of the garden you may freely eat; but of the tree of the knowledge of good and evil you shall not eat, for in the day that you eat of it you shall surely die."*

Genesis 3:1-6 *Now the serpent was more cunning than any beast of the field which the L*ORD *God had made. And he said to the woman, "Has God indeed said, 'You shall not eat of every tree of the garden'?" And the woman said to the serpent, "We may eat the fruit of the trees of the garden; but of the fruit of the tree which is in the midst of the garden, God has said, 'You shall not eat it, nor shall you touch it, lest you die.'" Then the serpent said to the woman, "You will not surely die. For God knows that in the day you eat of it your eyes will be opened, and you will be like God, knowing good and evil." So when the woman saw that the tree was good for food, that it was pleasant to the eyes, and a tree desirable to make one wise, she took of its fruit and ate. She also gave to her husband with her, and he ate.*

STUDENT NOTES

12. As you compare the command that God gave to Adam (Genesis 2:16–17) with Eve's version of God's command, how are they different?

_____

_____

_____

_____

_____

_____

_____

_____

_____

_____

_____

13. How exactly did Satan manage to turn Eve against her loving and wise Creator?

_____

_____

_____

_____

_____

_____

_____

_____

_____

_____

_____

_____

_____

_____

_____

_____

_____

_____

Personal Application

_____

_____

_____

_____

_____

_____

_____

_____

_____

_____

_____

_____

_____

John 21:15-19

So when they had eaten breakfast, Jesus said to Simon Peter, "Simon, son of Jonah, do you love Me more than these?" He said to Him, "Yes, Lord; You know that I love You." He said to him, "Feed My lambs." He said to him again a second time, "Simon, son of Jonah, do you love Me?" He said to Him, "Yes, Lord; You know that I love You." He said to him, "Tend My sheep." He said to him the third time, "Simon, son of Jonah, do you love Me?" Peter was grieved because He said to him the third time, "Do you love Me?" And he said to Him, "Lord, You know all things; You know that I love You." Jesus said to him, "Feed My sheep. Most assuredly, I say to you, when you were younger, you girded yourself and walked where you wished; but when you are old, you will stretch out your hands, and another will gird you and carry you where you do not wish." This He spoke, signifying by what death he would glorify God. And when He had spoken this, He said to him, "Follow Me."

14. In this, one of the really great personal conversations recorded in Scripture, how many times is the word "love" used, and what different Greek forms of the word does John explain in the video?

_____

_____

_____

_____

_____

_____

_____

_____

_____

_____

_____

_____

15. Why is Jesus' prophetic word about Peter's future a significant part of this conversation?

_____

_____

_____

_____

_____

_____

_____

Personal Application

_____

_____

_____

_____

_____

_____

_____

_____

_____

_____

_____

_____

_____

_____

Exposing the Truth

Use the following questions to help reach conclusions regarding the Scriptures and insights from the session.

16. How did the arguments between the disciples over who was the greatest affect your understanding of the problems we get into when we compare ourselves to other believers in spiritual achievements and personal growth?

_____

_____

STUDENT NOTES

_____

_____

_____

_____

_____

_____

_____

_____

_____

_____

17. How does pride, as illustrated in Peter's attitude and experience, create an environment in which Satan gets permission to sift people?

_____

_____

_____

_____

_____

_____

_____

_____

_____

_____

_____

_____

_____

Now pride attracts the enemy, like love attracts the Holy Spirit. Are you with me? So now, Satan's got permission. He has asked to sift Peter as wheat. What opened that door? Pride. Now the word "sift" in Luke 22:31 there, is from the Greek word, *siniazo*. Now listen to this. This means to sift, shake as in a sieve; figuratively, by inward agitation. And this is one translation, or the Greek dictionary renders it, "to try one's faith to the verge of overthrow." So Jesus says, "Simon, Simon, indeed Satan has asked for you, but will sift you as wheat." Jesus goes on to say in verse 32, "But I prayed for you." Now watch Jesus' prayer, "That your faith should not fail. And when you have returned to me, strengthen your brethren." Now today, many people would go, "Hey guys, Satan wants to sift our brother Simon. We need to pray and bind the devil right now." But yet Jesus does not pray that the devil would be bound. Jesus prays rather, that his faith doesn't fail. Why? Because Jesus knows that right now Peter does not have what it takes to strengthen the brethren. He's got revelation knowledge. But his confidence is being built off of his personality and his soulish strength, and not on the Lord. So Jesus said, "I'm going to allow you to go through this shaking to the verge of overthrow in order to shake out all the dead. To get rid of all the darkness. All the things that would keep you from being a strong leader."

—John Bevere, adapted from Video Session 7

18. How do the experiences of Peter, Judas, and Eve illustrate the significance of revealed knowledge in a person's life?

STUDENT NOTES

_____

_____

_____

_____

_____

_____

_____

_____

_____

_____

_____

God showed my wife, Lisa, five purposes for shaking an object:

1. To bring it closer to its foundation
2. To remove what is dead
3. To harvest what is ripe
4. To awaken
5. To unify or mix together so it can no longer be separated

Any thought process or heart attitude that is rooted in selfishness or pride will be purged. As a result of this tremendous shaking, all of Simon Peter's self-confidence would be gone, and all that would remain was God's sure foundation. He would be awakened to his true condition, the dead would be removed and the ripe fruit harvested, bringing him closer to his true foundation. He would no longer function independently but would be interdependent on the Lord.

> Peter boldly countered Jesus' words: "Lord, I am ready to go with You, both to prison and death." This statement was not born of the Spirit but out of his own self-confidence. He could not see the foreshadowing of this shaking.
>
> —John Bevere, *The Bait of Satan*, pp. 82-83

Applying the Lesson

Use the following specific directions to internalize the principles in the session and put them into practice.

19. Review the quoted text above and write down some thoughts about the ways God has used shaking and sifting to clarify His relationship with you. How have you grown from sifting and shaking?

   _____

   _____

   _____

   _____

   _____

20. What are the specific areas of your life for which you are presently asking God for revealed knowledge as you make choices and decisions?

   _____

   _____

   _____

   _____

   _____

21. Write down at least one sifting experience from your past that you know did not bring you godly results. Make those experiences a matter of focused prayer. Ask God to help you review those events and give you revealed knowledge about what He wanted or wants to accomplish in you through those difficult times.

_____

_____

_____

_____

Bait Warnings

A final opportunity for prayerful submission to the truth of the session.

What happened folks? Peter was shaken right down to the core. He now was not boasting in his own abilities any more. He's saying, "Jesus, there is nothing hidden from You. Now I know. I know I don't have the love to lay my life down. I know I love you affectionately." But let me tell you something. Jesus said, "This is what I see in you, Peter. You're going to feed my sheep." And then He says to him, "There will come a day that they will lead you where you don't want to go." And this is the death that He spoke of, that he would glorify Jesus. And church history shows that Peter, when he went to be crucified, looked at the men and said, "I am not worthy to die the death of my Lord." And so the Romans turned the cross upside down, and all his guts came up to his throat and that's how he glorified God in his death. He now had the love that it took to lay his life down. It wasn't in his own strength. He got shaken right down to the foundation and off of *that* foundation the Lord built upon his life.

That is what God desires to do with you. If you're walking in your own soulish ability and your confidence is not in Him, God says, "I know how to shake it up to get you down to the place where you can trust wholly in Me." And when you have that foundation, Jesus says, "You will not be offended."

—John Bevere, adapted from Video Session 7

Video Script for Lesson 7
All That Can Be Shaken Will Be Shaken

Luke's Gospel the twenty-second chapter please. Let me read you one verse of Scripture out of Hebrews, chapter 12. Just listen up. This is from the New Living Translation, Paul writes, *"He makes,"* He being God, *"[God] makes another promise."* He says, *'Once again I will shake not only the earth, but the heavens also.' This means that the things on earth will be shaken, so that only eternal things will be left."* How many of you know that God is in the shaking business?

What does shaking do? Five things. Number 1, brings whatever is being shaken closer to its foundation. Number 2, it removes what is dead. Number 3, it will harvest what is ripe. Number 4, it will awaken. And number 5, it will unify, or mix together, so that it can never be separated again. Interesting, huh?

Now, I want to show you an example here, another test for Simon Peter. Are you in Luke's Gospel the twenty-second chapter? I want to look at the twenty-first verse please. Well let's just read from verse 20: *"Likewise Jesus also took the cup after supper saying, 'This cup is the new covenant of my blood, which is shed for you.'"* Now verse 21 read carefully. *"But behold, the hand of my betrayer is with me on the table. And truly the Son of Man goes as it has been determined, but woe to that man by whom he is betrayed."* Look up at me please. This is the Last Supper, and He's just served them communion, He's washed their feet and then we would say it like this: He drops a bomb. Okay? Because here's the twelve guys, His closest associates that have been with Him for three and a half years, and He looks at all of them and says, "One of you is going to betray me." Can you imagine the feelings in that room? Can you just imagine? I mean the appetites are gone, the air is thick, they're stunned with silence for a

moment, they don't even know how to respond. They have watched Him heal the sick, raise the dead, feed them with just a few loaves; they watched Him teach them the most profound things that anybody had ever taught, they know He is Christ, the Son of God, and yet He looks at them and says, "One of you is going to betray Me." After the time of silence, now they begin to question each other. Because look at verse 23, *"Then they begin to question among themselves, which of them it would be that would do this thing."* Now, they begin to question among themselves. Who can do this? Who could possibly betray the Lord? But the thing is, they're questioning among themselves, did not confirm a pure motive. Because look at the very next verse. Look at verse 24, *"Now there was also a dispute among them as to which of them should be considered the greatest."* Jesus drops the bomb. They're stunned with silence and then they start saying, "Who could do this?" And that "who could do this" conversation turns into "who's the greatest." Now I'm going to tell you how it turns out into who's the greatest when they start saying who could do this. I mean they are really going who, who, which one of us would do this? And then all of a sudden, they start going, "Well it wouldn't be me. I certainly wouldn't do it. Because I've been faithful, and I've done this and I've done that and I've done this." And the other one goes, "Yeah, and I've done this and I've this it wouldn't be me." Now I'm going to tell you who's been the most outspoken of the whole group. Guess who? Peter. I mean he looks at all of them and says, "Hey guys, now wait a minute, let's talk about this. It wouldn't be me. Because I am the one who got the revelation that He is Christ, the Son of the living God." Now they all kind of look at him with these glaring eyes, you know. "Come on now, you know I am one of the three that went up on the mountain of Transfiguration. Come on. And I'm the one that offered to build the three tabernacles. And guys, let me remind you of something, I remember you eleven guys were sitting in the boat and I walked on the water. Now come on." So, you know, he's got the personality, that's the D. Have you ever heard of the Disc personality? D means driver, he's the dominant. And so he dominates the conversation. And he's got a track record to prove it, but you know what? Listen, his life we can see now is not being built off the foundation of revealed knowledge and the love of God. Because the Bible says we are to be rooted and grounded of the love of God. It's being built off of his past experiences and his own personality.

So Jesus immediately says in verse 25, Jesus has to say to all of them, He interrupts this conversation and says, "[Hey look guys,] *the kings of the Gentiles exercise lordship over them, and those who exercise authority over them are called benefactors. But not so among you, on the contrary, he who is greatest among you let him become the younger and he who governs is he who serves. For who is greater? He who sits at the table or he who serves, is it not he who sits at the table? Yet I am among you as one who serves.*" So He immediately says, "You guys, your whole motive is wrong." I mean can you believe these guys? He tells them He's about to be betrayed and out of this, they are arguing, "Who is the greatest?" I mean they're acting like a bunch of kids. Right? So Jesus has to get out of the mold of "Hey, I'm to be betrayed," and start teaching mood and about what it's about true humility and serving.

But then what's amazing is, look at verse 31, "*And the Lord said, 'Simon, Simon.'*" Now isn't this interesting, because He's not calling him Peter now. *"Simon, Simon,"* He said, "*Indeed Satan has asked for you that he may sift you as wheat.*" Now folks, what gave Satan the permission to ask for Simon? Come on say it. Say it. (Pride.) You see,

folks, let me make this statement. The Bible says that the angels of darkness are chained to darkness. They can only operate in the realm of darkness. That's why confession is so powerful. Because what you bring to the light, comes into the domain of the light. What you keep hidden in the dark stays under the domain of darkness. That's why the enemy always goes to your mind. He wants, what are strongholds? Strongholds are thoughts; each thought is like a brick, and if he can build a house, he can build a place he can inhabit. Demon-possessed people are just people that have, through their thought life, developed a place where Satan can inhabit, demonic powers can inhabit.

Now, pride attracts the enemy, like love attracts the Holy Spirit. So now, Satan's got permission. He is asked to sift Peter as wheat. Now the word "sift" in verse 31 there, is from the Greek word, *siniazo*. Now listen to this. This means "to sift, shake, in a sieve." Figuratively, by inward agitation, to try one's faith to the verge of overthrow. So Jesus says, "*Simon, Simon, indeed Satan has asked for you, that he sift you as wheat.*" Jesus goes on to say in verse 32, "*but I have prayed for you.*" Now watch Jesus' prayer, "*That your faith should not fail and when you have returned to me, strengthen your brethren.*" Now today, many people would go, "Hey guys, Satan wants to sift our brother Simon. We need to pray and bind the devil right now." But yet Jesus does not pray that the devil would be bound. Jesus prays rather, that his faith doesn't fail. Why? Because Jesus knows that right now Peter does not have what it takes to strengthen the brethren. He's got revelation knowledge. But his confidence is being built off of his personality and his soulish strengths, and not on the Lord. So Jesus said, "I'm gonna allow you to go through this shaking to the verge of overthrow, in order to shake out all the dead. To get rid of all the darkness, the things that would keep you from being a strong leader."

Now Peter is very, very, very courageous in his soul. Because we know, because Jesus later goes on to say, "One of you are going to betray me," and do you know what Peter says in a different Gospel? He said, "Lord, if everybody betrayed you and fled from you" because Jesus said they would all flee tonight, he said, "Not me," he said, "I would die." And I mean, he says it so boldly, all the rest of them are going, "Yeah, yeah, yeah, that's right, that's right." And Jesus looks back at Peter, I mean, He just doesn't stop, Jesus looks back and says, "Oh yeah, before the rooster crows twice, and you'll deny me three times." Peter goes, "No, no, no, I'd die before I'd deny You." He says "OK." So He goes to Gethsemane. And in Gethsemane the Bible says Jesus' soul was sorrowful even to the point of death. And so what did He do? For three hours Jesus prays. Now you know what's amazing, is in Luke's Gospel, we find that Peter, James, and John were close to Jesus. Their souls are also sorrowful, because you know why, you know what's happening? They sense the conflict that's about to happen. Jesus prays; they sleep. And Jesus says to them, *"Can't you tarry for one hour? The spirit is indeed willing but the flesh is weak."* And Jesus said, "Hey yeah, you're willing Peter. You said you'd die, but your flesh is weak and you need to bring your flesh under," but he's not praying. So the whole thing is, he's operating off of his personal strength, his soulish strength.

Now, a lot of people would say that Peter was a chicken. Why? Because he denied the Lord three times, in front of a servant girl. Isn't that right? I mean when we think of Peter we think, okay, big talker, but he's really a chicken because he denied the Lord in front of the servant girl. Right? But can I make this statement? How many chickens do you know that when they're standing in front of a fully armed army will take a sword, which they only have two swords, and attack the head of the army's right-hand man, and try to cut his head off but miss and cut his ear off? I don't know many chickens that would do that. But his

strength is out of his soul. Folks, let me make this statement. There are people that have strong souls, and there are people who have strong spirits. If you read in Luke's Gospel, chapter 2, I believe it is verse 80—I will never forget, I was flying home on an airplane coming back from an overseas nation, I read these words. *"So the child grew and became strong in spirit and was in the desert until the day of his manifestation."* That child being John the Baptist. And the words, "strong in spirit," jumped up off the page and hit me between the eyes. I thought *Wow! There is a strength God wants us to carry in our spirits.* And I began to think, you know, there are people with strong souls, and there are people with strong spirits. What's the difference? The only way you can tell the difference is when the pressure comes. Because the person of the spirit will react correctly, and the person strong in soul will do something soulish, prideful, or some other kind of thing wrong. Pressure will reveal where it is coming from.

Now, Jesus said, *"I prayed for you, that your faith should not fail."* I want to look at Judas and Simon. I want to look at the difference between these two. Now this is sounding pretty bleak right now for Peter, but you know, let's just look at Simon Peter and let's look at Judas. They have a couple similar things. Number 1, they both stayed all the way to the end. If you remember in John chapter 6, many of His disciples left, but Judas stayed, and Simon stayed both, right? They both basically denied Jesus in His toughest hour. Isn't that true? But that's where the similarities end.

The two had fundamental differences. Judas basically had his own agenda the whole time he was walking with Jesus. If you look at his words in all the Gospels, you'll find some interesting statements.

Matthew 24, verse 16, Judas said, *"What are you willing to give me if I . . . ."* so therefore he's basing everything on himself. He lied and flattered to gain advantage in Matthew 26. He also took money from the treasury, isn't that right? Now, the thing is, both men after Peter had denied Him and Judas had betrayed Him, both men were sorry for what they did. But Judas didn't have the foundation Peter had. Matthew 27:3–5, *"Then Judas, his betrayer, seeing that he was condemned was remorseful and brought back the thirty pieces of silver to the chief priests and the elders."* Now, folks, stop there and think about this. When he saw that Jesus was condemned, first of all, Judas really believed that Jesus would somehow get out of it. He would get out of it, but it would also give Judas thirty pieces of silver. You seeing his motives? When he saw that Jesus was condemned, Judas was remorseful. So, here's sorrow, but it's not godly sorrow, it's worldly sorrow. *"And he brought back the thirty pieces of silver to the chief priests and the elders saying 'I have sinned by betraying innocent blood.' And they said, 'What is that to us. You see to it.' Then he threw down the thirty pieces of silver in the temple and departed and he went and hung himself."* Now, notice this statement, "He said to the priests, 'I have sinned by betraying innocent blood.'" If Judas had known Jesus as Simon Peter, he would never have said I've betrayed innocent blood. He would have realized he betrayed the Lord, the Christ. The very fact that Peter knew who He was kept him going. It was a foundation. Judas had never had that revelation knowledge that He was the Christ, the Son of the living God. To Judas, He was an innocent man. If the revelation would have been in Judas of who He really was, he would have went back and asked for mercy.

That's why Saul never asked for mercy. Saul said, "Now Samuel, worship with me, because you've embarrassed me in front of my elders." He was still more interested in the fact that I have been embarrassed; the sorrow was focused on himself. David, however, cried out to the Lord and said, "I've sinned against You and You only, and I throw myself at Your mercy." Because David had such a revelation of who God was. Saul didn't. Peter had the revelation of who Jesus was, Judas didn't. What's the difference? Peter was hungry; Judas wasn't. Judas was in it for his own motives, his own self-serving motives; Peter was hungry for Him. When Peter first saw Jesus, he said, *"Depart from me Lord, for I am a sinful man."* He saw Him for who He was. It was revealed in him who He was. That's why, folks, I'll be very honest with you, I can go to church after church after church, and then come back years later and there's this person that's left and that person that's left. They're not even in church anymore; they're not even serving God. But then I'll look at somebody else and they have been through one battle after another battle after another battle but they're still there. Why? Because they know who He is. When you have that revelation, Jesus said, *"Listen, upon this rock I will build my church."* That rock speaks of stability, and he who believes will not act hastily. So now, watch this. If we go to Mark 4:16-17 again, *"And these are they likewise which are sown on stony ground when they have heard the word, immediately receive it with gladness and have no root in themselves."* Again, what is the root, or the foundation? Revelation knowledge. *"And so endure for a time but afterwards when affliction or persecution arises for the word's sake immediately they are offended."* What are we to be rooted in, the love of God. Amen?

We cannot lay our life down for someone we don't trust, isn't that true? We have to have a revelation of who He is; when we really understand who He is we come to understand that He is love. And when we know that He is love, we can trust Him. Folks, I had to deal with this issue one time. I thought about this, I thought, "How can the devil get Eve to turn on God?" Now think about it. She's living in the garden and His presence is right there. She's never been abused by a boss, a husband, or a father. She's living in a perfect society. How does the devil get her to turn on God?

Do you ever wonder about that? I mean, have you ever thought about that? Put your marker right there in Luke and go over to Genesis 3 and I'll show you. Genesis the third chapter.

Look at chapter 2:16. You get the command. *"And the Lord God commanded man, saying, 'Of every tree of the garden you may freely eat, but of the tree of the knowledge of good and evil you shall not eat. For in the day that you eat of it you shall surely die.'"* Now, read again verse 16, *"And the Lord God commanded man, saying, 'Of every tree of the garden you may freely eat.'"* Would you please look at the emphasis of His command? The emphasis is, you can eat of every tree in the garden. The exception is, except for the tree of the knowledge of good and evil. So the emphasis is, look at all you can eat. But God didn't want robots, He wanted people that could choose to obey and love Him, isn't that right? So, He says, "Except that tree." Now watch what happens. Look at chapter 3:1. *"Now the serpent was more cunning than any beast of the field which the Lord God had made, and he said to the woman, 'Has God indeed said, "You shall not eat of every tree of the garden?"'"* The serpent comes and the first thing he says to her is, "So, you can't eat from every tree, can you?" So, what does he do? He gets her eyes off of all she can eat over to look what she can't eat. So he ignores the generosity, the emphasis, and gets her eyes on the exception. Now, she answers him, but I'm sure while she's answering him the thought's going through her mind, "Hey, wait a minute." Because she's inspecting that fruit, she goes, "Wait a minute. That's good fruit! And it will make me wise. And it's desirable to my eyes." And she's judging this fruit. She's looking at it and saying, "Wait a minute. That's good fruit! Hold it! If that's good fruit, He's withholding something good from me. And if He's withholding something good from me, what else is He withholding from me?" So all of a sudden the enemy comes in real quick and says, "You're not going to die." She says, "That's good.

It will make me wise. He's withholding something from me." What is the enemy doing? He's perverting the character of God in her eyes. He's making God look like a taker now instead of the giver that He is. As soon as he can pervert the character of God in her eyes, she turns on Him.

Did you ever wonder why, in the New Testament, James says, *"Do not be deceived, every good and every perfect gift comes down from the Father of lights, of whom there is no variableness neither shadow of turning."* What James is saying is, "There is nothing good for you outside of God's will." Don't be deceived like Eve was. There is nothing good for you outside of His perfect will for your life. It may look good, she may look good, it may feel good, it may this, this, and this—it's not. Don't be deceived. That's what makes a person easy prey for an offense.

Judas had the character of Jesus—never had it right in his eyes. Peter, on the other hand, knew who He was. And that was the foundation that would keep him through this shaking to the verge of overthrow. I mean, folks, let me tell you something. Peter was on the verge of giving up. Do you know that Paul talked about pressures that came against him in Asia that he said that he despised even life? Do you know, do you realize that the word "tribulation" literally means anything which brings pressure to the soul? This shaking of Peter was so violent that it looked like everything was done. He gave up, folks. I mean, if you look at Mark 16:7, listen to what the angel said, *"But go and tell his disciples, and Peter, that he is going before you into Galilee."* Peter gave up, folks. He thinks, "I'm through." But yet, what is it that brought him back? The revelation knowledge of who He was.

That's why Jesus could look at him and say, "All right, Peter. Do you love Me?" Do you remember in John 20, *"Do you love me?"* You know the Greek word that He uses for love there is *agapeo* which means "the love of God which lays its life down"? Jesus says, "Do you love Me enough, Peter, to lay your life down?" He asks him again. Go over there. John 21. Look at verse 15. *"So when they had eaten breakfast."* This is after the resurrection. *"Jesus said to Simon Peter, 'Simon, son of Jonah, do you love me* (that word love is *agape) more than these?'"* Now notice He says, "more than these." Now do you know who He's talking about? He's not talking about the fish; He's talking about the rest of the disciples, because they had an argument a little while ago about who was the greatest. So Jesus says, "Okay, do you love Me enough to lay down your life for Me, more than these guys?" He said to Him, *"Yes, Lord, you know that I love you."* But you know the word that Peter comes back with is not *agape*; it's *phileo*. Peter says, "I love you affectionately, but no, I don't have the love that it takes to lay my life down, because I've already proven that." And Jesus said, *"Feed my lambs."* Then Jesus said to him a second time, *"Simon, son of Jonah, do you love me?"* He uses *agape* again. "Do you love Me enough to lay your life down for Me?" He said, "Lord, I love you affectionately—*phileo*." In other words, "I don't have the love it takes to lay my life down." And Jesus said to him, *"Tend my sheep."* Verse 17, He said the third time, *"Simon, son of Jonah, do you love me?"* And now the word that Jesus uses is *phileo*, "Do you love me affectionately?" *"And Peter was grieved because he said to him a third time, 'Do you love me.'* And he said to Him, "Lord, you know all things. You know

that I love you affectionately—*phileo*." Jesus said to him, *"Feed my sheep."*

What happened folks? He was shaken right down to the core. Peter now was not boasting in his own abilities any more. He's saying, "Jesus, there is nothing hidden from You. Now I know. I know I don't have the love to lay my life down. I know I love You affectionately." But let me tell you something. Jesus said, "This is what I see in you, Peter. You're going to feed my sheep." And then He says to him, *"There will come a day that they will lead you where you don't want to go."* And this is the death that He spoke of, that he would glorify Jesus. And church history shows that Peter, when he went to be crucified looked at the men and said, "I am not worthy to die the death of my Lord." And so the Romans turned the cross upside down, and all his guts came up to his throat and that's how he glorified God in his death. He now had the love that it took to lay his life down. It wasn't in his own strength. He got shaken right down to the foundation and off of that foundation the Lord built upon his life.

That is what God desires to do with you. If you're walking in your own soulish ability and your confidence is not in Him, God says, "I know how to shake it up to get you down to the place where you can trust wholly in Me. And when you have that foundation, Jesus says, "You will not be offended."

Lesson 8

The Rock of Offense

Therefore it is also contained in the Scripture, "Behold,
I lay in Zion a chief cornerstone, elect, precious, and he
who believes on Him will by no means be put to shame."
Therefore, to you who believe, He is precious; but to
those who are disobedient, "The stone which the
builders rejected has become the chief cornerstone,"
and "A stone of stumbling and a rock of offense."
They stumble, being disobedient to the word,
to which they also were appointed.
(1 Peter 2:6–8)

Summary of *The Bait of Satan,* Chapter 9

Bevere begins this chapter with some commentary on
the way the word "believe" is used today. "In the eyes
of most," he notes, "it has become a mere acknowl-
edgment of a certain fact." Using the Scripture above,
he points out that "believe" and "disobedience" can be
used as opposites. That means there is a very close
relationship between "believe" and "obey" in biblical
language. The Jesus we believe in must be the same
Jesus we obey.

Because many of the people in His day refused to
believe in Jesus to the point of obedience, they
responded with offense. This was predicted by prophets,
including old Simeon who held Jesus as a tiny child and

declared, "Behold, this Child is destined for the fall and rising of many in Israel" (Luke 2:34). John points out that the "fall and rising" mentioned by Simeon described the extreme effect Jesus had on those around Him—He caused them to stumble in continued unbelief or rise to a new way of living.

Bevere continues to describe the one-sided views of Jesus often presented to children that "do not give the whole picture" (p. 97). Jesus certainly spoke forcefully and directly to those who were living falsely, whether they were self-righteous Pharisees or half-hearted followers. As Bevere summarizes, "Jesus did not compromise truth in order to keep people from being offended" (p. 94).

Bevere illustrates from Samuel's relationship with Saul and his own experiences in ministry situations how dangerous it can be to compromise the truth in order to avoid offense. The matter of offense clearly became a purging aspect of Jesus' ministry. He offended people in His hometown who couldn't accept His divinity. He offended His own family members who forgot His uniqueness. His own staff (His disciples) were not immune to offense. Each of these trouble areas boiled down to Jesus' fierce allegiance to the truth. Lastly, even His closest friends and John the Baptist passed through the valley of offense in order to clarify their faith. Jesus risked every friendship and all His prestige in exchange for His ultimate purpose—to be Savior and exercise His Lordship. To that end, He accepted the added role of being seen as a rock of offense.

Warm-Up Questions

Use the following questions to prepare your heart and mind for the personal and/or group study in which you will participate.

1. What were the earliest lessons that you remember learning about Jesus?

_____

_____

_____

_____

_____

2. When should friends risk offending friends?

_____

_____

_____

_____

_____

3. Briefly describe a situation in which a friend risked offending you in order to communicate the truth to you.

_____

_____

_____

_____

_____

Teaching by John Bevere

Watch the eighth session video presentation.

Personal Notes on Video Session 8

Use the following lines to keep notes as you view the video.

_____

_____

_____

_____

_____

_____

_____

_____

_____

_____

We're saved by grace. Now let me say this to you: No man, no woman, no child will ever be able to look at God and say, "My good works have earned me a place in your kingdom." We are saved by grace and only by grace. It's a gift that cannot be earned. However, James comes along and says you really have grace, you really have faith. Show me your grace without your works and I'll show you my grace *by* my works, or show me your faith without your works and I'll show you my faith *by* my works. In other words, the evidence that I've really got the grace of God in me is the fact that I obey. The evidence that I am a true believer is the fact that I have obedience in my life. You show me a person that consistently, repeatedly rebels and disobeys, I'll show you a person that really doesn't know God. Now in the ministry of Jesus, He is called the Rock of offense. You will notice that everywhere Jesus went, He went offending people. Who were the people that He was offending? He was

STUDENT NOTES

offending people that were not true believers, not obedient, and also He was offending people that had the wrong foundations in their life.

—John Bevere, adapted from Video Session 8

Teaching Review

Use the following questions to consider some of the central points made by John Bevere during this video session.

4. Early in the video presentation, how did Bevere describe the problem we create by the way we use the word "believe"?

5. Why is Jesus called "the Rock of offense"?

_____

_____

_____

_____

_____

_____

_____

_____

_____

_____

_____

_____

6. What were the specific groups in Jesus' life that He offended in one way or another?

_____

_____

_____

_____

_____

_____

_____

_____

7. What mistakes does Bevere point out that preachers today often make when they try to avoid offenses by "lightening" or "softening" the message of Jesus?

STUDENT NOTES

_____

_____

_____

_____

_____

_____

_____

_____

_____

_____

_____

_____

_____

_____

_____

_____

Exploring God's Word

Revisit the key passages from which John Bevere develops his teaching.

1 Peter 2:6–8 *Therefore it is also contained in the Scripture, "Behold, I lay in Zion a chief corner-stone, elect, precious, and he who believes on Him will by no means be put to shame." Therefore, to you who believe, He is precious; but to those who are disobedient, "The stone which the builders rejected has become the chief cornerstone," and "A stone of stumbling and a rock of offense." They stumble, being disobedient to the word, to which they also were appointed.*

8. As Peter quotes from prophetic passages in the Old Testament, how many different descriptions or titles for Jesus does he find?

    _____

    _____

    _____

    _____

    _____

    _____

    _____

9. What does Bevere have to say about the contrast between the two groups of people in these verses?

    _____

    _____

    _____

    _____

    _____

    _____

    _____

    _____

    _____

    _____

    Personal Application

    _____

    _____

    _____

_____
_____
_____
_____
_____

Hebrews 3:12-19 *Beware, brethren, lest there be in any of you an evil heart of unbelief in departing from the living God; but exhort one another daily, while it is called "Today," lest any of you be hardened through the deceitfulness of sin. For we have become partakers of Christ if we hold the beginning of our confidence steadfast to the end, while it is said: "Today, if you will hear His voice, do not harden your hearts as in the rebellion." For who, having heard, rebelled? Indeed, was it not all who came out of Egypt, led by Moses? Now with whom was He angry forty years? Was it not with those who sinned, whose corpses fell in the wilderness? And to whom did He swear that they would not enter His rest, but to those who did not obey? So we see that they could not enter in because of unbelief.*

10. Describe the warning that the writer of Hebrews is giving to his readers. Who were they and what was he concerned about?

_____
_____
_____
_____
_____

STUDENT NOTES

_____

_____

_____

_____

_____

_____

_____

_____

11. How are the terms "unbelief" and "obey" used in this passage?

_____

_____

_____

_____

_____

_____

_____

_____

_____

_____

_____

Personal Application

_____

_____

_____

_____

_____

_____

_____

_____

_____

_____

_____

Luke 2:25-35 *And behold, there was a man in Jerusalem whose name was Simeon, and this man was just and devout, waiting for the Consolation of Israel, and the Holy Spirit was upon him. And it had been revealed to him by the Holy Spirit that he would not see death before he had seen the Lord's Christ. So he came by the Spirit into the temple. And when the parents brought in the Child Jesus, to do for Him according to the custom of the law, he took Him up in his arms and blessed God and said, "Lord, now You are letting Your servant depart in peace, according to Your word; for my eyes have seen Your salvation which You have prepared before the face of all peoples, a light to bring revelation to the Gentiles, and the glory of Your people Israel." And Joseph and His mother marveled at those things which were spoken of Him. Then Simeon blessed them, and said to Mary His mother, "Behold, this Child is destined for the fall and rising of many in Israel, and for a sign which will be spoken against (yes, a sword will pierce through your own soul also), that the thoughts of many hearts may be revealed."*

12. How does this passage prophesy that Jesus will be the Rock of offense?

_____

_____

_____

_____

_____

_____

_____

_____

_____

_____

_____

_____

_____

_____

_____

13. How does this passage and Bevere's comments on it also demonstrate again the significance of revealed knowledge in comparison to observed knowledge?

_____

_____

_____

_____

_____

_____

_____

_____

_____

_____

_____

_____

_____

Personal Application

_____

_____

_____

_____

_____

_____

_____

_____

_____

_____

Matthew 15:7-14 *"Hypocrites! Well did Isaiah prophesy about you, saying: 'These people draw near to Me with their mouth and honor Me with their lips, but their heart is far from Me. And in vain they worship Me, teaching as doctrines the commandments of men.'" When He had called the multitude to Himself, He said to them, "Hear and understand: Not what goes into the mouth defiles a man; but what comes out of the mouth, this defiles a man." Then His disciples came and said to Him, "Do You know that the Pharisees were offended when they heard this saying?" But He answered and said, "Every plant which My heavenly Father has not planted will be uprooted. Let them alone. They are blind leaders of the blind. And if the blind leads the blind, both will fall into a ditch."*

14. Jesus potentially offended three different groups in this passage. Who were they and what did Jesus say to each of them?

_____

_____

_____

_____

_____

_____

_____

_____

_____

_____

_____

_____

_____

_____

_____

15. Why did Jesus level such harsh charges against the Pharisees and yet command the disciples to honor them?

_____

_____

_____

_____

_____

_____

STUDENT NOTES

_____

_____

_____

_____

_____

_____

Personal Application

_____

_____

_____

_____

_____

_____

_____

_____

_____

_____

_____

_____

_____

Exposing the Truth

Use the following questions to help reach conclusions
regarding the Scriptures and insights from the session.

16. Why is it crucial to understand that Jesus is the
    Rock of offense?

_____

_____

_____

STUDENT NOTES

_____

_____

_____

_____

_____

_____

_____

_____

_____

_____

17. What has Bevere learned about the natural effects of preaching the truth?

_____

_____

_____

_____

_____

_____

_____

_____

_____

_____

_____

_____

18. Review the box below and describe what Bevere learned about preaching a truth instead of preaching the truth God wanted him to preach?

_____

_____

_____

_____

_____

_____

_____

_____

_____

_____

I was in a big conference . . . and the Spirit of God told me to preach on offenses and the bait of Satan, and I remember I was writing other books—there were other hot issues in my heart—and I didn't want to preach it because I felt like I'd preached it so much, it wasn't that exciting. I remember going into that meeting that night and preaching what was hot in my heart, and you know what? People got excited, they were getting excited, they were standing and going "Yes!" like that—you know what to do. And you know, by the end, they were on the floor, and we had a great meeting.

The next morning when I woke up, I didn't get out of bed. I rolled out on my knees. Because, I mean, the Spirit of God was all over me, and not in a happy way.

And I remember saying, "Lord, I didn't preach what you wanted me to preach last night, did I?" And He goes, "No, you didn't."

And I said, "Oh God, forgive me." And I started pleading for forgiveness. The load didn't lift. I felt like I was going to die. So I go to the airport, and I fly to the West Coast. The whole time I'm going, "God, please forgive me. I feel like I am going to die." Finally we fly out to San Diego and we start circling the city of San Diego, and all of a sudden that heaviness, that heavy, heavy guilt feeling, just lifts off of me like this. It goes whish, just like that.

The Spirit of God speaks to me and says, "This is a new city, now obey Me!"

I said, "Lord, I've been pleading for forgiveness ever since this morning, and I even went a two-hour time change and had two more hours to put up with this. Why did You let me carry this the whole day?"

And the Spirit of God said, "Because I wanted you to know the seriousness of what you did. There were pastors in that meeting last night that needed to hear what I had put in your heart on offenses, and you preached what you wanted to, and now they missed what I wanted them to get."

And I said, "God, I will never, ever do this again." But you see, here is the thing that is really scary. You got these mainline denominational ministers like what I experienced, and then you got other ministers and what they're doing is making happy seeker-friendly messages and making sure that everybody gets in there and lives in sin and still feels comfortable.

—John Bevere, adapted from Video Session 8

Applying the Lesson

Use the following specific directions to internalize the principles in the session and put them into practice.

19. In what ways have you experienced Jesus' role as the Rock of offense in your own life?

_____

_____

_____

_____

20. As you watched John's presentation in this session, what did God's Spirit say to you about the connection between belief and obedience in your life right now?

_____

_____

_____

_____

21. In what areas of life do you desire God's help in becoming more open and willing to stand with Jesus, the Rock of offense?

_____

STUDENT NOTES

Bait Warnings

A final opportunity for prayerful submission to the truth of the session.

> So as leaders, we've got to understand something. There are times that God will give us something to preach. It's just plain, simple truth. I'm not talking about a revelation that is not in the Bible. I'm talking about just truth! He will upset people. And they may leave. But Jesus' attitude was "Let them go." Amen? Now you would think, "That's not very loving." That *is* loving. Because you can't mix wheat and tares. You cannot mix serpents and sheep, wolves and sheep. Are you with me? And the Word of God will expose what is in people. Shall we say, when the fire comes, the snakes come out. Snakes don't like fire.
>
> —John Bevere, adapted from Video Session 8

Video Script for Lesson 8
The Rock of Offense

Lesson number 8, we're talking about the rock of offense, and I want to read from 1 Peter, chapter 2, verse 6. *"Therefore it is also contained in the scripture, 'Behold I lay in Zion. A chief cornerstone elect precious, and he who believes on Him will by no means be put to shame.'"* Verse 7, *"Therefore to you who believe he is precious, but to those who are disobedient the stone which the builders rejected, has become the chief cornerstone."* Now notice in verse 7 again, *"Therefore to you who believe he is precious, but to those who are disobedient,"* notice that Peter contrasts the word "believe" and "disobedient." You see that? He says they are opposites.

Now I want to make a statement today, tonight, that today in our English language we have reduced the word "believe" down to what it is not. In the days of Bible writers, the word "believe" meant to "obey." Today, the word "believe" means that you acknowledge and you believe in somebody's existence but it doesn't necessarily mean to obey. I mean if you said the opposite of the word "believe" is "disobedient" today on the S.A.T., you'd flunk the question. Hebrews the third chapter. This is so important that we understand this. Today we have so misrepresented this word because we teach that all you have to do is believe that Jesus existed, died on Calvary, and rose again and you're saved. Everything is great. You're in good standing with God. But I want to show you that the word "believe" means "to obey." Hebrews, chapter 3, look at verse 12. The writer of Hebrews says, *"Beware brethren."* Notice he is talking to believers, *"Beware brethren, lest there be in any of you an evil heart of unbelief and departing from the living God."* Now if we take that word "unbelief" and we put it in today's context, to believe just means that you acknowledge in somebody's existence. Right? Or you believe that the

Lord exists and died on the cross. Well, how are they going to have an unbelieving heart? Everyone of these people knew that God existed. Verse 15, *"Today if you will hear his voice do not harden your heart as in the rebellion."* Verse 16, *"For who having heard, rebelled. Indeed was it not all who came out of Egypt led by Moses? Now with whom was he angry those forty years? Was it not with those who sinned whose corpses fell in the wilderness?"* Now look at verses 18 and 19 carefully, *"And to whom did he swear that they would not enter into his rest but to those who did not obey."* Now look at verse 19, *"So we see that they could not enter in because of unbelief."* So do you notice that He says that unbelief, and not obeying, are synonyms? Now look at verse 19, *"So we see that they could not enter in because of unbelief."* In other words unbelief is not to obey. To believe is to obey and to not believe is to not obey. Now we have got to get this firmly established in our hearts, because today what we have in the church is a gospel that says that you just believe He existed, and died on the cross, and everything is fine. Doesn't matter, you can disobey, live however you want to, but you see folks, that is a lie. And we've got to preach the gospel.

I have found that today, when people take the word "grace" it's all perverted the same way. They look at grace as the big cover-up. In other words, I know I'm not obeying, and I'm not living the way I should, but thank God for His grace. And yet Jesus said, *"Not everybody who says to me, 'Lord, Lord' is going to enter the kingdom and he who does will be with my Father."* It's not just confessing Jesus that gets a person into heaven. It's confessing and doing.

Now let me say this to you. No man, no woman, no child will ever be able to look at God and say,

"My good works have earned me a place in Your kingdom." We are saved by grace and only by grace. It's a gift that cannot be earned; however, James comes along and says, "You really got grace? You really got faith? Show me your faith without your works and I'll show you my faith by my works." In other words, the evidence that I've really got the grace of God in me is the fact that I obey. You show me a person that consistently, repeatedly rebels, and disobeys; I'll show you a person that really doesn't know God. Now in the ministry of Jesus, He is called the Rock of offense. You will notice that everywhere Jesus went, He went offending people. Who were the people that He was offending? He was offending people that were not true believers, not obedient, and also He was offending people that had wrong foundations in their life.

He made the statement, He said one of two things are going to happen. Either you're going to fall on the rock and be broken or the rock's going to fall on you and grind you to powder.

In Luke's Gospel, the second chapter we read in verse 25, "And behold there was a man in Jerusalem, whose name was Simeon. And this man was just, and devout, waiting for the consolation of Israel and the Holy Spirit was upon him. And it had been revealed to him by the Holy Spirit that he would not see death before he saw the Lord's Christ. So he came in by the Spirit—into the temple and when the parents brought the child Jesus [now Jesus at this time was thirty-three days old] to do for him according to the custom of the law, he took him up into his arms and he blessed God and he said, 'Lord now you are letting me depart in peace because my eyes have seen the Messiah.'" Now I find this an amazing thing. This man walks into the temple where there's thousands of people, finds a couple from Nazareth, picks up their thirty-three-day-old baby, lifts Him up and says, "the Messiah." Yet thirty-three years later, the Pharisees, who could quote the first five books of

the Bible from memory and watching them cast out devils and they don't even know who He is. What's the difference? He came in "by the Spirit." He knew God intimately. Now look what he goes on to say, verse 33, "And Joseph and his mother marveled at those things that were spoken of him. Then Simeon blessed him and he said to Mary his mother, 'Behold this child is destined for the fall and the rising of many in Israel, and shall be a sign which will be spoken against." Yes, now watch this prophecy, "A sword will pierce through your own souls also that the thoughts of many hearts will be revealed." I want to walk you through the Gospels and show you how that prophecy literally came true.

Jesus, everywhere He went, you will find Him offending people. He was the sword that pierced through people's souls. Go with me please to Matthew, the fifteenth chapter. In Matthew, the fifteenth chapter, I want to look at the seventh verse. Jesus made this statement to the leaders. He said, "You hypocrites, He said well that Isaiah prophecy about you saying these people draw near to me with their mouths, and they honor me with their lips, but their heart is far from me. And in vain they worship me, teaching as the doctrines of the commandments of man." Look at verse 10, "When He called the multitude to himself, he said to them, 'Hear and understand not what goes in does not defile men but what comes out of the mouth that defiles the man.'" Verse 12, "Then his disciples came and said to him, 'Do you know that the Pharisees were offended when they heard this saying?'" Now of course they were. He looked at them and said, "You're a bunch of hypocrites. You draw with Me with your mouth, but your heart is far from Me," and this offended the Pharisees, who were the religious leaders. So these guys came to Jesus, "Hey now listen Jesus, what You preached really upset these guys." But I want you to notice what Jesus said, now look at the next verse, verse 13. But He answered and said, "Every plant, which *my heavenly Father has not planted, will be uprooted. Let them alone, the blind leaders of the blind let the blind lead the blind and let them both fall into a ditch."* What is Jesus saying here? Jesus is saying that God, the Father, will actually use offense to root people out that really aren't planted in His kingdom.

What we have today is, we have a bunch of preachers that are lightening the message in order to keep more people in the church. It's very simple, you broaden the message, you increase the people that come to your church. Now here's the deception. The thought in the minister's mind is this, they want so badly to see people escape hell and go into heaven, they're thinking, "I don't want to say words that are going to drive people away from Jesus." Yet I find Jesus driving people away constantly with His words. With truth. Let me tell you again, what the Bible calls Him; it calls Him the Rock of offense, or stumbling stone, which means huge rock. Can I be honest with you? The way we preach Jesus in America, He's no more a stumbling stone. We've reduced Him down to a little pebble that anyone can walk right over.

I remember I was in a first year that we were traveling. Lisa and I went to a mainline denominational Spirit-filled church. And on Sunday morning I preached, a much nicer message than what I preached here today, to be honest with you. I'm a lot stronger here today than I was that Sunday morning. It was a basic message of repentance. And after the service we were at the cafeteria eating. The pastor looks at me and he goes, "Well brother," he said, "you know what? Some of the things you were saying this morning, God has really been speaking to my heart. My people just weren't ready for them." He said, "Because if I would've started preaching, I would've lost a third of my congregation." Now before I could even respond to him, Lisa blurts out of her mouth, she goes, "Since when did you become the pastor and not Jesus?" And he looks at my wife, and he drops

his head, and he looks back up and says, "Well that's what the Lord said to me a month ago. He said, 'I know what these people can handle.'" Now you know what's amazing is the next four days I preached in that church and you know what? I guess things were getting exposed. You know, many times when you're being prophetic, you don't even know you're being prophetic. You think you're just speaking from your heart, but God's just nailing things. Do you understand what I am saying? And that's where I learned that religious spirits are vicious. They're vicious. And I remember, after I left that place, the guy gave me that honorarium check.

What means more to me than the offering given to me is that smile. That is the Holy Spirit saying, "I'm pleased you said what I wanted said." Because let me tell you something. I've gotten big offerings in the cities and there wasn't a smile, and I remember the one time in particular that I'm talking about. I was in a big conference, with five major pastors there, and the Spirit of God told me to preach on offenses and *The Bait of Satan*, and I remember I was writing other books there were other hot issues in my heart and I didn't want to preach it because I felt like I'd preached it so much, it wasn't that exciting. I remember going into that meeting that night and preaching what was hot in my heart, and you know what? People got excited, they were getting excited, they were standing and going, "Yes" like that, you know what to do. And you know, by the end, they were on the floor, and we had a great meeting.

The next morning, when I woke up, I didn't get out of bed; I rolled out on my knees. Because, I mean, the Spirit of God was all over me, and not in a happy way. And I remember saying, "Lord, I didn't preach what You wanted me to preach last night, did I?" And He goes, "No, you didn't." And I said, "Oh God, forgive me." And I started pleading for forgiveness. Well, it didn't lift. I felt like I was going to die. So I go to the airport, and I fly to the West Coast city the whole time I'm going, "God, please forgive me. I feel like I am going to die." Finally we fly out to San Diego and we start circling the city of San Diego, and all of a sudden, that heaviness, that heavy, heavy guilt feeling just lifts off of me like this. It goes *whish*, just like that. The Spirit of God speaks to me and says, "This is a new city, now obey Me!" I said, "Lord, I've been pleading for forgiveness ever since this morning, and I even went two-hour time change in this thing and had two more hours to put up with this." And I said, "Why did You let me carry this this whole day?" And the Spirit of God said, "Because I wanted you to know the seriousness of what you did. There were pastors in that meeting last night that needed to hear what I had put in your heart, on offenses, and you preached what you wanted to, and now they missed what I wanted them to get." And I said, "God, I will never, ever do this again." But you see, here is the thing that is really scary. You got these mainline guys like what I experienced, and then you got other guys and what they're doing is making happy seeker-friendly message and make sure that everybody get in there and live in sin and still feel comfortable. Let me tell you something. Truth will pierce and penetrate. He is the Rock of offense. He is the stumbling stone. But instead, what people want to do is they want to create a "come to Jesus and get" message today in the United States. Let's get people hungry for what God can do for you. So then what you have is people coming and seeking God for what He can do for me, and not for who He is. And that it's like a woman marrying a man for his money. She's not marrying him for who he is, she marries him for what he can do for her.

Now a person, who preaches truth, is a person who preaches the character of God. He is the person that is more interested in seeing people becoming conformed to the image of Jesus Christ. That is the goal of Christianity folks. The goal of Christianity is to be conformed to His image. When you have somebody that is in the Spirit and he is speaking the Word of God, let me tell you something, it will discern what is in your heart. It will pierce in your heart. If it just makes your soul feel real nice and good, I don't think it came from the Rock of offense.

So as leaders, we got to understand something. There are times that God will give us something to preach, its' just plain simple truth. I'm not talking about a revelation that is not in the Bible. I'm talking about just truth! He will upset people. And they may leave. But Jesus' attitude was "Let 'em go." Now you would think, "That's not very loving." Yes that's loving, because you can't mix wheat and tares, you cannot mix serpents and sheep, wolves and sheep. And the Word of God will expose what is in people. Go with me please to Matthew, chapter 13, Matthew 13, verse 55. Jesus is in His own hometown. Now this is where He offended His own hometown. Watch this. Verse 54, *"When he had come to his own country, he taught them in their synagogue so that they were astonished and said, 'Where did this man get this wisdom? And what mighty works. Is this not the carpenter's son? Is not his mother called Mary? And is not his brothers, James, Joses, Simon and Judas? And are not his sisters not all with us? Where did this man get all of these things?' So they were offended at him, but Jesus said to them, 'A prophet is not without honor, except in his own country and in his own house.'"* What offended them? It was the truth He was preaching. It was the miracles He was doing. Now what's interesting was, they were not offended with Him when He was the nice carpenter's son, when He was walking around the hills of Galilee, meditating and praying. They weren't offended then. It was when He started coming out and speaking the Word of God. They were offended. So He offended His hometown. And we find in another Gospel that they were so offended, they tried to bring Him to the cliff of a hill and throw Him off the cliff and kill Him, that is how upset they were at Him. I'll tell you, religious people are vicious. I said they're vicious. He offended His own family members.

If you go to Mark's Gospel, chapter 3, verse 21 please. *"But when his own people"*—in the NIV it says, *his own family.* You know when I got saved, I was a Catholic boy, and when I got saved when I found out that Jesus had brothers and sisters, it just about blew me out of the water. He had four brothers and a bunch of sisters. It doesn't take away from the virgin birth. She was a virgin when she had Jesus, but that didn't mean she couldn't have babies after that. *"When his own people heard about this, they went out and lay hold of him and said 'He's out of His mind.'"* This is His family. His family says, "He's out of His mind, He's gone deranged." Now go to verse 31. *"Then his brothers and his mother came standing outside,"* they wouldn't even come in, and they sent in, calling to Him, because they thought He was out of His mind and they wanted to take Him home; they wanted to grab Him. *"And a multitude was sitting around beside him and they said, 'Look your mother and brothers are standing outside seeking for you.' He said, 'Who is my mother and brothers?' And he looked around in the circle and said, to those who sat about him, and said, 'Here are my mothers and brothers. For whoever does the will of God is my brother, and my sister, and my mother.'"* I remember when I got saved, my family wasn't very enthusiastic. I mean they weren't, and I remember it got to the point where they actually didn't invite me to some of my dad's parties, his retirement party and stuff like that, because they thought I would preach to everybody. And then when I dropped the bomb, and I said that I was going to Bible College, my mom said, "You are going to Bible College over my dead body." And I had an engineering degree. And they had hopes for me and all this. And they said, "If you are going into ministry, you're going to be a priest," and I said, " No, Mom and Dad, God's call-

ing me to Bible school." And I said, "Mom, I respect you and I love you, but this is what God is calling me to do." And she said, "Alright, but you are paying for it by yourself." And I said, "Fine, I'll pay for it myself." And you know, what's amazing is, I made the decision, with my whole family rejecting me, which they did, I was going to serve God. Now you know what? Jesus' family rejected Him, but you know what is really neat? You will find His mother and His brothers up in the Upper Room. And that was what God used to minister to me. I said, "Lord, if I obey You, You'll take care of my family." And you know what is really neat is now my mom and my dad read my books and watch my videos. And you know what? When my dad was 79 years old (he is 82 today), I had the privilege of praying with him to receive Jesus Christ. And you know what is really neat? When my grandfather, my mom's dad, he's Mr. Italian man. He's a very strong devout Catholic. He persecuted me more than anybody else in my family. I mean he really laid into me. And I remember the Lord just saying, "Love him, love him, love him, love him," and I kept loving, and you know what? When he was 89 years old, I led him to the Lord. And do you know, it was such a powerful conversion, it was such a powerful conversion, every time I came to his apartment he would sit there and weep and drop his head into his hands. And he would say to me, "What's wrong with me?" He said, "I feel like I am losing my mind because I am weeping all the time. And I only weep when I pray, and when you come over." And I said, "Do you know what it is?" I said, "You lived 89 years apart from the love of God, and now the love of God, and the presence of God in your life, and when the presence of God comes, you just break down like a little baby." And it was so beautiful, because when he was 89, he told me, "The Lord told me that I got two more years to live," and you know what? At 91 years old he went home to be with the Lord. So you know when you obey God, God says, "I'll take care of your family." Just live the life before them.

We saw already tonight that He offended His own staff by His preaching. He preached something so strong His staff said, "We've had it, we can't handle it, we're leaving." When they left, He didn't run after them saying, "Guys, you got to come back." He turned to the rest of them and said, "You want to go too?" He was ready to start all over again by Himself.

If you're noticing something, He is offending people with truth. Now He also offended, His close friends. If you go over to John, chapter 11, you will find out that Lazarus, who was a friend of His, and Martha and Mary. Lazarus becomes sick and Martha and Mary send messengers to find Jesus. Now you got to understand. Jesus was someplace in Judea. And He's teaching in a house. And these guys got to search everywhere. They finally found Him in the house, and they say, "Jesus, you got to come really quick. Your really good buddy, Lazarus, is sick. He's going to die." And you know what the Bible says? When He heard that he was sick, He stayed there two more days. Now you know what the Lord told me? Do you know what you would've done? You would've jumped in your car and got your Bible, robe on, and rubbed oil all over his head, and said, "Be healed in Jesus' name," and never looked inside to see what I was saying. But He said, "I only do what I saw My Father do, and My Father wanted Me teaching." So He said, "I just kept teaching." Can you imagine those messengers going, "He doesn't care"? And I'm sure a couple of them went back to Martha and Mary and said, "Look man, He's just sitting there; He's not doing anything." Lazarus meantime dies. Now if you go read this carefully, you would be amazed. You know what the first words out of Martha and Mary, I'm talking about the real Mary, the Gospel the Woman's Aglow lady, okay? The one who sits at His feet. The first words out of both of their mouths, you know what it is? "If You would have been here, Lazarus wouldn't have died." They're offended. I mean you go read it. That's the first words out of

their mouths. "Lord, if You would have been here, he wouldn't have died." They're having to deal with this offense.

Now you want to know who else He offended? John the Baptist. Go with me to Luke's Gospel, the seventh chapter and you will be amazed at this. Luke's Gospel, the seventh chapter, look at verse 18. *"Then the disciples of John reported to him, concerning all these things. And John calling two of his disciples and sending them to Jesus saying, 'Are you the coming one or do we look for another?'"* What? What do you mean, "Are you the coming one or do we look for another?" This is John the Baptist. This is the one who recognized Jesus when He was in His mother's womb! He jumped! I mean this is the one, when you baptized Him, the Lord, he saw the Spirit of God ascending upon Him like a dove and the Lord spoke to Him and said, "Whomever you see the Spirit of God descending upon Him like a dove, this is the one whom will baptize with the Holy Ghost and fire." This is the Christ, the Lamb of God, right? What do you mean, "Are you the coming one?"

Why is he doing this? Because, remember what I said in the first lesson? We set ourselves up for an offense when we have expectations. Now John gave up his life to serve God. Not only that, he has got this diet of locusts and wild honey, and he's wearing a camel hair with a leather belt holding it together. Jesus was wearing a seamless robe. Now you got to understand, that's a nice robe. It's so nice that Roman soldiers are going to gamble over it to see who gets it. That's how nice it is. He's eating with sinners. He's drinking at their parties with them. And He's not coming to visit John in prison. And John's going, "Hold on! This is not what I expected." So look what Jesus does here. He says, now watch this, verse 20, *"When the men had come to Jesus, they said, 'John the Baptist has sent us, saying are you the coming one or should we look for another?'"* And Jesus is going, "Oh boy." So verse 21, *"That very hour, he cured many infirmities and afflictions, evil spirits and to many blind he gave sight."* Verse 22, *"Jesus answered and said to them, 'Go and tell John, the things you have seen and heard. That the blind see, the lame walk, the lepers are cleansed, the deaf hear, and the dead are raised, and the poor have the gospel preached to them.'"* He's quoting Isaiah, alright? And then He says, "P.S." Verse 23, *"Blessed is he who is not offended because of me."* Wham! Let me tell you something. He is the Rock of offense. And I'm going to tell you this. He is absolute truth, He is truth. And when you have a confrontation sometimes with truth and things aren't quite aligned right in your life, you get the opportunity to fall on truth and be broken. You know a horse that is broken, is a horse that's been submitted.

These people, John the Baptist, Martha, Mary, Lazarus, Martha, Mary, His disciples, they loved Him. But they all had to confront, they all had to deal with confrontation, the Rock of offense. Even Peter's going, "Where else shall we go?" But you know what? He loves us so much, He's not willing for us to stay the same that we are. Just keep that in mind, the next time you meet up with the Rock of offense.

Lesson 9

Lest We Offend Them

*Therefore let us not judge one another anymore,
but rather resolve this, not to put a stumbling block
or a cause to fall in our brother's way.*
(Romans 14:13)

Summary of *The Bait of Satan,* Chapter 10

This chapter represents a reversed look at the issues we've been considering until this point. Now, rather than dealing with how we respond to offenses by others, we will be thinking about the matter of causing offense to others. As John highlights at the beginning of the chapter, "Jesus offended some people by obeying His Father, but He never caused an offense in order to assert His own rights." Once again, a conversation between Jesus and Peter offers the perfect illustration for the principle that we should choose humility over unnecessary offense to others.

Bevere spends a good deal of time clarifying the tension between freedom in Christ and the challenges of servanthood that flow out of that freedom. He highlights the differences between a slave mentality and a servant mentality. A former slave who insists on asserting his rights in every situation demonstrates that, though free, he retains a slave mentality. He is not free to serve because he is a slave of his freedom.

STUDENT NOTES

In contrast, believers demonstrate that they understand their freedom in Christ when they are willing to lay down their rights in the service of others. Bevere points to 1 Corinthians 8:9 as one of the clear guidelines for this principle, "But beware lest somehow this liberty of yours become a stumbling block to those who are weak." John then shares a personal lesson in the way a simple right asserted can cause unnecessary offense to other believers.

Bevere closes the chapter with a brief lesson on the "edification test," a helpful guide in discerning between exercising our rights and considering how our actions may affect others negatively. As John states the challenge, "We should make it our aim not to cause another to stumble because of our personal liberty" (p. 119). We actually reach a deeper level of freedom when we don't feel bound to exercise it, but can forgo what we consider ourselves free to do because we have a deep appreciation for how it may wound another brother or sister. The point of the "edification test" is not simply to avoid offending others unnecessarily, but to seek ways in which we can build others up by willingly sacrificing a right we would feel completely free to exercise in another setting. As Bevere puts it, "Use your liberty in Christ to set others free, not to assert your own rights" (p. 119).

Warm-Up Questions

Use the following questions to prepare your heart and mind for the personal and/or group study in which you will participate.

1. Last session, we talked about the fact that Jesus offended a lot of people during His ministry. How would you say Jesus offends people today?

_____

_____

_____

_____

_____

2. What example from your life would you use to illustrate the point that sometimes we offend others completely unintentionally?

_____

_____

_____

_____

_____

3. What do you think is the first question people ought to ask themselves when they discover that they have unintentionally offended someone else?

_____

_____

_____

_____

_____

_____

Teaching by John Bevere

Watch the ninth session video presentation.

Personal Notes on Video Session 9

Use the following lines to keep notes as you view the video.

_____

_____

_____

_____

_____

_____

_____

_____

_____

_____

In the last session we actually saw that Jesus is called the Rock of offense. And we discovered that He offended people everywhere He went. It's an amazing thing when you see how many people He offended. Truth will offend, if you can be offended. And God will use that to either help you grow or you'll stumble. But we saw in the last session how Jesus offended the Pharisees when He made a statement and they didn't like it very much. The disciples came to Him and said, "Did You know that You offended the Pharisees when You said that?" And He said, "Let the blind lead the blind into a ditch." He said, "Every plant that My Father has not planted will be uprooted." So He said that when truth is preached, it will bring offense and that offense God will use to uproot those who really aren't His.

And then we saw He offended His own hometown by what He preached. And they were so offended they wanted to push Him off the brow of the hill. And then we saw He offended His own family members, which to me is absolutely amazing. We saw that He offended even His close friends.

Jesus was offending people everywhere He went. In this lesson, I want to look at the reverse. I want you to see the totally opposite side of what Jesus did when it came to offenses.

—John Bevere, adapted from Video Session 9

Teaching Review

Use the following questions to consider some of the central points made by John Bevere during this video session.

4. What was Peter's response when an official caught him off guard with the question about whether Jesus paid the temple tax?

_____

_____

_____

_____

_____

_____

5. In His dialogue with Peter, what point did Jesus make very clear about His status as a taxpayer?

_____

_____

STUDENT NOTES

_____

_____

_____

_____

6. What specific reason does Jesus give Peter for agreeing to pay a tax for which He, as the Son of God, was not liable?

_____

_____

_____

_____

_____

_____

_____

7. Drawing from what you heard John say, and the chart on page 114 of *The Bait of Satan,* fill out the following comparisons between a slave and a servant:

A. _____

B. _____

_____

C. _____

D. _____

E. _____

F. _____

_____

Exploring God's Word

Revisit the key passages from which John Bevere develops his teaching.

> **Matthew 17:24–27** *When they had come to Capernaum, those who received the temple tax came to Peter and said, "Does your Teacher not pay the temple tax?" He said, "Yes." And when he had come into the house, Jesus anticipated him, saying, "What do you think, Simon? From whom do the kings of the earth take customs or taxes, from their sons or from strangers?" Peter said to Him, "From strangers." Jesus said to him, "Then the sons are free. Nevertheless, lest we offend them, go to the sea, cast in a hook, and take the fish that comes up first. And when you have opened its mouth, you will find a piece of money; take that and give it to them for Me and you."*

8. How many different discoveries about Jesus did Peter learn or have confirmed by this brief episode over the temple tax?

_____

_____

_____

_____

_____

_____

_____

_____

_____

_____

_____

9. How would not paying the temple tax be an unnecessary offense that Jesus was unwilling to cause the officials in charge of the collection?

10. How does Bevere use the passage that immediately follows this one (Matthew 18:1–8) to demonstrate how seriously Jesus took this principle of not offending others unnecessarily?

Personal Application

_____
_____
_____
_____
_____
_____
_____
_____
_____
_____

This return to Capernaum would be Jesus' last visit prior to his death. All Jewish males (age twenty and older) had to pay a temple tax every year (Exodus 30:11–16). The amount was equivalent to about two days' wages for the average worker. The money went for public sacrifices and then for the upkeep of the temple. If any was left over, it would be used for the upkeep of Jerusalem, which was considered part of the temple property. This tax was even collected from Jewish males who lived outside of Palestine. Enormous sums of money came in from such places as Egypt where there were 8 to 10 million Jews. Tax collectors set up booths to collect these taxes. Only Matthew records this incident—perhaps because he had been a tax collector himself. These collectors of the temple tax were probably the temple commissioners who went through Palestine annually (these were not the same people who collected the Roman tax, such as Matthew). These collectors came to Peter. He may have been seen as a leader in this band of

STUDENT NOTES

Jesus' followers, or he may have been approached because he was "head of the household" and a home-owner in Capernaum (Mark's Gospel records that Jesus and the disciples were in the house, presumably Peter and Andrew's; see Mark 1:29; 9:33). These men asked Peter if Jesus (your teacher) would be paying the temple tax. To not pay the tax indicated a desire to separate from the religious community.

—from the Life Application Commentary, Matthew[1]

Galatians 5:13 *For you, brethren, have been called to liberty; only do not use liberty as an opportunity for the flesh, but through love serve one another.*

11. What does Paul mean when he warns the Galatians not to "use liberty as an opportunity for the flesh"?

_____

_____

_____

_____

_____

_____

_____

_____

12. How does the phrase "serve one another" capture an essential part of freedom?

STUDENT NOTES

_____

_____

_____

_____

_____

_____

_____

_____

_____

_____

_____

_____

_____

Personal Application

_____

_____

_____

_____

_____

_____

_____

_____

_____

_____

Do you want to know how to get promoted? First of all, recognize the favor of God on your life. Then, start serving instead of working. Start serving. That means work until 7:30 at night one time and the boss will say, "Why are you here so late?" And you'll say, "Because this has to be done and I love working

here." Do something that you're not expected to do like sweep the floor or clean the toilets or something like that. Believe me, you'll get promoted like that. Because bosses are always looking for servants, not hirelings.

—**John Bevere, adapted from Video Session 9**

Romans 14:1, 12–19 *Receive one who is weak in the faith, but not to disputes over doubtful things . . . So then each of us shall give account of himself to God. Therefore let us not judge one another anymore, but rather resolve this, not to put a stumbling block or a cause to fall in our brother's way. I know and am convinced by the Lord Jesus that there is nothing unclean of itself; but to him who considers anything to be unclean, to him it is unclean. Yet if your brother is grieved because of your food, you are no longer walking in love. Do not destroy with your food the one for whom Christ died. Therefore do not let your good be spoken of as evil; for the kingdom of God is not eating and drinking, but righteousness and peace and joy in the Holy Spirit. For he who serves Christ in these things is acceptable to God and approved by men. Therefore let us pursue the things which make for peace and the things by which one may edify another.*

13. How does Paul drive home the important issues that lie behind the way we treat each other as Christians?

_____

_____

_____

_____

_____

_____

_____

_____

_____

_____

_____

_____

_____

_____

_____

_____

_____

_____

_____

_____

14. How many different ways does Paul get across the
idea behind the expression "stumbling block"?

_____

_____

_____

_____

_____

Personal Application

_____

STUDENT NOTES

_____

_____

_____

_____

_____

_____

_____

_____

So Paul is saying, don't judge one another. Don't judge the person who's weaker in faith and the weaker in faith should not judge the one who's stronger in faith. But what you should resolve is not to put a stumbling block; a stumbling block is a cause that brings offense. Look at verse 17, "For the kingdom of God is not eating and drinking but it's righteousness and peace and joy in the Holy Spirit." So Paul is making this really clear. There is something more important than your own rights. Are you seeing this? You may wonder why Jesus went around offending people everywhere He went. On the other hand, He proves that He's tax-free but says, "Lest we offend them, let's go pay taxes." Let me tell you the difference. The only time you will find Jesus offending is to obey the Father in truth. Whenever it came to preaching truth, He would offend because truth will naturally offend people if they don't want to embrace it. You will never find Jesus offending somebody for His own personal right. There's the difference. That's the whole difference right there.

—John Bevere, adapted from Video Session 9

1 Corinthians 8:4-13 *Therefore concerning the eating of things offered to idols, we know that an idol is nothing in the world, and that there is no other God but one. For even if there are so-called gods, whether in heaven or on earth (as there are many gods and many lords), yet for us there is one God, the Father, of whom are all things, and we for Him; and one Lord Jesus Christ, through whom are all things, and through whom we live. However, there is not in everyone that knowledge; for some, with consciousness of the idol, until now eat it as a thing offered to an idol; and their conscience, being weak, is defiled. But food does not commend us to God; for neither if we eat are we the better, nor if we do not eat are we the worse. But beware lest somehow this liberty of yours become a stumbling block to those who are weak. For if anyone sees you who have knowledge eating in an idol's temple, will not the conscience of him who is weak be emboldened to eat those things offered to idols? And because of your knowledge shall the weak brother perish, for whom Christ died? But when you thus sin against the brethren, and wound their weak conscience, you sin against Christ. Therefore, if food makes my brother stumble, I will never again eat meat, lest I make my brother stumble.*

15. Although both of the last two passages quoted are about eating habits and the effects they can have on others, how is this passage from 1 Corinthians different?

_____

_____

_____

_____

_____

_____

_____

_____

_____

_____

_____

16. How can exercising a freedom in Christ wound a weak conscience (see verse 12)?

_____

_____

_____

_____

_____

_____

_____

_____

_____

_____

_____

Personal Application

_____

_____

_____

_____

_____

_____

_____

_____

_____

_____

Exposing the Truth

Use the following questions to help reach conclusions regarding the Scriptures and insights from the session.

17. During the video presentation, Bevere made this statement: "Sometimes people don't understand when we as believers are supposed to have offensive behavior and when we're not. Because you know what? If the Rock of offense lives on the inside of you, you're going to end up offending someone. But you have to know when it is right to offend and when it is not right to offend." So, when is it right to offend and when is it not right to offend?

_____

_____

_____

_____

_____

_____

_____

_____

STUDENT NOTES

_____

_____

_____

_____

_____

_____

_____

18. If Christians can't do whatever they desire out of their freedom in Christ, why is freedom so important?

_____

_____

_____

_____

_____

_____

_____

_____

_____

_____

19. What is Bevere talking about when he uses the term "edification test" in both his book and the video presentation?

_____

_____

_____

_____

_____

_____

_____

_____

_____

> If you live in a city like Chicago or Dallas or L.A., you can drive a certain car and live in a certain house. That's fine. But if you live in a small town and you drive a certain car and you live in a certain house, you may cause believers to stumble—because those believers have weak faith. They don't realize that God wants them blessed. So you know the thing I do is say, "Well, what's going to be smart here?" What's going to keep a believer from stumbling because you know, let me tell you something. My right to have something is not as important as causing one person to stumble and possibly go to hell.
>
> —John Bevere, adapted from Video Session 9

Applying the Lesson

Use the following specific directions to internalize the principles in the session and put them into practice.

19. In comparison with the life you led before you met the Lord Jesus Christ, what do you see in your life right now as a great example of freedom in Christ?

_____

_____

20. Note at least one relationship in which you realize you are going to have to re-evaluate whether the offenses have been caused because you have been speaking the truth in love or because you have been exercising a freedom that is unnecessarily offensive to someone else.

_____

_____

_____

_____

21. How have you benefited from another believer who you now realize set aside a personal freedom in order to edify you in your Christian life? Consider expressing your deep gratitude to that person for treating you in such a Christlike way.

_____

_____

_____

_____

Bait Warnings

A final opportunity for prayerful submission to the truth of the session.

> If we're going to walk with Jesus, we're going to offend people when we speak the Word of God. I've spoken to people before what God says and they were so mad they walked out of the room. But it was the truth because they were in sin or needed some instruction. But they just literally walked right out.

STUDENT NOTES

And I've offended them. And I've had people offended when I preach. I've had people come up to me so many times and they've said to me, "We didn't like you at all when we first heard you. But now we love you because we heard what you were saying." And it wasn't my life that was offending them. It was me, just speaking the truth. But then we have to turn around the flip side and say, "Hey, my priority is not my New Testament rights. My priority is to not offend."

—John Bevere, adapted from Video Session 9

Take time to pray for the group as you close. Lift up the matters that have been discussed in the group, particularly those relationships where unwise exercise of New Testament liberty may have caused unintended offense. Read, or ask someone to read, the final word of challenge from John Bevere.

Video Script for Lesson 9
Lest We Offend Them

We are ready to begin, "Bait of Satan" video curriculum lesson number 9. Now, let me review a little bit what we discussed last night. Last night we actually saw that Jesus is called the Rock of offense. And we discovered that He offended people everywhere He went. I mean, it's an amazing thing when you see how many people He offended. Amen. Truth will offend, if you can be offended. Amen. And God will use that to either cause you to grow or you'll stumble. Amen. But we saw last night how Jesus offended the Pharisees when He made a statement and they didn't like it very much and the disciples came to Him and said, "Did You know that You offended the Pharisees when You said that?" And He said, "Let the blind lead the blind into a ditch." He said, "Every plant that My Father has not planted will be uprooted." So He said, He literally showed us that when truth is preached, that it will bring offense and that offense God will use to uproot those who really aren't His. And then we saw He offended His own hometown by what He preached. And they were so offended they wanted to push Him off the brow of the hill. And then we saw He offended His own family members, which to me is absolutely amazing. His brothers, His mother, His half-sisters thought He was deranged and had gone out of His mind, and they went to lay hold of Him and He made the statement, "But who are My mother and brothers and sisters but those who hear the Word of God and do it?" And then we saw that He offended His own staff. That to me is an amazing thing. He preached something and His staff got offended and said, "This is a very hard saying." So then He looked at His staff and said, "Oh yeah?" and started preaching it even stronger. And then finally His own staff, many of them, the Bible says, not some, not a few, but *many* departed and walked away, and no longer walked with Him. So He didn't look to the rest of them and said, "Hey

guys, we got to buckle up because we just lost half our staff." He said, "Guys, do you want to go too?" when He turned to Peter and the rest.

And so we saw that He offended even His close friends. We saw when Lazarus was sick unto death they sent messengers, Mary and Martha. When they arrived all of a sudden Jesus was teaching. They said to Him, "Jesus, you've got to come with us right away." And the Bible says that when Jesus heard Lazarus was sick He stayed there two more days. And so when He finally got there a few days later the first thing Mary and Martha said to Him was, "Lord, if You would have been here our brother wouldn't have died."

So we see that Jesus was offending people everywhere He went. In this lesson tonight, I want to look at the reverse. I want you to see tonight the totally opposite side of what Jesus did when it came to offenses, and you'll understand when we talk about it. Now in Matthew 17, we're beginning tonight in the twenty-fourth verse. We find that Jesus, now let me just give you a little lesson here. Jesus based His traveling ministry out of Capernaum. A lot of people don't realize that. His hometown was Nazareth where He grew up, but He based His traveling ministry out of Capernaum. And so Peter, you know when you're in your home country, your hometown, you pay taxes, correct? We're used to that. Well, Peter was at the temple and he was amongst the people who collected the temple tax. And the officials looked at Peter and said, "Hey, your teacher, the guy that you're following around, does He pay the temple tax?" And Peter got a little nervous about it and said, "Sure, sure, sure, sure. He pays temple tax." And so he came back right away and he walked into the place that Jesus was sitting and Jesus anticipated Peter and He anticipated what he was going to say. Because, you know many times Jesus operated under a powerful word of knowledge.

So Jesus said to Peter, look at this, verse 25, *"And Peter said, yes, and when he had come into the house, Jesus anticipated him saying, 'What do you think, Simon? From whom do the kings of the earth take customs or taxes from, their sons or from strangers?'"* He is making just a simple statement here that everybody here should know but I'm going to make it really clear. Jesus looked at Peter and said, "Look, we've got kings of nations of kingdoms and who do they collect taxes from? Do they collect it from their own children, the princes and princesses, or do they collect the taxes from strangers?" Now that's a pretty simple question isn't it? And Peter answered back saying, "Well, they collect the taxes from strangers, not from the princes and the princesses." As a matter of fact, the princes and the princesses get greatly benefited by the taxes. They have the best wardrobes of any kids in the country. They live in the best houses of anybody in the country. They're benefited from the taxes that the strangers pay. So now watch this, verse 26. *"Peter said, 'From strangers.'"* Jesus said to him, *"Then the sons are free."* Jesus asked that question to make a point. He said, "So they do take the taxes from strangers." And Peter answered that, and so Jesus then said, "Alright then, the princes and princesses, the sons and daughters of the kings, they live for free." They live totally free. They are tax exempt. They do not have to pay taxes. So what is He doing? He's saying, "Hey Peter, guess what? My Father owns that temple. I'm His Son. I don't have to pay taxes." "The strangers are the ones that have to pay taxes. I'm tax exempt. I'm tax free. I don't have to pay taxes." Hallelujah. Right? Everybody starts getting happy and starts dancing at this point, especially when they are working for Him.

But then look at verse 27, *"Nevertheless, lest we offend them,"* lest we offend them . . . lest we offend them. *"Go to the sea, cast a hook, take the fish that comes up first and when you open its mouth you will find a piece of money. Take that and give that to them for me and you."* Now wait a minute. Is this the same Jesus we saw in the last lesson that was offending everybody everywhere He went? And yet now He makes this careful statement, "Alright Peter, I'm free, but nevertheless, lest we offend them, go pay the tax." Now, what is going on here? On one hand we see Him offending people everywhere He's going. On the other hand He says, "Well, I don't want to offend them so let's do it even though we're free."

Well, look with me please in Galatians, the fifth chapter. And this is what I want to cover and this entire lesson tonight because you know, sometimes people don't understand when we as believers are supposed to have offensive behavior and when we're not. Because let me tell you something, if the Rock of offense lives on the inside of you, you know what? You're going to end up offending someone. But you have to know when it is right to offend and when it is not right to offend. And we're going to make that very clear between the last lesson and this lesson.

Galatians, the fifth chapter, look at the thirteenth verse. Paul says, *"For you brethren, have been called to liberty only do not use liberty for an opportunity for the flesh."* In other words, liberty is privilege. You have been called to privilege; therefore, do not use privilege as an opportunity to serve, what? Yourself. But use it to serve one another through love. Because love lays down its life.

Now let me say this very, very boldly. There is freedom in serving, but there is bondage in slavery. A slave is one that has to serve, while a servant is one who gets to serve. Paul makes it very, very clear that we are to use our privilege to serve one another through love. I wrote down some differences between a slave and a servant. A slave has to, a servant gets to. Let this sink in a few minutes. This is one of the wonderful lessons we parents get to teach our children. But now we need to apply it to ourselves when we become adults, especially believers. Amen? A slave *has to* do something; a servant *gets to* do something. A slave does the minimum requirement; a servant does the maximum potential.

Do you want to know how to get promoted? First of all, the favor of God is on your life. Can I tell you how to get promoted? Start serving instead of working, start serving. That means work until 7:30 at night one time and the boss will say, "Why are you here so late?" And you'll say, "Because this has to be done and I love working here." And you do something that you're not expected to do like sweep the floor or clean the toilets or something like that. Believe me, you'll get promoted like that. Because bosses are always looking for servants, not hireling. A slave is a hireling. Or I should say a hireling is a slave.

The slave goes one mile and the servant gets to go two miles. He enjoys serving. The slave feels robbed; the servant gives. The slave is bound; the servant is free. Think about that. The slave fights for his rights. The servant lays down his rights.

Now, turn with me, please, to Romans, the fourteenth chapter. I'm going to go through a ton of Scriptures here to make a point tonight. Romans chapter 14, because I want this so seared in your heart that there is no question when you are to offend and when you are not to offend. Romans chapter 14, verse 1, Paul says, "*Receive one who is weak in the faith, but not to dispute over doubtful things, for one believes he may eat all things, but he who is weak eats only vegetables.*" Now, what is Paul talking about here? Back then the believers were very aware that there were certain meats that were offered to idols in temples. Jesus makes it clear in Mark's Gospel, I believe it was the seventh chapter, the eighteenth or nineteenth verse, that all meats were clean, that it is not what goes into a man that defiles him, but what comes out of a man's mouth that defiles him.

And thereby Mark's Gospel says that He made all meats clean. However, there were still Christians there, the Bible says were weak consciously or weak in faith. In other words, they just could not put themselves up to eating any meat that they thought was offered to an idol, even though the Bible clearly says that meat is sanctified by the Word of God in prayer. So, Paul is saying, "Receive a brother who is weak in the faith. Don't judge him. Don't dispute with him. But receive him." A lot of times we like to get in arguments over certain things. There are certain things I will have discussions with people about. But there are certain things we do not die on hills together with, do you understand what I'm saying? You have to choose the hills you're willing to die on. Now, I want to read you out of 1 Corinthians, the eighth chapter, verses 4, 6, and 7. Paul said to the Corinthians because they were having the same problem, "*Therefore concerning the eating of things offered to idols. We understand that an idol is nothing in the world.*" Isn't that true? "*Yet to us there is one God, the Father of all things, and through him, Jesus Christ, through whom are all things, and through whom we live. However, there is not in everyone that knowledge.*" In other words, those who are weak in faith. "*For some, with consciousness of the idol, until now, eating it is a thing offered to an idol and their conscience, being weak, is defiled.*" Paul is saying, "Hey listen, you've got to realize that there's some people who don't have the faith level that you have. Receive them, but don't receive them to argue with them."

Now, what Paul is dealing with here are Christians that were stronger in faith and it would seem that these believers that were stronger in their faith were bent on holding on to their rights rather than serving each other. They were really, really strong on the fact that hey, all meat is clean. Jesus cleansed it for me, He said it's clean, I can eat this, it doesn't matter what people believe. What Paul is saying is, "You're considering yourself more than you're considering your brother who has weak faith."

Now read Romans chapter 14, verse 12, please. *"So each of us shall give an account of themselves to God."* Verse 13, *"Therefore, let's not judge one another anymore but rather resolve this, not to put a stumbling block or cause to fall in our brother's way."* So Paul is saying don't judge one another. Don't judge the person who's weaker in faith, and the weaker in faith should not judge the one who's stronger in faith. But what you should resolve is not to put a stumbling block. Look at verse 17, *"For the kingdom of God is not eating and drinking but it's righteousness and peace and joy in the Holy Spirit."* So Paul is making this really clear that, "Hey there is something that is more important than your own rights." Now, you may wonder why Jesus went around offending people everywhere He went. But yet, on the other hand, He proves that He's tax free but says, "Lest we offend them, let's go pay taxes." Let me tell you the difference. The only time you will find Jesus offending is to obey the Father in truth. Whenever it came to preaching truth He would offend, because truth will naturally offend people if they don't want to embrace it. But you will never find Jesus offending somebody for His own personal rights. There's the difference. That's the whole difference right there.

Whenever we insist on hanging on to rights or privileges at the expense of offending somebody, we cause that brother to sin because listen to 1 Corinthians, chapter 8, verse 9. It says, *"But beware, lest somehow this liberty of yours becomes a stumbling block to those who are weak."* 1 Corinthians 8:11-12: *"And because of your knowledge shall the weak brother perish for whom Christ died? But when you thus sin against the brethren*

and wound their weak conscience, you sin against Christ."

Now hold your markers right there because we're going to come back and go to Matthew 18. Now immediately after the taxes, He goes right into the eighteenth chapter and starts talking about you must become like a little child. He warns immediately in verse 6, *"But whoever causes one of these little ones who believe in me to sin."* Now let's read this over again in 1 Corinthians 8, *"Because of your knowledge should the weaker brother perish for whom Christ died? But when you thus sin against brethren and wound their weak conscience, you sin against Christ."* When you wound a weak brother's conscience you sin against Christ. Jesus said in verse 6, *"But whoever causes one of these little ones who believe in me to sin, it would be better for him . . ."* Now look what Jesus says, this is strong language, *"If a milestone were hung around his neck and he was drown in the depths of the sea. Woe to the world because offenses must come, but woe to the man from whom the offense comes. If your hand or foot causes you to sin, cut it off."* Now I'm going to say something: If the privilege that you have as a New Testament believer is causing another brother to sin, cut it.

Let me give you an example of what happened with Lisa and I. A few years back I was about, it was about ten years ago, I took Lisa and our three sons, because at that time Arden wasn't born. Addison was six, Austin was three, and Alex was one. I took Lisa, Addison, Austin, and Alex, and a babysitter over to Indonesia. Now Indonesia is a long way away. Basically, you fly there and you keep going you start coming back. Okay, it's that far away. So it took thirty hours probably to get there and I'm telling you when we arrived in Bali, Indonesia, we were exhausted. We get off the plane, we're picked up by the pastor, and he has arranged for us to stay at one of the elder's hotels of the church. Now you have to understand that Bali is a beautiful place; it is a resort island. But this guy's hotel was not the most nice hotel that you'd even seen and it was in a pretty rough neighborhood. And I remember when we got in there, the walls were paper thin and there were dogs outside in the streets barking all night long. Well, my wife hardly slept at all. My kids hardly slept at all. So the next morning when we woke up, we were totally exhausted. But we had to catch a flight into Java and we immediately started preaching two times a day at least for two weeks, except for one day of rest in that two weeks. And I remember there was one day we actually preached five times in one day. It was a church of 30 thousand members, and today they're actually 85 thousand members. It's a magnificent church. Their midweek services are 7 P.M., 10 P.M., and 1 A.M. Their midweek service is over at four in the morning. I did the 7 and the 10 P.M. and there was seven thousand people in that one. And then they had seven services on Sunday, and so it was a very, very busy ministry schedule. You know what's beautiful about that church? Sixty percent of that church are converted Muslims.

But anyways, we get done after that two weeks and I remember we were sitting in Java at the breakfast table getting ready to catch our flight back to Bali because we were going to stay there two days and then fly home. And we were sitting at breakfast with a very wealthy woman. And the woman looked at us and she kind of found out about the hotel that we were staying at and that was where we were supposed to stay at again, the dog-barking hotel. And so she looked at my wife and I and said, "You know what, I want to bless you guys. There is a five-star resort hotel right on the beach at Bali." And you remember, Bali is like a Hawaii, okay? She said a five-star hotel. "I want to get you guys two rooms and I want to put you up and I want to pamper you guys the next two days." And I was like, "Praise God!" And my kids were excited. Our interpreter was excited but my wife said, "Well, honey, I don't really feel good about it." And I said, "No, no it's okay. Don't worry about it." But she said, "But John, you know the pastor and this is one of his elders and this is his hotel." I said, "He won't mind. This lady's blessed us. There's no problem with this. No problem. Just leave it to me."

So we're on the plane flying back to Bali and my wife says to me again, "Honey, I'm just not comfortable with this." I said, "Lisa, don't worry about it. This guy wants us to be blessed. He's a loving pastor. He'll be fine with this." And so we land and we're at the baggage claim and she said, "Honey, I don't feel good about this." I said, "Honey, don't worry about it. Just leave it to me." So I get in the car with the pastor and I said, "Hey pastor, I've got great news." I said, "Someone really blessed us with a beautiful five-star hotel. She's going to pay two nights for us there, two rooms. So we won't need to stay at the other hotel that we stayed at when we got here." Well, he got real quiet, didn't say a thing. And finally I said, "So is that okay?" And he said, "Well, I'm going to be very honest with you." And I said, "Well, I hope you would." "Well, you will really offend this man if you stay at that hotel. Because this man's hotel was booked tonight and he saved his best two rooms for you and your wife and your children." And I saw immediately what I'd done. I said, "Pastor, I will cancel the five-star hotel. We will gladly go to the elder's hotel," because I had already seen that I had probably offended the pastor.

Now, was it my right to stay at the five-star hotel when somebody was going to bless me with it? Absolutely. But it was going to cause a couple brothers to stumble. It was going to cause an offense. And I would much rather not bring somebody an offense like that than hang on to my right to go to a five-star hotel. See that's why Jesus said when you go into a town and they put you up someplace, bless it and stay there. Don't jump from house to house. Eat what's set before you. He is trying to tell you how to avoid offensive behavior.

Now you know what's wonderful? God blessed those two days and we had a blast. But it was a lesson I hope I never have to learn again. Paul made a statement to the Corinthians. He said, "The Lord has commanded that those who preach the gospel should live from the gospel, but this is a right of mine to choose not to take it. I work on my own. I've got my tent-making business. I've got other churches that are sowing and supporting me," but he sensed that somehow taking his rights from them was going to cause them to stumble. So he said, "I'm going to pass it up so you know where my heart is with you." You see there are certain rights we have as New Testament believers that we sometimes have to say, "You know what, I'm going to bypass this for one reason, because I'm more concerned about serving my brother than I am about receiving my rights."

Now when you live like that, God is pleased. Because God sees that you're not using your privileges to serve yourself but through love serving one another. So this is the thing we've got to do. We've got to ask ourselves sometimes: Is it something that's a New Testament privilege? Yes. Will it cause people to stumble? It may, it may not.

You know, I was so blessed the other night. I was just in Portugal preaching last week and the pastor was so considerate of me because he wanted to order a bottle of wine but he knew I was American. He said, "Will it offend you if I drink a bottle of wine?" I said, "No sir, it won't. Enjoy it, but I won't drink it, but will enjoy having fellowship with you. It won't bother me a bit." I said, "In America, people drink to get drunk. In Europe, people drink to be social. There's a big difference." And it really blessed me that that pastor was concerned about me because he knew

me being an American preacher. Europeans are just different in their mentality. And so this is the thing that we've got to determine.

If we're going to walk with Jesus, we're going to offend people when we speak the Word of God. I've spoken to people before what God says and they were so mad they walked out of the room. But it was the truth because they were in sin or this, that, or the other. They just literally walked right out. And I've offended them. I've offended people when I preach. I've had people come up to me so many times. They've said to me, "We didn't like you at all when we first heard you, but now we love you because we heard what you were saying." And it wasn't my right that was offending them. It was me just speaking the Word, the truth. But then we have to turn around the flip side and say, "Hey, my priority is not my New Testament rights. My priority is to not offend."

If you live in a city like Chicago, or Dallas, or L.A., you can drive a certain car and live in a certain house. That's fine. But if you live in a small town and you drive a certain car and you live in a certain house, you may cause believers to stumble because those believers have weak faith. They don't realize that God wants them blessed. So you know the thing I do is say, "Well, what's going to be smart here?" What's going to keep, because you know, let me tell you something. My right to have something is not as important as causing one person to stumble and possibly go to hell.

This is the way we have to look at everything. That's what Paul was saying to the Corinthians, "I have the right to take an offering from you. I have the right because the Lord commanded that those who preach the gospel should live from the gospel. But I'm passing that right up because I want you to know that I love you like a father, and I don't want any of you to stumble. I don't want any of you to ever have a reason to think that I'm preaching to you for money."

So you see, let me say something to you. You have people here in this church, always keep before you that we are called through love to serve one another and never give offense in our behaviors and hang on to our rights. Let me say this to you ushers: Remember that every single person that walks into this church, you may be the difference between heaven and hell to that person. That person may be coming in here for the first time and if they get a rude treatment, if you don't treat them as welcome into the house of God, we care about you with a smile; you understand what I'm saying? You might have that person turn right around and walk out and not walk into a church again. Do you understand what I'm saying?

If you're a security person, remember yes we've got to take care of the speakers; we've got to make sure that they're well cared for and protected, but you know what? That means that we also treat the other people because Jesus died for them just as much as the speaker. Now don't get me wrong, we always honor the men and women of God. The Bible teaches that. There's a blessing in that. God tells us to do that so we can get blessed. However, He died for every one of us. The least in the body of Christ is every bit as important to God and He's every bit as much in love with the least in the body of Christ as He is with the greatest in the body of Christ. So when we keep this before us, the law of love that we through love serve one another . . . guess what? We will not bring offense because Paul says in 2 Corinthians, chapter 6 this was his edification test. He said, "We give no offense in anything that our ministry may not be blamed." And let me read this to you out of 1 Corinthians, chapter 10, verses 22, 23, 33. He said, "*All things are lawful for me but not all things are helpful. All things are lawful for me but not all things edify. Let no one seek his own, but each one the other's well being.*" "*Therefore, whether you eat or drink, or what-ever you do, do all to the glory of God. Give no offense either to the Jew or to the Greeks or to the church of God, just as I also please all men in all things, not seeking my own profit, but the profit of many that they may be saved.*" 1 Corinthians 10:32-33.

Romans 14:19, "*Therefore, let us pursue the things which make for peace and the things by which one may edify one another.*" There's your edification test, Amen? Remember, through love serve one another and do not offend people with your own rights.

Lesson 10

Forgiveness: You Don't Give, You Don't Get

Therefore I say to you, whatever things you ask when you pray, believe that you receive them, and you will have them. And whenever you stand praying, if you have anything against anyone, forgive him, that your Father in heaven may also forgive you your trespasses. But if you do not forgive, neither will your Father in heaven forgive your trespasses.
(Mark 11:24–26)

Summary of *The Bait of Satan,* Chapter 11

In the first paragraph of this chapter, Bevere states his objectives for the remainder of the book when he writes, "I want to turn our attention to the consequences of refusing to let go of offense and how to get free from it" (p. 129). Because of the startling nature of the passages to which he will refer, John continues by pointing out that though we live in a culture that typically devalues a person's word, we can't afford to do that when we hear God speak. God says what He means and means what He says—the first time. When God makes a conditional promise or warning, usually stated in the formula, "If you do this, then the following will occur," we can be absolutely sure that God will keep His word.

Bevere then highlights a group of Jesus' statements that too many believers do not take to heart. Among these, he lists Matthew 6:12–15 and Luke 6:37. These and other passages underscore the point that an unwillingness to forgive cuts us off from God's forgiveness. John then shares several testimonies that confirm the principle that serves as the title to this chapter— forgiveness: you don't give, you don't get.

The heart of this chapter is a detailed study of Matthew 18:21–35, the Parable of the Unmerciful Servant. Bevere demonstrates how both the master and the first servant had genuine causes for offense. The first servant owed an enormous debt to the master, a debt that he could never pay. That servant, in turn, was owed a much smaller, but not insignificant, debt by a second servant. The call for forgiveness from the parable is not based on the idea that the servant should have been willing to forgive because someone owed him a smaller debt. In human terms, it wasn't small. The servant's real error was in ignoring the forgiveness that he had received for his own huge debt. His failure to forgive clearly shows that he did not appreciate or understand the gift of forgiveness he had received.

Bevere ends by spelling out the point of the chapter— forgiveness isn't an option. Jesus' own explanation of the parable warns those who claim to believe and testify to God's forgiveness that they run the risk of finding no

welcome in the kingdom if they themselves have per-
sisted in unforgiveness.

Warm-Up Questions

Use the following questions to prepare your heart and
mind for the personal and/or group study in which you
will participate.

1. How would you explain forgiveness to someone from
   each of the following age groups?

    A. Ten year olds

       _____

       _____

       _____

       _____

       _____

    B. Thirty year olds

       _____

       _____

       _____

       _____

       _____

2. What would you say forgiveness feels like: a) to
   those who give it, and b) to those who receive it?

_____

_____

_____

_____

_____

3. What's the toughest part of giving consistent
    discipline to children? Do you agree or disagree with
    John's description of parenting errors on pages
    129–130 of the book, quoted in the shaded box
    below? Why or why not?

    _____

    _____

    _____

    _____

    _____

    _____

We live in a culture where we don't always mean what
we say. Consequently we do not believe others mean
what they say to us. A person's word is not taken
seriously.

It begins in childhood. A parent tells a child, "If you
do that again, you'll get a spanking." The child not
only does it again but several times more after that.
Following each episode the child receives the same
warning from his parent. Usually no corrective action
is taken. If correction does take place, it is either
lighter than what was promised or more severe
because the parent is frustrated.

Both responses send a message to the child that you
don't mean what you say or what you say isn't true.
The child learns to think that not everything authority figures say is true. So he becomes confused about
when and if he should take authority figures seriously. This attitude is projected onto other areas of

his life. He views his teachers, friends, leaders, and bosses through this same frame of reference. By the time he becomes an adult he has accepted this as normal. His conversations now consist of promises and statements in which he says things he doesn't mean.

—John Bevere, *The Bait of Satan*, pp. 121-122

Teaching by John Bevere

Watch the tenth session video presentation.

Personal Notes on Video Session 10

Use the following lines to keep notes as you view the video.

_____

_____

_____

_____

_____

_____

_____

_____

_____

_____

_____

_____

Teaching Review

Use the following questions to consider some of the central points made by John Bevere during this video session.

4. At the beginning of the video presentation, Bevere asked his audience how many could admit they were thinking that someone had offended them and hurt them in such a grievous way that forgiveness seemed impossible. If you agreed with that statement, write down the initials of the people's names below that you think might be impossible to forgive.

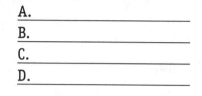

A. _____

B. _____

C. _____

D. _____

5. How does Bevere describe the suggested answer that Peter offered Jesus when he asked how often he ought to forgive someone?

_____

_____

_____

_____

_____

_____

_____

6. You'll be studying Matthew 18:21–35 in a moment. For now, what was the figure Bevere quoted that represented the approximate debt owed by the first servant? How large was the second servant's debt?

_____

_____

_____

_____

7. Bevere repeatedly makes the point that he can find a lot more Scriptures that predict punishment for one particular sin in much harsher terms than against sins such as murder, adultery (or what people usually call the "major sins"). What sin is that?

_____

_____

_____

_____

_____

Exploring God's Word

Revisit the key passages from which John Bevere develops his teaching.

> **Colossians 3:12–13** *Therefore, as the elect of God, holy and beloved, put on tender mercies, kindness, humility, meekness, longsuffering; bearing with one another, and forgiving one another, if anyone has a complaint against another; even as Christ forgave you, so you also must do.*

8. The apostle Paul lists five character traits that the "elect of God, holy and beloved" should exhibit among themselves. Beside each of these traits, write how they contribute to the twin actions of bearing with one another and forgiving one another.

A. Tender Mercies— _____

_____

_____

STUDENT NOTES

B. Kindness—

C. Humility—

D. Meekness—

E. Longsuffering—

9. How many of the qualities you have just been
   thinking about did Jesus demonstrate when He hung
   on the cross? In what ways?

_____

_____

_____

_____

10. According to the God's Word, what is the bottom-
    line standard that we should use to decide whether
    or not to forgive?

_____

_____

_____

_____

_____

_____

Personal Application

_____

_____

_____

_____

_____

_____

_____

_____

_____

_____

_____

STUDENT NOTES

Matthew 18:21–35 *Then Peter came to Him and said, "Lord, how often shall my brother sin against me, and I forgive him? Up to seven times?" Jesus said to him, "I do not say to you, up to seven times, but up to seventy times seven. Therefore the kingdom of heaven is like a certain king who wanted to settle accounts with his servants. And when he had begun to settle accounts, one was brought to him who owed him ten thousand talents. But as he was not able to pay, his master commanded that he be sold, with his wife and children and all that he had, and that payment be made. The servant therefore fell down before him, saying, 'Master, have patience with me, and I will pay you all.' Then the master of that servant was moved with compassion, released him, and forgave him the debt. But that servant went out and found one of his fellow servants who owed him a hundred denarii; and he laid hands on him and took him by the throat, saying, 'Pay me what you owe!' So his fellow servant fell down at his feet and begged him, saying, 'Have patience with me, and I will pay you all.' And he would not, but went and threw him into prison till he should pay the debt. So when his fellow servants saw what had been done, they were very grieved, and came and told their master all that had been done. Then his master, after he had called him, said to him, 'You wicked servant! I forgave you all that debt because you begged me. Should you not also have had compassion on your fellow servant, just as I had pity on you?' And his master was angry, and delivered him to the*

*torturers until he should pay all that was due to
him. So My heavenly Father also will do to you if
each of you, from his heart, does not forgive his
brother his trespasses."*

11. Bevere does the math for us and tells us Jesus
    responded to Peter's question about forgiving his
    brother seven times by saying He expected His
    followers to forgive up to 490 times (seventy times
    seven). What can you say about the quality of
    forgiveness that would keep count of forgiving
    490 times?

    _____

    _____

    _____

    _____

12. Describe the similarities and differences between
    the conversation the master had with the first
    servant and the conversation the first servant had
    with his fellow servant.

    _____

    _____

    _____

    _____

    _____

    _____

    _____

    _____

    _____

STUDENT NOTES

_____

_____

_____

_____

_____

_____

_____

_____

13. How does Jesus Himself draw the application point of this parable for His listeners?

_____

_____

_____

_____

_____

_____

_____

_____

_____

Personal Application

_____

_____

_____

_____

_____

_____

_____

_____

Proverbs 6:16–19 *These six things the L*ORD *hates, yes, seven are an abomination to Him: A proud look, a lying tongue, hands that shed innocent blood, a heart that devises wicked plans, feet that are swift in running to evil, a false witness who speaks lies, and one who sows discord among brethren.*

STUDENT NOTES

14. What principle did Bevere illustrate from these verses?

_____

_____

_____

_____

_____

_____

_____

_____

_____

_____

_____

_____

_____

_____

_____

_____

15. How does "sowing discord among brethren" affect the matter of forgiveness?

_____

_____

_____

STUDENT NOTES

Personal Application

Matthew 6:12–15 *"And forgive us our debts, as we forgive our debtors. And do not lead us into temptation, but deliver us from the evil one. For Yours is the kingdom and the power and the glory forever. Amen. For if you forgive men their trespasses, your heavenly Father will also forgive you. But if you do not forgive men their trespasses, neither will your Father forgive your trespasses."*

Mark 11:25–26 *"And whenever you stand praying, if you have anything against anyone, forgive him, that your Father in heaven may also forgive you your trespasses. But if you do not* *forgive, neither will your Father in heaven forgive your* trespasses."

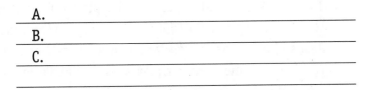

STUDENT NOTES

16. What three different types of forgiveness do these verses mention?

    A. _____

    B. _____

    C. _____

    _____

17. In each of these verses, who initiates forgiveness and why is this important?

_____

_____

_____

_____

_____

_____

_____

_____

Personal Application

_____

_____

_____

_____

_____

_____

_____

_____

_____

_____

Exposing the Truth

Use the following questions to help reach conclusions regarding the Scriptures and insights from the session.

18. In Jesus' conversation with Peter (Matthew 18:21–35), He challenges His disciple to be willing to forgive repeatedly (490 times a day). Why did Jesus choose that much larger number rather than the smaller one (seven times a day) that Peter suggested?

_____

_____

_____

_____

_____

_____

_____

_____

_____

_____

_____

_____

_____

19. Bevere has based much of this teaching on Luke 17:1, "Then He said to the disciples, 'It is impossible that no offenses should come, but woe to him through whom they do come!'" How could you restate that verse to demonstrate what it has to do with forgiveness? Keep the parable from Matthew 18 in mind.

_____

_____

_____

_____

_____

20. According to the passages you have just studied
    from God's Word, what is the biggest obstacle
    between believers in Jesus and their development
    of a continual attitude of forgiveness toward
    others?

_____

_____

_____

_____

_____

_____

_____

_____

_____

_____

_____

_____

_____

_____

**This guy goes to find the other servant who owes him
100 denarii. What is 100 denarii? Well, the first thing
you have to understand is that a denarii is one day's**

STUDENT NOTES

wage. So 100 denarii is 100 days' wages or one-third of a year's salary because when you take away holidays and weekends you work about three hundred days a year.

So this guy took from him one third of a year's salary. Now let's say you make 45 thousand dollars a year. This guy has taken from you 15 thousand dollars. Is that one of those little offenses? Is that one of those little offenses where you just go, "Oh, sorry man, no problem. Don't even think about it." Is that one of those kind of offenses? No. What Jesus is communicating is, this guy really did his fellow brother dirty. Because that's huge when someone takes one-third of what you make in an entire year and doesn't pay it back. Are you with me? But in relationship when you compare 15 thousand to 3 billion, it's not even a drop in the bucket. That is what Jesus is communicating to us when He says that the very worst thing that we can do to one another is not even a drop in the bucket to what we did to God. That is why I said a person who cannot forgive is a person who's forgotten what they've been forgiven of.

—John Bevere, adapted from Video Session 10

Applying the Lesson

Use the following specific directions to internalize the principles in the session and put them into practice.

21. What would you say is your biggest personal challenge: a) to deepen your appreciation for the height, breadth, depth, and length of God's

forgiveness toward you, or b) to forgive those who
have genuinely caused you offense in some way?

_____

_____

_____

_____

_____

_____

_____

22. Summarize your understanding of how God has
forgiven you.

_____

_____

_____

_____

_____

_____

_____

23. What attitudes or issues of unforgiveness has God's
Spirit revealed to you during this session? As you
note them, include what you plan to do about
them.

_____

_____

_____

_____

_____

_____

_____

Bait Warnings

A final opportunity for prayerful submission to the truth of the session.

> You see this is the whole problem, folks. We have categorized sin. I got news for you, folks, this is what we deserve—we deserve hell. We deserve to burn in the lake of fire forever. When Adam sinned against God, God the Father could have looked at the Son and said, "Alright. They chose the Devil over us. Let them all go to hell and burn forever. Let's go over and create another universe and create somebody that loves us." And you know what? He would have been totally just, because we deserved to burn in hell forever. You know, I think every Christian ought to hang over hell for thirty seconds. I think then you'll never have any trouble forgiving anybody again in your life . . .
>
> But here's the good news. I'll say it one more time. The Bible says that when we're born again, He has shed abroad His love in our hearts and that is the love that forgave us of the unpayable debt. You have, if you are saved, the ability to forgive as He forgave you.
>
> —John Bevere, adapted from Video Session 10

Video Script for Lesson 10
Forgiveness: You Don't Give, You Don't Get

Colossians, the third chapter and also find Matthew 18. We'll begin in Colossians 3 and then we'll go immediately to Matthew 18. In Colossians 3, I want to look at the twelfth and the thirteenth verses please. Colossians 3:12-13, *"Therefore, as the elect of God, holy and beloved, put on tender mercies, kindness, humility, meekness, and long-suffering."* Verse 13, *"Bearing with one another and forgiving one another. If anyone has a complaint against another, even as Christ forgave you, so you also must do."* "Should do" or "must do"? Must do. It is not a suggestion. It is a command for us to forgive one another.

So the rest of these lessons I want to focus in on the subject of forgiveness and how important it is. Now, how many of you have ever heard somebody make this statement when it comes to forgiveness, "But you just don't know what they did to me." How many of you have ever said that? "You just don't know what they said about me. You just don't know what they did to me." You know what I say to a person who says that? "No, *you* don't know what you did to Jesus." A person who cannot forgive is a person who has forgotten what they've been forgiven of. Let me say that again. A person that cannot forgive is a person who has forgotten or never really realized what they've been forgiven of. Amen?

Let me show you that. Go to Matthew 18. Now in Matthew 18, I want to look at verse 21. *"Then Peter came to Jesus and said, 'Lord how often shall my brother sin against me and I forgive him? Up to seven times?'"* Now would you look up at me please? Peter thinks he's being magnanimous here, okay? Now you have to understand, these guys, these disciples. What were they constantly doing? They were constantly jockeying for who's the greatest. Now, Peter's already two notches up

on the rest of them because he's already walked on the water and Jesus has already said, *"Blessed are you Simon, Bar-Jonah because flesh and blood have not revealed this to you,"* right? So Peter just thinks as big as he can. He just stretches it way out there, because you've got to understand folks, these guys lived under the law and the law says, "An eye for an eye and a tooth for a tooth." In other words, if you kill my dog, I get to kill your dog and do it legally. You punch me in the mouth, I get to punch you back in the mouth.

So Jesus has been teaching on this issue of forgiveness, and so Peter just says, "All right, I'm going to just stretch it. I'm just going to go as big as I can think." So he just really gets out there and says, "Alright Jesus, if my brother does me wrong seven times and I forgive him, that's enough, right?" And he's just waiting for Jesus to say, "Blessed are you, Simon!" I mean, he's just waiting for it. He's just, "Come on, come on. This is going to be the third notch." And what does Jesus say? Verse 22, Jesus said to him, *"I do not say to you up to seven times, but up to seventy times seven."* That's 490 times. And in Luke's Gospel, He said "in a day." Now for you to sin against me 490 times in one day you would have to do it once every three minutes provided you and I don't go to sleep.

Now I don't know anyone who can sin that good. Do you? So what is Jesus saying? He's saying, "Hey, Peter, your forgiveness is to be inexhaustible like your Father in heaven's forgiveness is." So He says, "Alright, let Me make this really clear and tell you a parable about it to make sure you get the point." So look at verse 23, *"Therefore, the kingdom of heaven is likened unto a certain king who wanted to settle accounts with his servants. And when he had begun to settle accounts, one was brought to him who owed him ten thousand talents."* What in the world is ten thousand talents? Now, the first thing you have to understand is a talent is not a measure of money; it's a measure of weight. One talent is approximately seventy-five pounds. Now this is a debt. So we can safely assume it's either gold or silver.

Ten thousand talents would be 750 thousand pounds of gold. Now, I checked it just on Friday. Gold is running right now at about 315 dollars an ounce. In gold weight, it's twelve ounces to a pound, not sixteen ounces to a pound, I don't know why they do that. So anyway, there's twelve ounces in one pound, and each ounce is worth 315 dollars. So if you multiply this out. If you multiply twelve ounces times 315 dollars times 750 thousand pounds, you know what this guy owed his master? Three billion dollars U.S. You have to understand I'm all over the world. I'm always dealing with these different currencies.

Three billion dollars! Now, how many of you would call that an unpayable debt? Anybody in here would call that a payable debt? So immediately we see who Jesus is correlating this king with, right? He's correlating this king with God the Father, because why? Because we were forgiven of an unpayable debt. Amen? The Bible said that Jesus took the handwriting of an ordinance that was against us and He nailed it to the cross. What was that handwriting of an ordinance? It was the note, the debt that was against us that we could never pay up. He nailed it to the cross. Hallelujah!

And He wiped us clean. Paid the debt in full. Forgave us of the unpayable debt. Amen? The claims of justice were satisfied. Verse 25, *"As he was not able to pay and his master commanded that he be sold with his wife and children and all that he had, and that payment be made, the servant fell down before him and said, 'Master, have patience with me and I will pay you all.' Then the*

master of the servant was moved with compassion, released him." See, that's forgiveness. When you release someone and they don't owe you anything anymore. *"He released him and forgave him of the debt."* Verse 28, *"And so that servant went out and found another servant who owed him one hundred denarii."* *"And he laid hands on him and took him by the throat and said, 'Pay me what you owe.' So the servant fell down at his feet and begged him saying, 'Have patience with me and I'll pay you all.'"* Verse 30, *"And he would not, but he went and threw him into prison until he should pay the debt."* This guy goes to find a fellow servant who owes him one hundred denarii. What is one hundred denarii? Well, the first thing you have to understand is a denarii is one day's wage. So one hundred denarii is one hundred days' wage or one-third of a year's salary because when you take away holidays and weekends you work about three hundred days a year.

So this guy took from him one-third of a year's salary. Now let's say you make 45 thousand dollars a year. This guy has taken from you 15 thousand dollars. Is that one of those little offenses? Is that one of those little offenses where you just go, "Oh, sorry man, no problem. Don't even think about it." Is that one of those kind of offenses? No. What Jesus is communicating is, is that this guy really did his fellow brother dirty. Because that's huge when someone takes one-third of what you make in an entire year and doesn't pay it back. But in relationship when you compare 15 thousand dollars to 3 billion, it's not even a drop in the bucket. That is what Jesus is communicating to us when He says that the very worst thing that we can do to one another is not even a drop in the bucket to what we did to God. That is why I said a person who cannot forgive is a person who's forgotten what they've been forgiven of.

You know what I think the whole problem is? I think the problem is we have categorized sins. We've got the big ones—adultery, drug abuse, murder, and one that's way above the others—homosexuality. And then we have what we have "weaknesses." Strife, gossip, jealousy, wrath, unforgiveness. Weaknesses. But you know what I find is amazing? Proverbs 6, *"These six things the Lord hates, seven is an abomination."* You know what's amazing? Homosexuality is not on the list. Adultery is not on the list. You know what the seventh one is that God says is an abomination? *"Those who sow discord among brothers."* Gossip. Treat gossip like you treat homosexuality and you'll probably get delivered.

Am I condoning homosexuality? Absolutely not. The Bible says, *"Those that practice such as this will not inherit the kingdom of God."* I think the big problem with this is that we put all these sins into categories. And it hinders people from coming to the Lord. I'll never forget the time I was in a church in Alabama and I did Sunday through Wednesday night set of meetings, and Tuesday night the place was packed. And this guy walks up to me on Tuesday night and said, "I need you to pray for me." So when service was over and I laid hands on him. The power of God hit that man and he was flat on his back on the floor. I left the building he was still on the floor. About a month later I got a call in my office, he gets ahold of me and this guy says, "I don't know if you remember me, but my name is J.R. and I was in a meeting with you about a month ago in Alabama." And I said, "I remember you. You were on the floor when I left the building." He says, "Oh, so you remember me. Well, you don't know about my life." I said, "Well, tell me about your life." And he goes off on some tangent for about ten minutes and he comes back again, he's real hard, real cold, and real distant. He says, "You just don't know about me; if you only knew about my life." I said, "J.R., tell me about your life." So he goes off on another tangent for about ten minutes. He said, "If you only knew about my life." I said, "J.R. stop right now. We're not going any further. We're not going to get anywhere unless you tell me about your

life." He says, "Alright. I'll tell you." He says, "I'm a homosexual." I said, "I know J.R." He got real quiet. He says, "You do?" I said, "Yeah, I knew when I was in Alabama." He says, "What do you think about me? Did you think, 'that pervert'?" I said, "No, J.R., I didn't think 'that pervert.' Let me tell you this." I said, "I got saved in my college fraternity. Prior to that I had an engineering degree. All the executives in my neighborhood said I'd be the most likely to succeed in my neighborhood." I said, "I loved girls. I was a normal guy according to society. I was not a homosexual, but I've got news for you, I would have been burning in hell right next to where you're going if I hadn't gotten saved."

And he got real quiet. And so for the next forty minutes I preached to that man and at the end of that forty minutes he got saved, filled with the Holy Spirit, and delivered from homosexuality. Now you know what happened? Five months later the pastor of that church in Alabama came to Orlando where I was living at the time, and we played some golf together. And the pastor said to me while we were playing golf, "Do you know this guy named J.R.?" I said, "Oh yeah, I remember. He called and got ahold of me five months ago and he got saved and delivered from homosexuality." He said, "Did he! John, that guy is bringing every homosexual in Tuscaloosa, Alabama, into our church and they're all getting saved."

Now, compare that to another church I went to. I go to this church of two thousand members in a city of 60 thousand people. That's a pretty significant church. And after the service, it's really tough preaching in this place, it's really tough. And after the service we're doing the dinner thing, and the pastor goes, "Uh, we're going through terrible persecution in this city." I said, "Oh yeah? How come?" He said, "Oh it's the homosexuals." I said, "What's going on?" He said, "Well, I told my whole congregation, if any institution has a homosexual working in it, if it's a store, restaurant, don't buy anything there, don't eat there, boycott it." I said, "Oh yeah, well pastor, why don't we boycott every store that's got somebody that lies and somebody that committed adultery and somebody that gossips and somebody that's in unforgiveness?" I said, "You won't be able to buy anything anywhere or eat anything anywhere." I said, "Why have you made that the sin above all others?"

You see this is the whole problem folks. We have categorized sins. I got news for you folks. We deserved hell. We deserved to burn in the lake of fire forever. When Adam sinned against God, God the Father could have looked at the Son and said, "Alright, they chose the devil over Us. Let them all go to hell and burn forever. Let's go over and create another universe and create somebody that loves Us." And you know what? He would have been totally just, because we deserved to burn in hell forever. You know, I think every Christian ought to hang over hell for thirty seconds. I think then you'll never have any trouble forgiving anybody again in your life, because that's what we deserved. I will never forget a pastor in the Caribbean. My wife and I were there preaching at a church, they've got a great church down there. And we were in his living room one night, and he shared with my wife and I. He said when we was eight years old how he fell into a construction ditch in the Caribbean (and his dad took him to church, he went every week). And the construction ditch was filled with water because it was the rainy season and he drowned and was dead—for forty-five minutes. He said, "John and Lisa, when I left my body it was like slipping your foot right out of a shoe."

He said, "All your senses are intact." He said, "When I left my body I started going down at a very rapid rate and everything was so dark. The darkness was so thick I could have done this with my hand and I wouldn't have seen anything. It was so thick I felt like I was wearing the dark-

ness." He said, "The farther I went down the worse the fear got." He said, "I thought nothing can get worse than the fear that I'm experiencing right now." He said, "But it would get worse every moment down. It would get worse and worse." He said, "We don't have fear to describe that kind of fear here on earth. There's no kind of fear."

He said, "I kept screaming, 'Why am I going this way for? I go to church.'" He said, "I knew exactly where I was going." Eight-year-old boy. He said, "Then I heard the screams." He said, "You know how there are screams and there are other screams that cause your blood to stand still?" He said, "That's the kind of screams I heard—filled with terror." He said, "John and Lisa, then I saw the lights from the flames and I came to the entrance of this place and I knew that if I went into this place that I would never, ever, ever come out."

He said, "And a being, some form of being, grabbed me by the shoulder." He said, "I couldn't look I was so scared. And started pulling me in backwards." And he said, "All of a sudden a voice spoke and shook everything and said, 'Let him go.' And the being said, 'No, he's mine.' And the voice said, 'Let him go! He's mine!'" And he said, "That being let me go and I was brought up, and when I came up I was outside of my body watching the paramedics work on my heart and my breathing and my lungs. And my father standing beside me praying these words, my dad was saying, 'God the Father, if You give me my son back' (because his father was a believer) 'I will give him to You forever.'" And now that young man is a pastor and he's been a pastor for years in the Caribbean.

Now, I talked with another woman who was in hell. Now listen to me, this woman, the Lord let her see hell in a vision. She said to me, she said, "John, that place is indescribable. We don't have any kind of torment or horror on this earth to describe that place." She said, "I had to sleep with the lights on in my house for two and a half months after seeing that place." Now that's what we deserved. That's what we justly deserve. There's nothing that we can do to one another that compares with that. What's the worst thing that you can think of that a person can do to another person? I thought about this and I personally think the worst thing that a person can do to another is child molestation. I remember when I was living in Orlando there was something that a father did; I mean it horrified the sinners in the gym. I mean, they were mad at this guy. For one week, Orlando was in shock because what had happened. We heard about it because every day in the gym they would play it on the radio. I mean, the disk jockeys were horrified by this. The city was horrified. It was one of the most horrific things I've ever heard a father do to a child. But this father had gotten just a little bit too upset at his one and a half little girl because she was crying too much . . . turns the broiler on, takes the scalding hot rack out, and starts bouncing the baby on the scalding hot rack. She had second to third degree burns from the crown of her head to the soles of her feet.

Now, I'm telling you that the sinners were mad. We were horrified. As horrific as that is, that is nothing compared to eternity in hell. But yet, that's what that little girl deserved. That's what I deserved. That's what you deserved. And yet, God chose to freely forgive us. That is why I said a person who cannot forgive is a person who has forgotten what they've been forgiven of.

Verse 29, *"So his fellow servant fell down at his feet and begged him saying, 'Have patience with me and I'll pay you all.' But he would not, but he went and threw him into prison until he should pay the debt. So when the fellow servants saw what had been done they were very grieved and came and told the master all that had been done. Then the master after he called him said, 'You wicked servant.'"* Notice he does not say, "You wicked hea-

then." This guy is a servant. He's already been forgiven of the unpayable debt. In the parable, he is a type of a Christian. Notice, he says, "You wicked servant," not wicked heathen. *"I forgave you of all the debt because you begged me. Should you not also have compassion on your fellow servant just as . . ."* what did we read in Colossians? "If we forgive just as God through Christ forgave us"? That's Ephesians. "Just as I have had pity on you." Verse 34, *"And his master was angry and delivered him to the torturers."* Look up at me—devils.

I'm going to share with you in the next couple of lessons, my personal testimony of this. I went through about a two-year time period where I would not forgive. I lived in torment. Here I am in the ministry. I mean, my wife and I were fighting things in the spirit like you can't believe. Day after day, night after night, and you know what? After we forgave, the whole thing stopped. I'm talking about we knew there was something wrong. We could sense demonic forces coming against us and we were binding continually things, but when we forgave it was all done. Look at this, *"And his master was angry and delivered him to the torturers."* *"Until he should pay all that was due to him."* Wait a minute. *All* that was due? Folks, that's an unpayable debt. Now look up at me and listen to my words because I'm going to choose very carefully my words.

What Jesus is saying is that a person in the church who refuses to forgive—I'm not talking about somebody who's working through it. I'm talking about somebody who says, "No! I will not forgive"—a person who refuses to forgive is a person that will cost them their salvation. Now, do you want to know why some of you may have choked at that? Do you want to know why? Because you've categorized sin. Suppose I told you there was a guy in here tonight and he was killing people. And the elders of the church got together and said, "Hey brother so and so, are you willing to stop taking guns and killing people?" And he said, "Nope, I like it. I'm going to do it." Would that guy inherit the kingdom of God? The Bible says don't be deceived, right? Murderers, adulterers will not inherit the kingdom of God. I can show you three times more Scriptures in the New Testament of how a person who refuses to forgive cannot inherit the kingdom of God than I can a murderer.

Mark, chapter 11, one of our favorite chapters where He talks about having the faith of God and then He comes down in verse 25, *"Whenever you stand praying, if you have anything against anyone, forgive him." "That your Father in heaven may also forgive your trespasses."* Is God Father to the sinner? No! He is God to the sinner; He is Father to the believer. And secondly, do sinners stand praying? No, He is talking prophetically to children. He's says forgive that your Father will forgive you. Look at verse 26, *"But if you do not forgive." "Neither will your Father in heaven forgive your trespasses."* Is that clear? I think it is.

Now, that's at the end of His earthly ministry, at the end of the three and a half years. Let's go to the beginning. Matthew 5. Look at verse 14 please. Jesus said, *"For if you forgive men their trespasses, your heavenly Father will also forgive you."* Again, He's talking to children. Verses 15, *"But if you do not forgive men their trespasses, neither will the Father in heaven forgive your trespasses."* Is that clear?

Let's talk about the Lord's Prayer. *"Our Father which art in heaven, hallowed be thy name. Thy kingdom come thy will be done on earth as it is in heaven. Forgive us this day, as we forgive those who trespass against us."* Do you want God to forgive you the way you forgive those who've done you wrong? The thing is that's exactly the way you are going to be forgiven. Now here's the good news; this is heavy but here's the good news. He has shed abroad His love in our hearts. His love, His love is what forgave us. We have the ability to forgive. This is the only parable; go back to Matthew 18, now this is an amazing truth right here.

Do you know with all the parables people would have to come up to Jesus and say, "Would you tell me what that meant?" How many can remember that? Not so with this one. This is the only parable in all four Gospels that He gives the interpretation of the parable without anybody asking. Because this thing is so far outside their box, their mentality, He has to make sure they get it. Verse 35, here's the interpretation, *"So my heavenly Father also will do to each of you, if each of you from his heart does not forgive his brother of his trespasses."* I've just showed you a lot more Scriptures about forgiveness than I could have about murder. But here's the good news. I'll say it one more time. The Bible says that when we're born again, He has shed abroad His love in our hearts and that is the love that forgave us of the unpayable debt. You have in you, if you are saved, the ability to forgive as He forgave you.

Lesson 11

Revenge: The Trap

*Repay no one evil for evil. Have regard for
good things in the sight of all men.*
(Romans 12:17)

Summary of *The Bait of Satan,* Chapter 12

If offense represents the finest bait Satan waves before
us, then revenge turns out to be his surest trap. The
hunger for justice may be a hint of the fact that we are
made in the image of God, but our fallen natures have
twisted our idea of justice. At the gut level, we want to
get even, and maybe a little more. We want the person
who hurt us to hurt. And if *we* can cause the hurt, all
the better. But Bevere reminds us that such feelings
lead us to try to take God's place in the scheme of
things, and that's a position we cannot handle.

As Bevere puts it, "It is unrighteous for us as children of
God to avenge ourselves. But that is exactly what we are
seeking when we refuse to forgive. We desire, seek, plan,
and carry out revenge. We will not forgive until the debt
is paid in full, and only we can determine the acceptable
compensation. When we seek to correct the wrong done
to us, we set ourselves up as judges" (p. 136).

For believers, the idea of revenge sounds so
unacceptable, yet we frequently fall prey to a form of
this trap. John borrows a term coined by Francis

STUDENT NOTES

Frangipane to describe the way in which Christians become ensnared in "unfulfilled revenge[1]" that takes on the form of bitterness. In fact, as John illustrates with the story of the woman who couldn't gain freedom from her ex-husband who had left her, we can talk the language of forgiveness while letting a root of bitterness flourish in our hearts. When we not only expect God to bring about judgment for wrongs done to us but also expect God to do it on our terms and to our satisfaction, we are attempting to switch places in the order of the universe with our wise Creator.

The story of Absalom from the Old Testament shows clearly how much damage and sorrow can be created by someone who takes offense and develops a deep root of bitterness against another. In the case of David's family, the results were devastating. Revenge was heaped on wrongdoing until brothers were killing each other and a father's heart was broken.

Having described the terrible effects of deep roots of bitterness caused by "unfulfilled revenge," John ends the chapter with an appeal to be watchful. "Do not be afraid to allow the Holy Spirit to reveal any unforgiveness or bitterness. The longer you hide it, the stronger it will become and the harder your heart will grow. Stay tenderhearted" (p. 143). Then he quotes Ephesians 4:31–32 as a prescription for tenderheartedness.

Warm-Up Questions

Use the following questions to prepare your heart and mind for the personal and/or group study in which you will participate.

1. How would you summarize in one sentence what you have learned so far in *The Bait of Satan* study?

_____

_____

_____

_____

2. What passage or passages from Scripture have taken on added significance in your life as a result of these sessions with John Bevere?

_____

_____

_____

_____

3. In your mind's eye, what does a "root of bitterness" look like?

_____

_____

_____

_____

Teaching by John Bevere

Watch the eleventh session video presentation.

Personal Notes on Video Session 11

Use the following lines to keep notes as you view the video.

_____

_____

STUDENT NOTES

_____

_____

_____

_____

_____

_____

TESTIMONY:

"The first book that I read was *The Bait of Satan*. It was about a year ago. When I read the first chapter, I put the book down and said arrogantly in my heart, 'Oh, I don't have an offense. This book is not for me, but for so-and-so.' And so the book sat on my shelf. Weeks later the Holy Spirit literally drove me to the book and I picked it up and began to read it again. This time I listened to God in my heart. It brought healing to my life and exposed an area that God had been trying to deal with me on."

—Pam, Hawaii

Teaching Review

Use the following questions to consider some of the central points made by John Bevere during this video session.

4. What was the main point of Bevere's reference to the book by Cole Stringer, *Take Your Hand Out of the Cage, Monkey*?

_____

_____

_____

_____
_____
_____
_____

_____
_____
_____
_____
_____

_____
_____
_____
_____

5. How does Bevere use the parable of the unforgiving
   servant to explain the concept of "unfulfilled
   revenge"? In other words, how do debts, offenses,
   and "unfulfilled revenge" relate to each other?

_____
_____
_____
_____
_____
_____
_____
_____

6. To review the basic facts of the story from 2 Samuel,
   with what two significant people in his life did
   Absalom hold deep offenses?

_____
_____

_____

_____

_____

7. Bevere told a story of a divorced woman. In spite of her repeated claims that she had forgiven her ex-husband, what did she and John uncover about her attitude that indicated that she was still "holding the banana in the cage" regarding her former husband?

_____

_____

_____

_____

_____

_____

_____

_____

Exploring God's Word

Revisit the key passages from which John Bevere develops his teaching.

Hebrews 12:14–15 _Pursue peace with all people, and holiness, without which no one will see the Lord: looking carefully lest anyone fall short of the grace of God; lest any root of bitterness springing up cause trouble, and by this many become defiled._

8. What two objectives does this passage instruct us to pursue? How do these objectives relate to the issue of offenses?

_____

_____

_____

_____

_____

_____

_____

_____

_____

_____

9. How does Bevere explain the nature of the root of bitterness?

_____

_____

_____

_____

_____

_____

_____

Personal Application

_____

_____

_____

_____

_____

STUDENT NOTES

2 Samuel 13:21–29 *But when King David heard of all these things, he was very angry. And Absalom spoke to his brother Amnon neither good nor bad. For Absalom hated Amnon, because he had forced his sister Tamar. And it came to pass, after two full years, that Absalom had sheepshearers in Baal Hazor, which is near Ephraim; so Absalom invited all the king's sons. Then Absalom came to the king and said, "Kindly note, your servant has sheepshearers; please, let the king and his servants go with your servant." But the king said to Absalom, "No, my son, let us not all go now, lest we be a burden to you." Then he urged him, but he would not go; and he blessed him. Then Absalom said, "If not, please let my brother Amnon go with us." And the king said to him, "Why should he go with you?" But Absalom urged him; so he let Amnon and all the king's sons go with him. Now Absalom had commanded his servants, saying, "Watch now, when Amnon's heart is merry with wine, and when I say to you, 'Strike Amnon!' then kill him. Do not be afraid. Have I not commanded you? Be courageous and valiant." So the servants of Absalom did to Amnon as Absalom had commanded. Then all the king's sons arose, and each one got on his mule and fled.*

10. The passage above records one of the turning points in a longer passage (2 Samuel 13:1–18:33)

of the story of Absalom. In this passage, what evidence do you find that shows Absalom has already moved beyond offense to develop and nourish a root of bitterness?

_____

_____

_____

_____

_____

_____

_____

_____

_____

_____

11. Based on your awareness of Absalom's story and the comments by Bevere, describe Absalom's attitude toward his own father.

_____

_____

_____

_____

_____

_____

_____

_____

_____

_____

_____

_____

STUDENT NOTES

_____

_____

_____

_____

Personal Application

_____

_____

_____

_____

_____

_____

_____

_____

_____

_____

_____

_____

_____

_____

Romans 12:17–19 *Repay no one evil for evil. Have regard for good things in the sight of all men. If it is possible, as much as depends on you, live peaceably with all men. Beloved, do not avenge yourselves, but rather give place to wrath; for it is written, "Vengeance is Mine, I will repay," says the Lord.*

12. Why does God insist, "Vengeance is Mine"?

_____

_____

_____

_____

_____

_____

_____

_____

_____

_____

_____

_____

_____

13. How does Bevere use James 4:12 and 5:9 to emphasize the points he makes about the verses above?

_____

_____

_____

_____

_____

_____

_____

_____

_____

_____

Personal Application

_____

_____

STUDENT NOTES

Matthew 5:38–42 *"You have heard that it was said, 'An eye for an eye and a tooth for a tooth.' But I tell you not to resist an evil person. But whoever slaps you on your right cheek, turn the other to him also. If anyone wants to sue you and take away your tunic, let him have your cloak also. And whoever compels you to go one mile, go with him two. Give to him who asks you, and from him who wants to borrow from you do not turn away."*

14. What title does Bevere give to this series of hard-hitting guidelines from the Lord?

15. When Jesus talked about life this way, what foundational quality was He seeking to build in those who call Him Lord?

_____

_____

_____

_____

_____

_____

_____

Personal Application

_____

_____

_____

_____

_____

_____

_____

_____

_____

_____

_____

_____

_____

Exposing the Truth

Use the following questions to help reach conclusions regarding the Scriptures and insights from the session.

16. What are the questions that Bevere read from the back cover of *The Bait of Satan* book that serve as a checklist to warn of the danger of a root of bitterness?

    A. _____

    B. _____
    C. _____
    D. _____

    _____

17. How does John describe the "Absalom and David" kind of conflicts and offenses that often occur within churches?

    _____
    _____
    _____
    _____
    _____
    _____
    _____
    _____
    _____
    _____
    _____

18. Why is expecting or demanding an apology before

we will extend forgiveness a dangerous misunder-standing of how to handle offenses? In other words, what's wrong with unfulfilled revenge?

_____

_____

_____

_____

_____

_____

_____

_____

_____

_____

_____

_____

_____

_____

_____

_____

_____

_____

_____

_____

_____

What happened to Absalom and what happens in modern ministries is a process that takes time. We are often unaware that an offense has entered our hearts. The root of bitterness is barely noticeable as it develops. But as it is nursed it will grow and be strengthened. As the writer of Hebrews exhorts, we

STUDENT NOTES

are to look "carefully . . . lest any root of bitterness springing up cause trouble, and by this many become defiled" (Hebrews 12:15).

We must examine our hearts and open ourselves to the correction of the Lord, for only His Word can discern the thoughts and intentions of our hearts. The Holy Spirit convicts as He speaks through one's conscience. We must not ignore His conviction or quench Him. If anyone has done this, repent before God, and open your heart to His correction.

A minister once asked me if he had acted as an Absalom or a David in something he had done. He had served as an assistant to a pastor in a city, and the pastor fired him. It seemed that the senior pastor was jealous and afraid of this young man because God's hand was on him.

A year later the minister who was fired believed the Lord wanted him to start a church on the other side of the city. So he did, and some of the people from the church he had left came over to join him. He was troubled because he did not want to act as an Absalom, but he was apparently not offended with his former leader. He started the new church from the leading of the Lord, not out of responding to the lack of care at the other church.

I pointed out to him the difference between Absalom and David. Absalom stole the hearts of others because he was offended with his leader. David encouraged others to stay loyal to Saul even though Saul was

attacking him. Absalom took men with him; David left alone.

—John Bevere, *The Bait of Satan,* p. 142-143

Applying the Lesson

Use the following specific directions to internalize the principles in the session and put them into practice.

19. As you heard and read about the heartache and pain caused by Absalom's root of bitterness, what events from your own life came to mind?

   _____

   _____

   _____

   _____

   _____

20. Which of the events you just listed are still un-resolved because you haven't been able to forgive or because you have been trying to forgive but hoping/demanding that the other party (or parties) apologize or realize what they have done to you?

   _____

   _____

   _____

   _____

   _____

21. Based on this particular session, what do you want God's Spirit to help you do?

_____

_____

_____

_____

You don't know how many people I've met in the church who have not dealt with certain offenses in their lives. And those offenses have been growing for years. And the sad thing is, folks, a plant is easy to pluck up when it's young because the roots are not very deep. But if you fester and you water that thing for years, it does take some effort to get it out. That is why the Bible says, "Do not let the sun go down on your wrath."

—John Bevere, adapted from Video Session 11

Bait Warnings

A final opportunity for prayerful submission to the truth of the session.

"Why do you want to hang around with the turkeys in the barnyard when I've called you to soar with the eagles? You need to think like I think, speak like I speak." That is why Jesus comes along in Matthew 5:38–42, "You have heard that it was said, 'An eye for an eye but a tooth for a tooth'." That is revenge. "But I tell you," now here comes the higher level of thinking, He says, "But I tell you not to resist an evil person." Did God resist you before you got saved? Come on, I asked a question, where's the answer? [No.] "But whoever slaps you on the right cheek, turn and offer him the other. If anyone wants to sue you and take away your tunic, let him have your coat also. And whoever compels you to go one mile, go with him two. Give to him who asks you and from him who wants to borrow from you do not turn away." This is kingdom-level thinking, folks. This is not revenge thinking. Revenge thinking is the way of the world— the way of darkness. It is sensual, demonic—it is earthly. It is the wisdom that ascended from below. Are you with me? But the wisdom that descends from above is first of all pure, gentle, easy in being treated, willing to yield, full of good fruits and mercy. God is saying, "Come up to My level of thinking. Come up to My level of living."

—John Bevere, adapted from Video Session 11

Video Script for Lesson 11
Revenge: The Trap

We are in lesson number 11. Can you believe we are this far in "The Bait of Satan" curriculum? Can I read you just a couple testimonies? Would that be all right? You know what the Bible says; *"They overcame by the blood of the Lamb and by the word of their testimony."* Amen? You know, I get these testimonies, and my staff shares them with me and I'm telling you. It just really blesses my life to see how God loves His people and touches His people and can use books to do it.

"The first book that I read was *The Bait of Satan*. It was about a year ago. When I read the first chapter I put the book down and said arrogantly in my heart. 'Oh, I don't have an offense. This book is not for me, but for so and so.' And so the book sat on my shelf. Weeks later the Holy Spirit literally drove me to the book and I picked it up and began to read it again. This time I listened to God within my heart. It brought healing to my life and exposed an area that God had been trying to deal with me on." That's Patty from Hawaii.

We have several. Just let me read one more. "Whether it's air rage, road rage, or put-down humor or sitcoms, society today has become more rampant with arrogance and indifference. I felt myself becoming drawn into it. Defending myself against perceived injustices—real and imaginary—and in the process realizing how unhappy I'd become. While visiting Pensacola and subsequently reading your book *The Bait of Satan*, your inspired words about dealing with the sin of offense were able to help me immeasurably not only with regard to authority but in everyday life solutions as well. From store clerks who don't say thank you to people who don't use their turning signals. I thought I'd grown up with strong Christian influences. I'd long since developed a disdain for Christianity because of the negativity

and control tactics I'd experienced. But your words have awakened me to the realization I had no longer had to extract my love and validation from others, rather through Jesus." That's Doug from Louisiana.

You know, we get these time and time again. And I'm telling you just to see how God has used this message all over the world, watching people coming forward in conferences 50 percent to 80 percent of people and then the testimonies that we get of how their lives have been changed. *The Bait of Satan* offense is literally the trap of the devil to destroy the call of God on your life in these last days. There is a man named Cole Stringer from Australia who wrote a book and I just read it two days ago, and it's called *Take Your Hand Out of the Cage, Monkey*. And this Australian discovered how the people out in the bush catch monkeys. Do you know how they catch monkeys? What they do is, now this is an amazing thing, they put a banana on the inside of the cage. There's no doors inside of the cage. It's just a little round cage. But the thing is, the cage is only wide enough for the monkey's hand to go through like this. And what the monkey does is grab the banana but when he grabs the banana he can't pull his hand back out because it's too narrow. And then when all these monkeys grab all these bananas in all these cages, then out comes the guys with the baseball bats and they start hitting the monkeys over the head and killing them. And these monkeys know exactly what these guys are doing. And they go right down the row killing them just like that or putting them out and bringing them to somewhere else or something like that. And they go right down the row and even though these monkeys are watching and know exactly what's going to happen, they won't let go of that banana.

Now that is such a perfect illustration of some-body who picks up an offense, especially after you've heard what you've heard these past several weeks in these lessons. You know the consequences. It's made so clear in the Word of God, but yet you have to hang on to that offense. Let go of it. "Get your hand out of the cage, monkey," is what he says, right?

Offense is a serious thing. I will review again. It is the bait of Satan to pull you into his trap. Luke 17 verse 1 says, *"It is impossible that offenses will not come."* But what you do with the offense will determine your future. Either you will become stronger or you will become bitter. An offense is from the Greek word *skandalon,* which is an old Greek word which was used to describe the bait stick of the trap that hunters used to catch small animals and birds in. They would put the bait on the *skandalon,* the animal would take it, and the cage would either capture it or kill it. Thereby an offense is the bait of Satan to pull you into captivity. You will have the opportunity to be offended but it will determine your future on how you handle it.

Tonight, I want to talk to you some more about what we've been talking about—not letting go of an offense. Now, when a person refuses to let go of an offense, the reason is because he feels that the person that has offended him owes him something. Do you remember the last parable that we talked about in the last lesson? Remember the unforgiving servant? When his fellow brother did him wrong, what did he do? He threw him into jail, until he should pay what he owed. When you hold an offense against somebody, you feel they owe you something. You feel that you have a debt that has not been satisfied. In actuality, you are setting yourself up to be the judge because you determine what is owed to you. But really there is only one Judge, the Bible says, and that is God.

When you hold on to that debt, you are holding on to unfulfilled revenge. Isn't that true? Because you want revenge and revenge is your payment. Isn't that true? Now, bitterness is nothing more than unfulfilled revenge. It is an offense that is allowed to take root in a person's heart; you have not had your revenge. And it takes root and it grows. When a bitter root grows in a person's heart, the Bible says that it will defile you. The Bible says that we are to *"examine our hearts carefully lest there be in us any roots of bitterness by which many have become defiled."* That is Hebrews 12.

Let me say it again. We are to *"examine ourselves carefully." "Lest there be in us any root of bitterness by which many have become defiled."* Now a root is something that starts out as a seed. The seed is offense. If that seed is watered, if it is nurtured, it will grow. What it grows into is a very destructive plant in your life. It will defile you. I think the person that exemplifies this better than anybody else is a young man named Absalom. If you look at David—remember we talked about David several lessons ago, how David was severely mistreated by Saul, but that David did not take the bait. He was not offended. When Saul was judged by God, what did David do folks? David taught all the men of Judah a love song. He grieved over Saul being put to death and he blessed his descendants. That is not the sign of a bitter man. That is the sign of man with a heart after God.

However, David had several sons. Later on he got the kingdom and had several wives and several sons from each of those wives. Go with me please to 2 Samuel. And we will start here talking about one of his sons; his name is Absalom. Second Samuel 13, verse 1, *"After this Absalom the son of David had a lovely sister whose name was Tamar. And Amnon the son of David loved her. Amnon was so distressed over his sister Tamar that he became sick for she was a virgin and it was improper for Amnon to do anything to her."* David's got several wives, alright. Amnon is his firstborn son by one wife. Absalom is his third-born son but he's through another wife. So both boys have the same father, David, but different mothers. Absalom has a sister that's gorgeous. Tamar. Amnon the firstborn son is lovesick over her. So he's losing weight, he's wanting her so bad, but it was not proper. She was his half-sister. So one of David's nephews, a very cunning man, says to Amnon, "Hey why are you losing weight? You're one of the king's sons. This is what you need to do. Pretend like you're sick and when David inquires about your sickness ask the king to please send Tamar in to feed you by her hand and that you will recover." So he listens to one of David's brother's son's advice and he does it. He pretends that he's sick. He's lying on the bed and the king comes to see him. He says, "Please have Tamar come and feed me." So the king orders Tamar to come and feed him. Tamar makes him a couple of cakes to feed him and Amnon then sends all of the servants out of his quarters and when he does, he locks the door and he forces Tamar and he rapes her. Now Tamar is trying desperately to stop him. She's saying, "Please ask the king," but he doesn't. He rapes her.

So after he rapes her, the Bible says that his hatred for her was even greater than his love for her before he raped her. Isn't that interesting? We could preach on that one for awhile. And so he puts her out. And she says, "No! Now what you're doing is worse than raping me." And he still doesn't listen and he throws her out. And when this happens to her, she takes a robe of many colors (because the king's virgin daughters wore beautiful robes), she tore her robe and put ashes on her forehead. And she went to her brother's home, Absalom, and she mourned. Now Absalom is seeing his sister raped by his half-brother Amnon and he was furious. And he hated his brother. So for two years he waited for David to avenge his sister, but David heard about it and was very angry but didn't do anything.

The fact that David didn't do anything infuriated Absalom. And so Absalom says, "My father's not done anything. I'm going to take matters into my own hands." And so Absalom plans a party for all the king's sons. He hires two scoundrels, it says, "When I give the signal, when Amnon's good and drunk, rise up and kill him." He waited, he does it, and Amnon is put to death. All the king's sons flee. Absalom then flees to a place called Geshur and stayed there for three years. After three years, Joab says, "Hey look, the king has been comforted about the death of his son Amnon. We really need to see Absalom come back because he's lost two sons. Let's get the one back." So Joab goes to the king and Joab through a wise woman persuades the king to bring Absalom back. Absalom is then brought back but the king says, "No way will I see his face." So for the next two years King David refuses to see the face of Absalom. So now it's been five years. So now you have to understand something. Absalom got his revenge on Amnon his brother, but he's still offended with Dad for not doing anything. And that offense has been in that boy's heart for five years. That offense has grown; it has taken root and grown and now it's festering worse and worse. It's never been dealt with.

You don't know how many people I've met in the church who have not dealt with certain offenses in their lives. And those offenses have been growing for years. And the sad thing is, folks, a plant is easy to pluck up when it's young because the roots are not very deep. But if you fester and you water that thing for years, it does take some effort to get it out. That is why the Bible says, "Do not let the sun go down on your wrath."

You do not want to allow a seed of offense to germinate in your heart overnight. You do not avoid offenses; you confront offenses. And we will talk about that in the next lesson. You have to deal with them. It's very simple. It's done before the throne of God but it's got to be dealt with.

Now Absalom has had this thing growing in his heart for five years. Five years. So you know what? He's still offended with Dad. And finally David says, "Alright, bring him before me." And he comes. Absalom bows down, kisses the king's hand, and now he's restored, but the offense is still there. So what does Absalom begin to do? Absalom begins to provide for himself horses and men to run before him. And he stands outside the gate of the city and all the people that are coming in who have cases that the king needs to hear, the king's busy. And Absalom says, "Oh, if I was ruler in Israel I would judge your case." So the Bible says that he stole the hearts of the men of Israel.

Do you know how many times this has happened in churches? Associate pastors picked up an offense with the senior pastor and they never dealt with it and they begin to steal men and women's hearts in the church and a few years later there's a church split. You don't want to be an Absalom because you're about to hear the outcome of an Absalom. Do you know what ran through Absalom's head? "My father, he sure does have the people deceived. Hides behind his fake worship of Jehovah. Ha! His own daughter gets raped and he doesn't even do anything about it. Well, no wonder he can't do anything about it because of what he did to his own servant's wife. Uriah the Hittite. Raped his wife and then murders Uriah to cover it up. Ha! And Saul, he lost his kingdom because he just spared one king and a few animals. My father rapes a woman and then kills her husband and covers it up. He's mister worship-man. He didn't do anything for my sister."

See, it's festered. He's been thinking about this for a long time. I want to read you the back of the book. "Are you compelled to tell your side of the story? Do you fight thoughts of suspicion and distress? Are you constantly rehearsing past hurts? Have you lost hope because of what somebody else did to you or somebody close to you?" This is

exactly what's going on. He had never dealt with the offense. So now he's stole the hearts of the men. Why? Because he's justified it. "My father is such a jerk, he's so hypocritical. There's no way he's qualified to rule. I mean, if Saul lost his kingdom for just sparing a king, why should my father have the kingdom?"

So he steals the men's hearts. And then he takes over Israel and marches on the throne with soldiers. And David's servants say to him, "Your son has stole Israel out from under you," and David has to leave. Of course, God's hand is on David and his men and shortly after that Absalom is put to death. I mean, even David gave the order, "Don't put him to death," but he was still put to death because I believe it was the judgment of God. It's very severe when you rise up against a father, folks. God does not take that lightly. I mean, David had the man executed who even said that he'd killed Saul, but he didn't do it. It's a very serious thing when you rise up against a father. And so Absalom is put to death.

So here is a young man who would have been a potential king, but his whole life was destroyed because of unfulfilled revenge. It wasn't embezzling funds, it wasn't homosexuality, it wasn't adultery, it wasn't murder, it wasn't rape. The whole root was an offense that grew into bitterness: unfulfilled revenge.

Several years ago I was preaching at a church in Florida. And I had just gotten done preaching on *The Bait of Satan*. A woman came up to me in church and said, "Pastor John, while you were preaching I just felt kind of an ache on the inside." She said, "Now, I'd forgiven my ex-husband and everything's fine, but I can't understand why I was feeling a little uncomfortable on the inside of me." And I mean the Spirit of God just really lead me and I said, "Well, that's because you haven't forgiven your ex-husband." She said, "Well, I have. I've forgiven him. I've cried, I've wept. I've released him." I said, "No, you haven't." She said, "Yes, I have!" She started getting a little upset. She said, "Yes, I have! I've released him. I've prayed. I've released him. I've cried. I've forgiven him!" I said, "No, you haven't." Well, then she started getting really upset. And she finally looked at me because I kept saying, "No, you haven't, no, you haven't." And she said, "Well, help me." And I said, "Why don't you tell me what your ex-husband did." She said, "Okay. We were pastors, he left me and ran away with a very prominent woman in our church, left me and my kids with nothing. John, he has blamed me all these years. He said I was a hindrance to his ministry and the call of God in his life and that God always intended for him to marry that woman and not me, and that it was the will of God that he should have married her." That's perverted as the day is long, but you know. So he really wounded this woman. She said, "Now I'm married. I have a new husband and he treats me fine. I have this good pastor now," whom she worked for, she was the secretary of a church. She said, "But, I have a hard time relating to my husband. I have a hard time relating to my pastor." I said, "Well, that's because you haven't forgiven your ex-husband." She said, "But I have." I said, "Well, keep going."

She said, "Well, all these years he's blamed me. But he's never come back once and said, 'I'm sorry.'" I said, "Stop right there. We've just hit the unfulfilled revenge." She looked at me and said, "What?" I said, "Listen, your unfulfilled revenge with your ex-husband is not alimony, it's not child support because you've got a new husband who's taking care of you, and taking care of your kids. It's not the house. What your unfulfilled revenge is, you just want him to come back and say, 'I was wrong,' for him to apologize." I said, "If Jesus would have waited for us to come back and say 'I'm sorry,' He never would have forgiven us at the cross." And she looked at me and her eyes got big like that. I said, "When He hung on the cross, He said, 'Father forgive them for they don't know

what they're doing.' He wasn't just talking about the soldiers or the Sanhedrin. He was talking about the next generation and the next generation and the next generation right down to you and me, because you and I put him there." I said, "He forgave us before we ever said, 'I'm sorry.'"

Do you know how many times I've had people come up to me and say, "Well, I'll forgive them when they apologize." If Jesus would have waited for you to apologize, He never would have forgiven you and you would have been in hell. Jesus chose to forgive you before you ever said, "I'm sorry." I said, "Your unfulfilled revenge is just wanting your ex-husband to come back and say 'I'm sorry. I was wrong.' And you know what? That's what's kept you in captivity all these years."

I want you to see this one more time before we go into the final lesson. Romans 12, we read in verse 17, *"Repay no one evil for evil. Have regard for good things in the sight of all men. If it is possible, as much as depends on you, live peaceably with all men."* Verse 19, *"Beloved, do not avenge yourselves but rather give place to wrath for it is written, 'Vengeance is mine. I will repay,' says the Lord."* God says, "Vengeance is mine." He says you are not to take vengeance. Why? Because He is the judge. When we determine that somebody owes us something, we put ourselves in the place of the judge. And according to James chapter 4, verse 12, and James chapter 5, verse 9, let me read it to you: *"There is one lawgiver who is able to save and destroy. Who are you to judge another? Do not grumble against one another brethren."* Folks, this is a command. *"Do not grumble against one another brethren, lest you be condemned."* Can I read that one more time? *"Do not grumble or gripe or complain against one another brethren, lest you be condemned. Behold the judge is standing at the door."*

Folks, God is the just Judge. He will pass the righteous judgment. He will repay according to righteousness, folks. If somebody has done wrong and genuinely repents, that means what? That Jesus will release them. If somebody will say, "Well, yeah, but what they did was against me! Not Jesus." But you have to remember what *you* did to Jesus. But He chose to freely forgive when you and I didn't deserve it. See folks, if you really want to know the truth, we are talking about the very foundation of Calvary. This is Christianity. This is when you release somebody who doesn't deserve to be released.

This is why Jesus comes along and says, "Hey, I want to change your whole way of thinking." See, do you know what the word "holiness" really means? Holiness is from the Hebrew word *kadosh*, which simply means this: "a cut above." Back in the days when ladies made outfits, if you went to a material store you'd have average fabric, nice fabric, very nice fabric, and then you'd have this one fabric that's a cut above all of them. When God says, "Be holy as I am holy," what He's speaking of His relationship to His creation. He is an infinite cut above His creation. So when He says, "Be holy as I am holy," He's saying, "I don't think like you, I don't talk like you, My ways are not like your ways. Come up to My level of living." What He's saying is this folks, because He's not talking about wearing your hair a certain way and not wearing makeup and having your hair in a bun. You can have a bun and a dress down to your ankles and have a seducing spirit up to your eyeballs—that is not holiness.

What He's saying is this: "Why do you want to hang around with the turkeys in the barnyard when I've called you to soar with the eagles? You need to think like I think, speak like I speak, and think like I think." That is why Jesus comes along in Matthew 5, verses 38-42, *"You have heard that it was said, an eye for an eye but a tooth for a tooth."* That is revenge. *"But I tell you,"* now here comes the higher level of thinking, He says, *"But I tell you not to resist an evil person."* Did God resist you before you got saved? *"Not to resist an evil person, but whoever slaps you the on the right cheek turn and offer him the other."* You know what Jesus is saying? Jesus is saying the way the love of God works is the love of God will risk being hurt again. Now, I'm going to get into reconciliation in the next lesson. We're going to make that real clear.

Now look at this, *"Turn the other also. If anyone wants to sue you and take away your tunic, let him have your coat also. And whoever compels you to go one mile, go with him two. Give to him who asks you and from him who wants to borrow from you do not turn away."* This is kingdom-level thinking folks. This is not revenge thinking. Revenge thinking is the way of the world, the way of darkness. It is sensual, demonic—it is earthly. It is the wisdom that ascended from below. But the wisdom that descends from above is first of all pure, gentle, easy in being treated, willing to yield, full of good fruits and mercy. God is saying, "Come up to My level of thinking. Come up to My level of living."

Lesson 12

Escaping the Trap

*"This being so, I myself always strive
to have a conscience without offense
toward God and men."*
(Acts 24:16)

Summary of *The Bait of Satan,* Chapters 13, 14, and Epilogue

In the last three sections of the book, Bevere gives his full attention to showing us how to avoid and disarm the bait of Satan. Chapter 13 provides a continuation to the teaching of chapter 12, where the desire and power of revenge are seen as the trap. Now John leads us in a teaching about escaping that revenge trap. The desire for the score to be settled when we are hurt represents a very powerful human drive. The deeper the hurt, the more that desire will continue to try to reassert itself— even when we have turned away from revenge, offered heartfelt forgiveness, and moved on. As Bevere confesses in this chapter, believers are often ambushed by their genuine desire to respond to hurts in a mature way. Sometimes the hurts are denied or downplayed because we want to be obedient. If we haven't faced the depth of our hurt, however, it will remain. The deeper the hurt, Bevere tells us, the more we will need the equivalent of physical therapy in our spirit.

A large part of reconstruction of what was damaged and wounded by a hurt or offense involves a disciplined prayer life in which we practice Matthew 5:44 toward those who have hurt us. We bless them. John makes it very clear from his own experience that praying for our enemies is neither a game nor a light thing. As God put it to John, "Pray the very things for him that you want Me to do for you!"

Chapter 14 covers the importance of loving, prayer-directed confrontation. This is not a stealth way of exacting revenge, but a humble movement toward reconciliation. John uses Matthew 5:21–24 to point out Jesus' teaching about the dangers of humiliating others with hateful comments and the value of initiating reconciliation when we know someone "has something against" us. The chapter takes us through various other Scriptures, primarily from the Gospels, in which Jesus continually directed those who believed in Him to take their relationships with others very seriously. The principle of reconciliation becomes a human picture of God's great reconciling work with us. We show that we understand what it took for God to be reconciled with us by becoming reconciled with one another. Peace-making based on the love of God is what Bevere calls "The Bottom Line." Based on Romans 12:18, we know that all may not be willing to live in peace, but there should never be a lack of willingness on our part.

The Epilogue of *The Bait of Satan* offers a thoughtful, deliberate action plan for applying the truth found throughout the book. John provides a helpful "prayer of release." As he has discovered in conference after conference, an overwhelming percentage of the people in his audiences admit that they are carrying offenses. You may well fit into that category. He appeals to us to not endanger our own walk with God or miss out on the blessings of living as peacemakers, practicing what the apostle Paul described in Acts 24:16 (see above).

Warm-Up Questions

Use the following questions to prepare your heart and mind for the personal and/or group study in which you will participate.

1. What are the two or three most significant examples of revealed knowledge that God has impressed upon you?

   _____

   _____

   _____

   _____

2. In what way would you say this study on offense has made a lasting impact on your life?

   _____

   _____

   _____

   _____

3. If you could ask John Bevere one question, what would it be?

   _____

   _____

STUDENT NOTES

_____

_____

_____

_____

_____

Teaching by John Bevere

Watch the twelfth session video presentation.

Personal Notes on Video Session 12

Use the following lines to keep notes as you view the video.

_____

_____

_____

_____

_____

_____

_____

_____

_____

_____

Jesus clearly delineates the consequences of offense in this portion of His sermon. He illustrates the severity of holding anger or bitter offense. If one is angry with his brother without a cause, he is in danger of judgment. He is in danger of the council if that anger bears fruit and he calls his brother "Raca!"

The word _raca_ means "empty-headed," or fool. It was a term of reproach used among the Jews in the time

STUDENT NOTES

of Christ. If that anger reaches the point where he calls a brother a fool, he is in danger of hell. The word *fool* means to be godless. The fool says in his heart there is no God (see Psalm 14:1). In those days to call a brother a fool was quite a serious accusation. No one would say such a thing unless the anger they bore had turned to hatred. Today it would be comparable to telling a brother, "Go to hell," and meaning it.

Jesus was showing them that not dealing with anger can lead to hatred. Hatred not dealt with would put them in danger of hell. Then He said that if they remembered their brother was offended with them, they were to make it top priority to find him and seek to be reconciled.

Why should we seek with such urgency to be reconciled—for our sake or for our brother's sake? We should go for his sake that we might be a catalyst to help him out of the offense. Even if we are not offended with him, the love of God does not let him remain angry without attempting to reach out and restore. We may have done nothing wrong. Right or wrong doesn't matter. It is more important for us to help this stumbling brother than to prove ourselves correct.

—John Bevere, *The Bait of Satan*, pp. 155-156

Teaching Review

Use the following questions to consider some of the central points made by John Bevere during this video session.

4. Several times in his presentations, Bevere has connected the idea of hunger and the importance of good, biblical preaching. What is that connection?

_____

_____

_____

_____

_____

_____

_____

5. What were John's stated reasons for choosing to base this final session on his personal testimony?

_____

_____

_____

_____

_____

_____

_____

_____

_____

6. What term does Bevere use to distinguish between offenses that are frankly easy to forgive and

offenses that must be dealt with intentionally in
our lives?

_____

_____

_____

_____

_____

_____

_____

_____

_____

7. There were at least seven stages that the Lord had
   to take John through before he could overcome the
   grievous and wounding offense that occurred in his
   life a number of years ago. How many of them can
   you describe below? (See also pages 146-150 in *The
   Bait of Satan*.)

   First, _____

   _____

   Second, _____

   _____

   Third, _____

   _____

   Fourth, _____

   _____

STUDENT NOTES

Fifth,

_____

_____

_____

Sixth,

_____

_____

Seventh,

_____

_____

Exploring God's Word

Revisit the key passages from which John Bevere develops his teaching.

Acts 24:10–16 _Then Paul, after that the governor had beckoned unto him to speak, answered, "Forasmuch as I know that thou hast been of many years a judge unto this nation, I do the more cheerfully answer for myself: Because that thou mayest understand, that there are yet but twelve days since I went up to Jerusalem for to worship. And they neither found me in the temple disputing with any man, neither raising up the people, neither in the synagogues, nor in the city: Neither can they prove the things whereof they now accuse me. But this I confess unto thee, that after the way which they call heresy, so worship I the God of my fathers, believing all things which are written in the law and in the prophets: And have hope toward God, which they themselves also allow, that there shall be a resurrection of the dead, both of the just and unjust. **And herein do I exercise myself, to**_

have always a conscience void of offence
toward God, and toward men." (KJV, emphasis
added)

8. What does Bevere point out about the importance of
   the word "exercise" in this statement Paul made in
   his self-defense before the ruling authority?

   _____

   _____

   _____

   _____

   _____

   _____

   _____

   _____

   _____

   _____

9. In Bevere's illustration, how do opportunities for
   offense provide us with exercises that develop in us
   the same objective that the apostle Paul said he
   pursued—"a conscience void of offence toward God
   and toward men"?

   _____

   _____

   _____

   _____

   _____

   _____

STUDENT NOTES

Personal Application

_____

_____

_____

_____

_____

_____

_____

_____

_____

Matthew 5:43–48 *"You have heard that it was said, 'You shall love your neighbor and hate your enemy.' But I say to you, love your enemies, bless those who curse you, do good to those who hate you, and pray for those who spitefully use you and persecute you, that you may be sons of your Father in heaven; for he makes his sun rise on the evil and on the good, and sends rain on the just and on the unjust. For if you love those who love you, what reward have you? Do not even the tax collectors do the same? And if you greet your brethren only, what do you do more than others? Do not even the tax collectors do so? Therefore you shall be perfect, just as your Father in heaven is perfect."*

10. What word of revealed knowledge did God give to Bevere when he asked Him what exercise he should practice to rehabilitate his spiritual life damaged by offense?

_____

_____

11. What four specific actions does Jesus spell out in
these verses that He expects His followers to do to
their enemies? How did Bevere struggle with this
truth?

_____

_____

_____

_____

_____

_____

_____

_____

_____

Personal Application

_____

_____

_____

_____

_____

_____

_____

_____

Psalm 35:1–13 *Plead my cause, O LORD, with
those who strive with me; fight against those who*

STUDENT NOTES

fight against me. Take hold of shield and buckler, and stand up for my help. Also draw out the spear, and stop those who pursue me. Say to my soul, "I am your salvation." Let those be put to shame and brought to dishonor who seek after my life; let those be turned back and brought to confusion who plot my hurt. Let them be like chaff before the wind, and let the angel of the LORD chase them. Let their way be dark and slippery, and let the angel of the LORD pursue them. For without cause they have hidden their net for me in a pit, which they have dug without cause for my life. Let destruction come upon him unexpectedly, and let his net that he has hidden catch himself; into that very destruction let him fall. And my soul shall be joyful in the LORD; it shall rejoice in His salvation. All my bones shall say, "LORD, who is like you, delivering the poor from him who is too strong for him, yes, the poor and the needy from him who plunders him?" Fierce witnesses rise up; they ask me things that I do not know. They reward me evil for good, to the sorrow of my soul. **But as for me, when they were sick, my clothing was sackcloth; I humbled myself with fasting; and my prayer would return to my own heart. I paced about as though he were my friend or brother; I bowed down heavily, as one who mourns for his mother.** (emphasis added)

12. What was John thinking and feeling when the Lord told him to read Psalm 35 and he got as far as verse 12?

_____

_____

_____

_____

_____

13. How did the Lord use verses 13 and 14 (in bold above) to change John's attitude?

_____

_____

_____

_____

_____

_____

_____

_____

_____

_____

_____

_____

_____

_____

_____

_____

_____

_____

STUDENT NOTES

Personal Application

_____

_____

_____

_____

_____

_____

_____

_____

_____

Romans 2:1–11 *Therefore you are inexcusable, O man, whoever you are who judge, for in whatever you judge another you condemn yourself; for you who judge practice the same things. But we know that the judgment of God is according to truth against those who practice such things. And do you think this, O man, you who judge those practicing such things, and doing the same, that you will escape the judgment of God?* **Or do you despise the riches of His goodness, forbearance, and longsuffering, not knowing that the goodness of God leads you to repentance?** *But in accordance with your hardness and your impenitent heart you are treasuring up for yourself wrath in the day of wrath and revelation of the righteous judgment of God, who "will render to each one according to his deeds": eternal life to those who by patient continuance in doing good seek for glory, honor, and immortality; but to those who are self-seeking and do not obey the truth, but obey unrighteousness—indignation and* *wrath, tribulation and anguish, on every soul of man who does evil, of the Jew first and also of the Greek; but glory, honor, and peace to everyone who works what is good, to the Jew first and also to the Greek. For there is no partiality with God.* (emphasis added)

14. Look back at the verses from Matthew 5 that you read a few minutes ago. One of Jesus' expectations of His followers is that we "do good to those who persecute" us. In this passage, Paul discusses the crucial part that God's goodness plays in our repentance. How do repentance and goodness relate to each other?

_____

_____

_____

_____

_____

_____

_____

_____

_____

_____

15. How did John learn the lesson of "doing good" as part of his reconciliation with the person who hurt him deeply?

_____

_____

_____

_____

STUDENT NOTES

_____

_____

_____

_____

_____

_____

_____

_____

_____

_____

_____

_____

_____

_____

_____

_____

_____

_____

_____

_____

_____

16. How did John's practice of Matthew 5 and his
     application of the goodness principle lead to a new
     understanding of love in his life?

_____

_____

_____

STUDENT NOTES

_____

_____

_____

_____

_____

_____

_____

_____

_____

_____

_____

_____

_____

Personal Application

_____

_____

_____

_____

_____

_____

_____

_____

_____

_____

_____

Exposing the Truth

Use the following questions to help reach conclusions regarding the Scriptures and insights from the session.

17. Whether or not offense has occurred, how do we need to exercise and train in order to be ready to escape the trap of offense?

_____

_____

_____

_____

_____

_____

_____

_____

18. Why, based on John's experience, is it important to state or express forgiveness even before we "feel" forgiving?

_____

_____

_____

_____

_____

_____

_____

_____

_____

_____

_____

_____

_____

_____

_____

_____

_____

_____

19. Why is it imperative that we deal with the reality
    of offenses and their wounds in our lives?

_____

_____

_____

_____

_____

_____

_____

_____

You see, folks, the Bible says in Isaiah, "Your sin has
separated you from Me." It doesn't say it separated Me
from you; it says it separated you from God. You have
got to understand that even though what was done to
you was a sin, two wrongs never make a right. The sin
of offense is not justified by how badly you were
treated because two wrongs don't make a right. When
you realize that you have sinned against God by holding the offense, then you open up the door to get free.
Amen? Amen. So the question is: Will you take the
bait? It is impossible that offenses will not come. You
will have the opportunity to be offended. What you do
with the offense will determine your future.

—John Bevere, adapted from Video Session 12

Applying the Lesson

Use the following specific directions to internalize the principles in the session and put them into practice.

20. Have you been reconciled with God? Are there offenses between you and God that you now know need to be settled? Based on what you've learned from God's Word in these sessions, what are they and what will you do?

   _____

   _____

   _____

   _____

21. What people do you now realize have offended or hurt you in the past over whom you have been experiencing unfulfilled revenge or holding in unforgiveness? Based on what you've learned from God's Word in these sessions, what will you do about those relationships?

   _____

   _____

   _____

   _____

22. What people do you now realize have something against you, even if you don't know what that is? Based on what you've learned from God's Word in these sessions, what are you going to do about those relationships?

   _____

   _____

Bait Warnings

A final opportunity for prayerful submission to the truth of the session.

Response Prayer

Close your eyes and focus on Jesus. Close your eyes. We are not looking for anything else other than a person and the Bible says that the Holy Spirit reveals Him to us. The Holy Spirit speaks to you in your heart.

Some of you have offense with God Himself because He didn't meet up to your expectation. Some of you, your offense is with a father; some of you it's with a brother, a pastor, a boss, a friend. Some of you it's with a child. Close your eyes and focus on Jesus. I'm asking the Holy Spirit to reveal Him in Jesus' name. If you could see His eyes right now, you would not see angry eyes. You would not see condemning eyes. You would see eyes with tremendous love and compassion. I mean, deep love, deep compassion. Some of you right now are getting a glimpse. Some of you are sensing His presence, and we haven't even prayed. What's happening? You're drawing near to Him, and He's drawing near to you.

I want you to pray together, "Father in heaven, in Jesus' name, I am so grateful to You for what You have given me these last few weeks. I have recognized

STUDENT NOTES

Your voice within Your servant and I have heard Your Word and I realize that I'm the one that's wrong. I have sinned. I've justified harboring my offense because of what was done to me and I realize after hearing truth that I am wrong. Lord, I ask Your forgiveness. I've sinned against You by not forgiving, by not releasing. But tonight I repent of my sin and I renounce the sin of unforgiveness and of offense and of bitterness and of all resentment. I ask You to cleanse me with Your blood. Wash me with the blood of Jesus. Even now, I receive. Now Father, from my heart I forgive _____." Now, before you say the person's name, I want you to see that person. When you see him or her, I want you to bring that person before the Lord and forgive right now. Say, "I forgive you right now. I release you."

—John Bevere, adapted from Video Session 12

Video Script for Lesson 12
Escaping the Trap

Now in this last lesson I want to share with you my personal testimony. Of course, the last eleven lessons in "The Bait of Satan" is not just a bunch of theory to me. It is something that I personally went through and I'm hoping that my testimony will help you tonight to overcome any kind of offense that may be in your life.

Before I got saved, it was very, very easy for me to forgive. I was really raised in a good family. I never had much problems forgiving people. After I got saved, it was even easier for me to forgive. And then what happened was there was a man who did some things to me, several things to me, and it took place over the course of a year. And it climaxed with some absolutely devastating things that happened at the end of that year. Now this man was a man that I highly respected. A man that was almost like a father figure, and when the things that happened at the end of the year climaxed with these events, people could see how obvious it was that I had been mistreated. So several people started coming to me and saying, "Are you okay?" I said, "I'm fine." They said, "Are you offended?" I said, "No, I'm not offended. I'm fine. I'm going on with the call of God on my life." Other people said, "Are you going to go to him?" I said, "No! I'm not going to him. I'm going on with the call of God on my life. I'm fine."

And so this went on for several months. Now folks, what the problem was is I was too proud to admit that I was offended. See for me to admit that I was offended, I saw a person being offended was a sign of weakness. And I was too proud to say that I was weak. So this went on for several months. And I'm going to tell you what happened, with each month that went by, my heart got colder and colder and colder. And it wasn't an all of a sudden thing. It was a very gradual thing.

I made an illustration in an earlier lesson: if you put a frog in a pan of water at room temperature and turn on the heat, if you gradually heat up that water to the point of boiling that frog will not jump out because he doesn't realize what's happening. If you put a frog in hot, scalding water he will immediately jump out.

The love was growing cold bit by bit by bit. I remember there were times when we would be riding in our car and we would have a worship tape on and my wife would be sitting next to me in the presence of God's honor, and I can see it and tears are coming down her eyes. And she would look over at me and I was just driving the car. And she one time looked over at me and she said, "John, why aren't you worshiping? Why aren't you enjoying yourself?" I said, "I'm meditating, I'm meditating. I'm fine. Please leave me alone." This went on for several months.

Now the thing that's really scary is this: I'm still preaching. I'm still laying hands on the sick and they're getting healed. I'm still laying hands on demon-possessed people and demons are coming out. But yet my heart is growing colder and colder and colder. That is the thing that is so alarming, is a person can be in a state of offense yet still have a powerful ministry because it's the anointing upon them that ministers to people, not their heart within them as much, although that will effect the ministry eventually. So months go by and it just keeps getting worse and worse and worse, and finally, one day I walked out to my back yard on my deck and I looked up to heaven and I said, "Father, am I offended?" And I heard this on the inside of me, "YES!"

That was about how loud it was. I almost jumped. And I remember saying this out in my back yard,

I said, "Father, I have prayed, I have done every-thing I know how to do. I can't get out of this one. I need your help." Now I was at the end of a four-day fast, and I went to a funeral for a secre-tary of this church and this man was conducting the funeral. And I remember I got there a little late so I had to sit in the very back of the church while he conducted the funeral. And I remember two-thirds or three-quarters of the way through the funeral I started weeping and I stretched forth my hands and I said, "I forgive you. I release you. I release you from everything I've done. I release you. I forgive you. I forgive you." And I'm just weeping the rest of the service and I said, "Okay, it's over." And I'm at the end of a four-day fast. I just wept. I released him. And I walked out of the church thinking, "It's over, it's done."

Well, two weeks later I saw him again. When I saw him the thought goes through my mind, "How could he be so blessed? He's done this to me. He's done that to me. He's done this to me. He said this. He's done that. He hasn't done this. He hasn't done that. He's done this to that person, this to that person. How can he be so blessed?" So I remember leaving that place where he was at and I went home driving home thinking about it. I thought about it at lunch that afternoon. I thought about it that afternoon. I talked about it with my wife at dinner. I thought about it that evening. I woke up thinking about it. I took a shower the next morning thinking about it. And then I got in my car to leave the house and all of a sudden I got scared. I thought, "Wait a minute. I forgave him and I wept and I wept and I wept. I forgave him, yet why am I still harboring these thoughts?"

Let me show you something. I need someone who goes to the gym on a regular basis. Come on, I need somebody real quick. Here we go, we've got a volunteer. What's your name brother? Joe, come on up here. Stand right here Joe. Alright, now watch this folks. I can walk up to Joe and do this.

You knew what I was going to do? Now, I hit him pretty hard. But you know what. After I hit him it's over. It's like water off a duck's back. He's fine. Nothing's wrong. But now, I could take this stand. Well, maybe not that stand, let me grab this stand. I could take this stand right here and I could take this thing and I could go as hard as I could and hit him. Now, what am I going to do if I hit him with this? Honestly? I'm going to hurt him. But let's go one step further. I'm going to wound him.

So here's the thing we have to understand. There are some offenses that hit us that like water off a duck's back. We don't like it, but when it's over, we're fine. There are other offenses that hit us that wound us. Wounds don't heal overnight, and if not properly treated, wounds never heal. As a matter of fact, they will eventually kill somebody, possibly.

Thanks, brother. Now, go with me to Acts 24, I want to show you something. Acts 24. I want to look at the sixteenth verse. Paul makes this state-ment. He says, *"This being so I myself always strive."* [or exercise] *to have a conscience without offense towards God and men."* The key word here is exercise.

Now, several years ago I went to Hawaii and I did some meetings and the meetings went really well, and I remember on the second to the last day of the meetings I was playing tourist. And I went to a place called [Wiameiah] Bay and they had a wall that said, "Do not climb the wall." And I climbed the wall. That was before I wrote *Under Cover*, okay? So I went to climb the wall and I lifted my right foot up to get on the wall, and it was an uneven wall because it was made of boul-ders. My foot wasn't even and I lifted up, I heard this crack on the inside of my knee. I mean that loud, and I went "Ahhh!" like that. And I sat there and took the stupid picture I wanted to take and I jumped down off the wall on my left leg. And my wife and the associate pastor were laughing at me in the car because when they saw me jump down, my wife said, "He can't walk!" So they rushed out of the car and they helped me back into the car. Well, I was in a wheelchair for the next four days. Now the next morning, the associate pastor's wife knew a guy who was a physical therapist who owned his own gym. His name was Alex. He was huge guy. Bald head, about six-foot-three, weighed about 230, solid muscle. Big guy, okay? Now he's got me in his gym and he is working on my knee and making it hurt.

And in the middle of working on my knee, he says this to me: "Do you want to know why you got injured? You know why most people who would have climbed that wall yesterday would not have injured themselves, but you did? Do you want to know why?" Now he almost offended me with that statement. I had said, "Why did I injure myself and most people wouldn't?" He said, "Cuz you're out of shape. You don't exercise." And all of a sudden I thought about it. I thought, "Wait a minute. That's true. There are some people, they don't exercise. They're not praying. They're not reading the Word of God. They're not diligently studying. Their spirit-men are weak."

Do you know why I asked someone in the gym and I had Joe come up here? Because Joe goes to the gym. I hit Joe purposely pretty hard. If I had chosen some of you that don't go the gym and are out of shape, and I had hit you that hard, you would have been at the chiropractor or doctor tomorrow, because I purposely hit him really hard.

But there are other people who are studying, praying, and seeking God and you know what? They don't get hurt when something hits them like that. See, I'll never forget, for years we lived next door to a WWF wrestler. We became very, very close with his family. The wife got saved. The children got saved. We did Bible studies in their home and our home, but he's another story, today. But anyway, I remember one day—we did all kinds of stuff together. We played street hockey with our kids. We played basketball. They were just really close friends—and one day he looked at me and he said, "John, please come watch my videos. Come watch me wrestle." I said, "Sure, I'll come watch you wrestle." So I went over to his house and I couldn't believe what I saw. You have to understand, this guy is about six-foot-four and weighs two hundred eighty pounds and had 6 percent body fat, and I mean his body is almost like a perfect V. And his arms are as big as my calves. And I'm watching this film on WWF wrestling. And I'm watching guys break chairs over his back. I watched a guy bust a guitar over his head. I watched a 450-pound sumo wrestler jump off the ring thing and land right on top of him. And he got up! And then I watched him being thrown off the eight-foot-high ring onto this little tiny mat. And I'm sitting here going "Wow!"

Now, if they had done that to you, you'd be in traction. Well, what I realized that there are some people who are so strong in the Spirit that they can have chairs thrown at them, guitars, and everything else as far as offenses go and they don't get injured. So I got on the airplane and I flew to Indonesia with my wife. It was the most hilarious thing you'd ever seen because I had my wife, the three boys, and the babysitter get off the airplane with all the carry-ons and here comes the man of God in a wheelchair. It was really funny. So anyways, when I get to Indonesia, there's another physical therapist guy over there who starts working on my knee and he says, "Do you want to know how you're going to get your knee healed?" And I said, "Yeah, I'd like to know how I'm going to get my knee healed." He said, "You need to exercise every day." And he starts showing me the exercises. And I started thinking about it, I thought, "You know, there are athletes that get hurt and physical therapists, what do they have to do? Focus exercise to get that part of the body stronger than what it was before the injury."

So that's what Paul says, *"This being so, I myself always exercise to keep my conscience free from offense of God or man."* So I said to the Lord, "What do I need to do? What is the exercise?" And the Lord spoke to me and He said, "Matthew 5:44." Now I've quoted it to you before. I'm just going to quote it again. Jesus said what? *"Pray for those who abuse you."* Listen to me again. *"Pray for those who abuse you."* And the Lord spoke to me and He said, "Son, pray for that man." So out of obedience I got up and I started praying. And this was the way my prayers went, "Father, in Jesus' name, bless him and give him a good day. Amen." Next day, I'm praying . . . the next day, "Father, in Jesus' name, by the way, bless him." The next day I'm praying, "Lord, if you can, bless him."

Now that's the way I prayed for him for the next four to six weeks. Now, as you obviously know, I got no better but rather grew worse. I was on another fast, and in the middle of that fast the Spirit of God spoke to me and He said, "I want you to read Psalm 35." I went over to Psalm 35. Go over to Psalm 35, I want to show it to you please. Psalm 35. Now I really didn't know what I was going to run into, so I started reading the first verse and I got down to verse 11 and all of a sudden my attention was attained; I was glued. David says in verse 11, *"Fierce witnesses rise up, they ask me things I do not know, they reward me evil for my good."* I said, "Hey, that's me! I did this guy good and I've been rewarded evil for it." So I'm getting excited. I'm thinking God's going to bless me. So verse 13, he says, *"But as for me."* *"When they were sick,"* these were the people that did him evil for his good, *"when they were sick my clothing was sackcloth. I humbled myself with fasting and my prayer would return to my own heart.*

I pace as though he were my brother, my friend or brother. I bow down heavy as one who mourns for his mother."

You know what David said? "These guys award me for my good. But when they were sick I prayed for them like my mother or my brother." And the Lord spoke to me. He said, "I want you to pray for that man what you want me to do in your life or basically your family." Now, that changed. And I remember I was in the house in the middle of this fast at the kitchen table. I got up from that kitchen table and I started walking back and forth. And I said, "Father, in Jesus' name, I lift up so-and-so to You and I pray that You would surround him with Your presence. I'm asking that he would know You the best a man can know You. I pray that he would please You the best a man can please You. I pray Father that You would reveal Your ways to him and I am asking in Jesus' name that You would increase the anointing of God upon his life. I'm asking You to surround him with angels, surround his family with angels. I'm asking You to protect his wife, protect his children. I'm also asking that You would surround him with godly men and women that Lord, not wicked and unreasonable men and women, but godly men and women who would speak the truth and speak the Word of God and the council of God into his life." And this is what I started praying.

And let me tell you something. It took everything in me to pray like that. Did you ever see a guy that's gotten injured? He's going through physical therapy. Takes everything in him to lift twenty pounds. But if he keeps doing it, what happens? He gets stronger and stronger. So now, I start praying like this several weeks and what happens is I start getting happy. I start getting passionate about the prayer. See, I'm doing it the first day totally by faith. Not any feelings in it. Totally by faith. But a couple weeks go by and now I'm starting to pray with passion.

Well, several weeks go by and I remember I was deep in prayer one morning in a remote place and this came out of my spirit, "So-and-so, I LOVE YOU!" I called his name out and when I said I love you; it was like junk came right out of my gut. And I sat there and I said, "I'm healed. I'm totally healed. I'm healed." I was so excited. I was so excited. So a couple of weeks later I saw him again, and then I felt a little "eh" on the inside of me and I thought, "Now what?" Now, my wife has no idea that this is going on. She's very prophetic. So she pulls me over to the couch and she says, "Honey, you need to go to him." I said, "No, no, no, no, I don't need to go to him. Everything's fine. I've prayed it through. I'm healed. It's fine. I don't need to go to him." She said, "Okay." So I went out and prayed and said, "Lord, do I need to go to him?" Lord said, "YES!" Now do you know when Jesus says if your brother sins against you, go to him? Can I show you the way most people handle that Scripture? Would you like to see it? Come here, Pastor Mark, I just want you to know you did this, you did this, you did this, you did this, but I forgive you!" [snidely]. Do you understand what I'm talking about? In other words, they use that Scripture to come vomit all over you and tell you how bad you treated me. "But I forgive you." Did you ever hear this: "Brother I love you BUT . . ."? Get ready, put up your umbrella, you're about to be vomited on. You understand what I'm talking about? That is not what Jesus had in mind when He said, "If your brother sins against you, you should go to him." So what did Jesus have in mind when He said if your brother sins against you, go to him? Reconciliation.

Now listen to me. There is a huge difference between forgiveness and reconciliation. How do we see the difference? Just look at the cross. When did Jesus forgive us? I went over this in the last lesson but I'm going to do it again. When did Jesus forgive us? At the cross, right? When He said, *"Father forgive them, they don't know what*

they're doing," He's speaking to the next generation, next generation, right down to us because we put Him there, right? He forgave us before we ever said, "I'm sorry." Some people say, "Well, I'll forgive when they apologize." No, if Jesus would have waited for you to apologize, He wouldn't have forgiven you from the cross.

When were we reconciled back to God? When we repented and said, "I'm sorry. You were right. I was wrong. Forgive me." At that point we were reconciled. A relationship cannot be reconciled unless there is repentance. What led us to repentance? The goodness of God. Romans chapter 2. The goodness of God. Did He cause the sun to shine on us before we got saved? Did He give us food and clothing, right? So you say why Jesus says go to your brothers? He's saying, "Go to your brother and create an atmosphere, an atmosphere that's kind and full of loving goodness that's going to want to make him say, 'I'm sorry.'" When you go up to him and say, "You did this and this and this and this, but I forgive you," you know what his attitude is? "Well, excuuuuse me!" Right? That is not creating an atmosphere that is conducive to reconciliation.

So you know what the Lord led me to do through my wife? Buy this guy a really, really nice gift. I'm talking about a gift I'd like to have, that kind of gift. So I bought this thing and I wrapped it up and made an appointment. I went into his office and I said, "You know what? I want to give this to you." He's looking at me and he opens this thing up and he goes, "Wow. Thank you." I said—now this is the way the Lord has me open this up because I'm trying to create an atmosphere of goodness, you see what I'm doing—I said, "You know, I've been in prayer and God has really dealt with me. I've been very critical and very judgmental of you and I'm wrong." He said, "Oh no, no, no you haven't been critical and judgmental of me!" I said, "Oh yes I have. I know when God has shown me my heart. Can you please forgive me?" He said, "Sure." And that opened him up. And he shared his frustration. At the end of that conversation, we came together like this. And we've been like this ever since.

And do you know what is amazing? A couple days later I looked at my wife and said, "You know, when I first met that man, he could do no wrong in my eyes. That's immature love." I said, "But then, he did things against me, I saw his faults and his faults were directed towards me and I didn't love him anymore. That's immature love. But now, I still see his faults, but I love him with the same intensity as when I first met him." I said, "Lisa, that's got to be the love of God because the love of God covers over the multitude of sins." My life, my ministry, everything changed from that weekend forward. I have never been the same since. I would not be standing here in front of you today had it not been for that.

I was getting ready to preach in Florida several years ago and before I got up to preach the leader of the meeting said, "We're going to have a man get up and testify before you preach tonight." I said, "Fine." I had no idea what he was going to testify about. Well, this man gets up, he's 36 years old. He's a construction guy. He's got a beard and some raggy clothes on and he's weeping. And he says, "All my life there's been a wall between me and God." He says, "I'd go to services and I'd watch people get touched by the presence of God and I would do everything I would think would be necessary and I wouldn't get touched with His presence. I'd try with my prayer closet and I wouldn't get touched with His presence. Then several weeks ago, somebody gave me this book, *The Bait of Satan*," what we're talking about here, the last twelve sessions.

He said, "I started reading that book and I couldn't stop until I was finished. When I got to the end of that book I realized that I had held unforgiveness against my mother for thirty-six years. My mother when I was six months old gave me away. I've hated her for it ever since. But when I read the book I realized that I had sinned against God by harboring this offense. I contacted my mother and I talked to her for the second time in thirty-six years." When she got on the phone he said, "Mom, I needed to call you because I've done wrong. I have held unforgiveness against you for thirty-six years because you gave me away." She starts weeping and says, "I've hated myself for thirty-six years for giving you away." The wonderful thing about the phone call is that he forgave her and she forgave herself. But listen, this is where it begins. Now the guy is weeping so profusely that the tears are dripping down off his beard onto his shirt, on his T-shirt. Now he looks at the congregation and says, "Now the wall that has been between me and God for thirty-six years is totally gone. I have been weeping like this for the past three weeks. I weep like this when I go into prayer. I weep like this whenever the presence of God comes into a church service." He said, "I have been weeping nonstop for almost three solid weeks because for the first time in thirty-six years I am experiencing the presence of God."

You see, folks. The Bible says, in Isaiah, "*Your sin has separated you from me,*" God said. Doesn't say it separated Me from you, it says it separated you from God. You have got to understand that even though what was done to you was a sin, two wrongs never make a right. The sin of offense is not justified by how badly you were treated because two wrongs don't make a right. When you realize that you have sinned against God by holding the offense, then you open up the door to get free. So the question is: Will you take the bait? It is impossible that offenses will not come. However, what you do with the offense . . . they will come; you will have the opportunity to be offended. What you do with the offense will determine your future. Amen? God bless you.

I want you to bow your heads because I am not going to preach twelve lessons and not give you the opportunity to forgive. This is the most important part of the twelve lessons. I realize tonight that I have sinned by harboring this offense, and I realize tonight that two wrongs don't make a right and I'm ready to deal with my sin of harboring the offense. I'm ready to confess it to God and I am ready to forgive." If that's you, I want you to raise your hands. Lift them up high. It's not different here than anywhere else in the world. Those of you with your hands raised, stand to your feet. I don't want to miss this opportunity. I'm looking at about 70 percent of you standing up right now.

New Testament repentance is not sackcloth and ashes, folks. It's a change of mind. A change of heart. Listen carefully, this is repentance. You've been thinking this way, living this way because of the way you think and all of a sudden, God's wisdom exposes the error of your thinking because God's wisdom says this is the right way. Here's repentance. I've been wrong. This is right. I'm letting go of this and embracing His ways. That's repentance. You can cry, you cannot cry. It doesn't make any difference. It's when you have that change of heart, change of mind and say, "I'm embracing His wisdom." If that's you and you're ready to forgive, ready to confess it and embrace His way of thinking, I want you to leave the sin at your seat and I want you to come down here and I want to pray with every one of you as a group. Come on down.

Some of you have offense with God Himself because He didn't meet up to your expectation. Some of you, your offense is with a father, some of you it's with a brother, a pastor, a boss, a friend. Some of you it's with a child. If you could see His eyes right now you would not see angry eyes. You would not see condemning eyes. You would see eyes with tremendous love and compassion. What's happening? You're drawing near to Him and He's drawing near to you. I tell you, the presence of God is in this place. I want you to lift up your hands in reverence to Him. I want you to pray this prayer with me. I don't want you to repeat words. I want you to speak these words from your heart. If you need to change my words, make them different so they come from your heart, that's fine.

Let's pray together. "Father in heaven, in Jesus' name, I am so grateful to You for what You have given me these last couple of days. I have recognized Your voice within Your servant and I have heard Your Word and I realized that I'm the one that's wrong. I have sinned. I've justified harboring my offense because of what was done to me, and I realize after hearing truth that I am wrong. Lord, I ask Your forgiveness. I've sinned against You by not forgiving, by not releasing, but tonight I repent of my sin and I renounce the sin of unforgiveness and of offense and of bitterness and of all resentment. I ask You, Lord, that You would cleanse me with Your blood, wash me with the blood of Jesus. Even now, I receive. Now Father, from my heart, I forgive." Now before you say it, I want you to see them and when you see them, I want you to bring them before the Lord right now and forgive them right now. Say I forgive them, say them out loud, and whisper so your ears can hear them right now. The Spirit of God right now is almost just sweeping this stuff right out of here. For some of you it's just like He's pulling a root right out of your heart, a sword right out of your heart. Just let it go in His presence; forgive them. Now lift up your hands right now and say this, "Father in Jesus' name, thank You. I ask You now to fill me afresh with Your Holy Spirit. Shed abroad Your love afresh in my heart, in my life. Let it consume me. In Jesus' name." Now thank Him for it right now. Thank Him.

End Notes

Lesson 9: Lest We Offend Them

1. Grant Osborne, ed., *Matthew* in the *Life Application Bible Commentary Series*, (Wheaton, IL: Tyndale House Publishers, 1996), 348–349.

Lesson 11: Revenge: The Trap

1. Francis Frangipane, *Three Battlegrounds* (Cedar Rapids, IA: Advancing Church Publications, 1989), 50.

THE BAIT OF SATAN

Fight Like a Girl
The Power of Being a Woman

Why is it that women often don't like women? What could possibly cause a large portion of us to reject our own gender? More often than not we lack an appreciation for women. We associate men with strength and women with weakness. We therefore attempt life in roles as men, only to find ourselves conflicted. But God is awakening and empowering His daughters to realize who they truly are, as well as their unique and significant contributions. In order to find our way we must first turn off the ever-present negative noise surrounding us as women. What does this static say?

"Women are a problem"

Have you heard it? Notice I did not say women can cause problems, for surely they can, but that women are a problem. This ancient lie has worked against us since the garden, but I have discovered for every lie there is an overriding truth.

"Women are not a problem, they are an answer"

As the curtains of time draw to a close, women will be restored to fight the battles they are called to wage and to confront the enemy who has robbed them for so long. It is time we stop hiding in the guise of male and begin to fight like a girl!

Driven by Eternity
Making Your Life Count Today & Forever

We were made for eternity. This life on earth is but a vapor. Yet too many live as though there is nothing on the other side. Scriptural laws and principles may be applied to achieve success on earth, but are we prepared for eternity? Have we failed to remember we will all stand before the Great Judge of Heaven and Earth?

Scripture tells us there will be various degrees of rewards for believers ranging from those who watch as all they accomplished is devoured in judgment to those who are awarded the privilege to reign with Christ. These judgments will determine how we spend our span of eternity.

Included in this book is a riveting allegory. It takes place in a world similar to our own, yet different. Lord Jalyn is the ruler of the Kingdom of Affabel. You will journey with six of his subjects through their lives, witness their judgment, and see how and where they will spend the rest of their lives. The teaching of this book revolves around the lessons learned from their lives.

DRIVEN by Eternity
INDIVIDUAL and GROUP KITS

INCLUDED IN THE INDIVIDUAL KIT:
* 12 - 40 MINUTE LESSONS ON 4 DVD'S
* DRIVEN BY ETERNITY HARDBACK BOOK
* HARDBACK DEVOTIONAL JOURNAL
* AUDIO NARRATION OF
  THE PARABLE OF AFFABEL

We have taken this powerful message, *Driven by Eternity,* and created an individual and group curriculum kit for further, in-depth study. You can now share this riveting message with friends and family, lead bible studies and church services.

A HEART ABLAZE

Jesus has never accepted lukewarmness. Rather, He calls for passion! But where do we get the fire to heat up our relationship with him? He never requires anything He doesn't equip us to do. If you have felt that a passionate relationship with Him is unattainable, this book will show you otherwise.

INCLUDES:
* **BESTSELLING BOOK**
* **PERSONAL WORKBOOK**
* **12 LESSONS ON 4 DVD'S**

World-renowned author and Bible teacher John Bevere challenges you to exchange a mediocre relationship with God for a vibrant, fiery one. *A Heart Ablaze* offers riveting insights woven with masterful teachings to help you ignite an maintain a passion for God. As you begin your mission, allow the Holy Spirit to transform you as the fire of God's holiness touches the very depths of your soul.

No matter where you are in your walk with God, if taken to heart these teachings will transform your life. A MUST FOR THOSE WHO DESIRE A STRONGER RELATIONSHIP WITH GOD!

UNDER COVER

The Promise of Protection Under His Authority

LET'S FACE IT, authority is not a popular word, yet by rejecting it, we lose the great protection, provision, promotion and freedom authority provides. If you embrace these principles, living under authority will liberate you rather then restrain you.

INCLUDES:
* **12 LESSONS ON 5 VHS TAPES**
* **2 DVD'S**
* **6 CD'S**
* **1 BESTSELLING UNDER COVER BOOK**
* **1 LEADER'S GUIDE**
* **1 WORKBOOK**

#1 Seller for Churches and Bible Studies

Please contact us today to receive your free copy of Messenger International's newsletter and our 32 page color catalog of ministry resources!

FREE
NEWSLETTER
&
CATALOG

MESSENGER INTERNATIONAL
www.messengerintl.org

The vision of MI is to strengthen believers, awaken the lost and captive in the church and proclaim the knowledge of His glory to the nations. John and Lisa are reaching millions of people each year through television and by ministering at churches, bible schools and conferences around the world. We long to see God's Word in the hands of leaders and hungry believers in every part of the earth.

UNITED STATES
PO Box 888
Palmer Lake, CO 80133-0888
800-648-1477 (US & Canada)
Tel: 719-487-3000
Fax: 719-487-3300
E-mail: mail@messengerintl.org

EUROPE
PO Box 622
Newport, NP19 8ZJ
UNITED KINGDOM
Tel: 44 (0) 870-745-5790
Fax: 44 (0) 870-745-5791
E-mail: europe@messengerintl.org

AUSTRALIA
PO Box 6200
Dural, D.C. NSW 2158
Australia
In AUS 1-300-650-577
Tel: +61 2 8850 1725
Fax +61 2 8850 1735
Email: australia@messengerintl.org

The *Messenger* television program broadcasts in 216 countries on GOD TV, the Australian Christian Channel and on the New Life Channel in Russia. Please check your local listings for day and time.